The Essential Galbraith

THE ESSENTIAL
Galbraith

John Kenneth Galbraith

SELECTED AND EDITED BY

Andrea D. Williams

A Mariner Original
HOUGHTON MIFFLIN COMPANY
BOSTON · NEW YORK
2001

For information about permission to reproduce selections from
this book, write to Permissions, Houghton Mifflin Company,
215 Park Avenue South, New York, New York 10003.

Visit our Web site: www.houghtonmifflinbooks.com.

Library of Congress Cataloging-in-Publication Data
Galbraith, John Kenneth, date.
The essential Galbraith / John Kenneth Galbraith.
p. cm.
Includes bibliographical references and index.
ISBN 0-618-11963-9
1. Galbraith, John Kenneth, 1908– 2. Economics —
United States. I. Title.
HB119.G33 A25 2001
330 — dc21   2001024986

Printed in the United States of America

Book design by Robert Overholtzer

QUM 10 9 8 7 6 5 4 3 2 1

CONTENTS

PREFACE

I send this book to press and on to my readers with one slight sense of concern. It is that someone will ask who decided that this was *The Essential Galbraith*. The author will be a plausible suspect. In fact, it was associates, my publisher and the wider professional and reading public who were responsible. The selection here is of writing that is thought to have had some durable impact on economic and other scholarly thought or on the world at large.

Thus, as later noted, the piece on Countervailing Power, an excerpt from *American Capitalism*, is still in print after nearly fifty years. The balance of power between buyer and seller therein described was considered a major modification of the traditional competitive supply-and-demand construct to which all who have studied economics were exposed. It is perhaps a measure of the enduring nature of the term "the Conventional Wisdom," as defined in the second essay, that one rarely gets through a newspaper today without encountering it. Though I try, however unsuccessfully, to convey an aspect of modesty, I am always pleased to have added this phrase to the language.

The Affluent Society, from which several chapters are here included, was the most widely published economic volume of its time. After his nomination for President in 1960, one of the first questions asked of John F. Kennedy was whether, if elected, he would be guided by the ideas expressed by his known supporter in that book. He responded favorably but also with a certain note of ambiguity.

Later in this collection come three pieces from *The Great Crash,*

1929, which was published in 1955, just after the twenty-fifth anniversary of that catastrophic event. It was a bestseller at the time; so it has remained to this day. Even now, as we are launched in a new century, there is inevitable unease about the future of the economy and therewith the stock market, so a knowledge of what happened in 1929 is, indeed, still essential.

There are other essays here which were similarly selected and thus selected themselves. The reader will, I think, have no trouble accepting their relevance either to history or to the present day, and I have added some headnotes to suggest my view of their particular significance then and now. I end with a paper given at the London School of Economics in 1999 on the unfinished business of the millennium; this had the largest circulation both here in the United States and around the world of any lecture I have ever given.

JOHN KENNETH GALBRAITH

March 2001

INTRODUCTION

If, as Professor Galbraith says in the preface, others are responsible for the contents of this book, it is of primary interest to inquire why he himself eschews the credit. It has been widely believed that he is not a man for whom modesty is a familiar virtue, so why does he find it necessary now to step back into the shadows? The answer seems to lie in the fact that what has been considered vanity could be better viewed as a deep sense of security. He is secure in his basic beliefs and secure that his readers, for whom he has the deepest respect, will be able to discern them. He is not given to self-analysis, and so, while he clearly understands what is the Essential Galbraith, he prefers that others define it.

It should first be noted that in the pages that follow, readers will find John Kenneth Galbraith the economist and the writer, with little trace of the diplomat, the art historian, the novelist, the book reviewer, the theater critic or even, except in the last essay, the lecturer. This is highly appropriate, because economics has, in fact, been his chosen field and writing his obviously innate talent. He has always believed that economics should be studied not in the abstract or as a mathematical construct but as it affects the lives of men and women every day. He is not afraid to overturn or at least reexamine strongly held beliefs of earlier generations, realizing that as technology, communications and business change, so too must the economist's interpretation of them. He has brought to the subject a new way of looking at the role of the great corporations as they faced the countervailing power of trade unions and consumer coalitions. He has identified those who are the guiding intelligence of the corporate world, naming them the technostructure, and has undermined belief in what he calls the myth of consumer sovereignty. A better balance between public and private expenditures has been a recurring theme in his writing, with its reminder that the affluence of our contemporary society should be made to extend to the poorest and most defenseless of our citizens. The uses of power and the persistence of financial euphoria in our public marketplace have consistently attracted his interest, as have the problems of the developing countries, notably India. Above all, the constant thread through his work is his concern with how economics affects the quality of our daily lives and how it will change that of succeeding generations.

These are some of the essentials of the Essential Galbraith, but there are more. There is his continuing fondness for certain of his economic predecessors — for the gift for language and the basic structure that Adam Smith gave to political economy, for the irreverence and unique perception of Thorstein Veblen, for the profound effect John Maynard Keynes and his *General Theory of Employment Interest and Money* had and continue to have on the economic world.

Finally, there is a writing style that illuminates and enhances all that is said: sardonic humor, felicitous phrasing, reasoned argument in reasonable words or, as he would say, clarity of thought reflected in clarity of prose.

So how can the Essential Galbraith be defined? He is a committed liberal, a compassionate optimist, a cautious but firm iconoclast and a writer whose words can change the way the world looks at its problems.

And none of that would he ever write about himself.

ANDREA D. WILLIAMS

March 2001

The Essential Galbraith

Countervailing Power

[*from* American Capitalism]

This is a chapter from one of my first books, the generously titled
American Capitalism, *which came out in 1952, barely into the second
half of the last century. Then, and for well over a hundred years before,
a near-sacred doctrine in the economic textbooks had been the
beneficent regulatory role of competition. It was the competition of
many sellers that protected the consumer and also the individually
powerless wage earner from the full economic effects of monopoly. The
preservation of competition through the antitrust laws — the fabled
Sherman Act in particular — was a vital element of public policy going
back to the latter part of the nineteenth century. Now, as I argued in*
American Capitalism, *a new process was at work: trade unions, a
countering organizational force, were the obvious response to the
greater power of the big corporations. Similarly, but less evidently,
when there was one expression of economic power — such as the large
producer of consumer staples — another one developed in the form of
the seller of those staples — the A&P or the latter-day Wal-Mart. The
numerous and technically competitive farmers found their best economic recourse in purchasing cooperatives when dealing with those
who bought and bargained for their product. Thus the answer to monopoly was less and less the rule of law and more and more the coercion
of countering bargaining power. Not exceptionally, perhaps, I carried
this idea somewhat to the extreme, but it did involve an impressive attack on established belief.*

  A substantial number of economists greeted my thesis with interest and approval when it was published, but a much larger number of defenders of the orthodox view were strongly at odds. At the annual meeting of the American Economic Association, the most prestigious gathering of economists, it was suggested by the head of the organization, the distinguished Calvin Hoover of Duke University, that there be a major reception for the book. This was quickly vetoed, but a special meeting to discuss it was added to the program. At lunch that day I heard someone at the next table say, "We must go now — it's time to hear them kill off Galbraith." It didn't prove to be quite that bad; there was even some supporting comment. The concept of countervailing power was allowed to pass into economics and in a small way into public instruction. The book has been continuously in print ever since — as I say, a matter of almost fifty years.

*   *   *   *

O N THE NIGHT of November 2, 1907, J. P. Morgan the elder played solitaire in his library while panic gripped Wall Street. Then, when the other bankers had divided up the cost of saving the tottering Trust Company of America, he presided at the signing of the agreement, authorized the purchase of the Tennessee Coal & Iron Company by the Steel Corporation to encourage the market, cleared the transaction with President Roosevelt and the panic was over. There, as legend has preserved and doubtless improved the story, was a man with power a self-respecting man could fear.

A mere two decades later, in the crash of 1929, it was evident that the Wall Street bankers were as helpless as everyone else. Their effort to check the collapse in the market in the autumn of that year is now recalled as an amusing anecdote; the heads of the New York Stock Exchange and the National City Bank fell into the toils of the law and the first went to prison; the son of the Great Morgan went to a congressional hearing in Washington and acquired fame, not for his authority, but for his embarrassment when a circus midget was placed on his knee.

As the banker as a symbol of economic power passed into the shadows, his place was taken by the giant industrial corporation. The substitute was much more plausible. The association of power with the banker had always depended on the somewhat tenuous belief in a "money trust" — on the notion that the means for financing the initiation and expansion of business enterprises was concentrated in the hands of a few men. The ancestry of this idea was in Marx's doctrine of finance capital; it was not susceptible to statistical or other empirical verification, at least in the United States.

By contrast, the fact that a substantial proportion of all production was concentrated in the hands of a relatively small number of huge firms was readily verified. That three or four giant firms in an industry might exercise power analogous to that of a monopoly, and not different in consequences, was an idea that had come to have the most respectable of ancestry in classical economics. So, as the J. P. Morgan Company left the stage, it was replaced by the two hundred largest corporations — giant devils in company strength. Here was economic power identified by the greatest and most conservative tradition in economic theory. Here was power to control the prices the citizen paid, the wages he received, and which interposed the most formidable of obstacles of size and experience to the aspiring new firm. What more might it accomplish were it to turn its vast resources to corrupting politics and controlling access to public opinion?

Yet, as was so dramatically revealed to be the case with the omnipotence of the banker in 1929, there are considerable gaps between the myth and the fact. The comparative importance of a small number of great corporations in the American economy cannot be denied except by those who have a singular immunity to statistical evidence or a striking capacity to manipulate it. In principle, the American is controlled, livelihood and soul, by the large corporation; in practice, he or she seems not to be completely enslaved. Once again the danger is in the future; the present seems still tolerable. Once again there may be lessons from the present which, if learned, will save us in the future.

As with social efficiency and its neglect of technical dynamics, the paradox of the unexercised power of the large corporation begins with an important oversight in the underlying economic theory. In the competitive model — the economy of many sellers, each with a small share of the total market — the restraint on the private exercise of economic power was provided by other firms on the same side of the market. It was the eagerness of competitors to sell, not the complaints of buyers, that saved the latter from spoliation. It was assumed, no doubt accurately, that the nineteenth-century textile manufacturer who overcharged for his product would promptly lose his market to another manufacturer who did not. If all manufacturers found themselves in a position where they could exploit a strong demand and mark up their prices accordingly, there would soon be an inflow of new competitors. The resulting increase in supply would bring prices and profits back to normal.

As with the seller who was tempted to use his economic power against the customer, so with the buyer who was tempted to use it against his labor or suppliers. The man who paid less than the prevailing wage would lose his labor force to those who paid the worker his full (marginal) contribution to the earnings of the firm. In all cases the incentive to socially desirable behavior was provided by the competitor. It was to the same side of the market — the restraint of sellers by other sellers and of buyers by other buyers, in other words to competition — that economists came to look for the self-regulatory mechanism of the economy.

They also came to look to competition exclusively, and in formal theory they still do. The notion that there might be another regulatory mechanism in the economy has been almost completely excluded from economic thought. Thus, with the widespread disappearance of competition in its classical form and its replacement by the small group of firms if not in overt, at least in conventional or tacit collusion, it was easy to suppose that since competition had disappeared, all effective restraint on private power had disappeared. Indeed, this conclusion was all but inevitable if no search was made for other restraints, and so complete was the preoccupation with competition that none was.

In fact, new restraints on private power did appear to replace competition. They were nurtured by the same process of concentration which impaired or destroyed competition. But they appeared not on the same side of the market but on the opposite side, not with competitors but with customers or suppliers. It will be convenient to have a name for this counterpart of competition and I shall call it *countervailing power.*[1]

To begin with a broad and somewhat too dogmatically stated proposition, private economic power is held in check by the countervailing power of those who are subject to it. The first begets the second. The long trend toward concentration of industrial enterprise in the hands of a relatively few firms has brought into existence not only strong sellers, as economists have supposed, but also strong buyers, as they have failed to see. The two develop together, not in precise step but in such manner that there can be no doubt that the one is in response to the other.

The fact that a seller enjoys a measure of monopoly power, and is reaping a measure of monopoly return as a result, means that there is an inducement to those firms from whom he buys or those to whom he sells to develop the power with which they can defend themselves against exploitation. It means also that there is a reward to them in the form of a share of the gains of their opponents' market power if they are able to do so. In this way the existence of market power creates an incentive to the organization of another position of power that neutralizes it.

The contention I am here making is a formidable one. It comes to this: competition, which, at least since the time of Adam Smith, has been viewed as the autonomous regulator of economic activity and as the only available regulatory mechanism apart from the state, has, in fact, been superseded. Not entirely, to be sure. I should like to be explicit on this point. Competition still plays a role. There are still important markets where the power of the firm as, say, a seller is checked or circumscribed by those who provide a similar or a substitute product or service. This, in the broadest sense that can be meaningful, is the meaning of competition. The role of the buyer on the other side of such markets is essentially a passive one. It consists in looking for, perhaps asking for, and responding to the best bargain. The active restraint is provided by the competitor who offers, or threatens to offer, a better bargain. However, this is not the only or even the typical restraint on the exercise of economic power. In the typical modern market of few sellers, the active restraint is provided not by competitors but from the other side of the market by strong buyers. Given the convention against price competition, it is the role of the competitor that becomes passive in these markets.

It was always one of the basic presuppositions of competition that market power exercised in its absence would invite the competitors who would eliminate such exercise of power. The profits of a monopoly position inspired competitors to try for a share. In other words, competition was regarded as a *self-generating* regulatory force. The doubt whether this was in fact so after a market had been pre-empted by a few large sellers, after entry of new firms had become difficult and after existing firms had accepted a convention against price competition, was what destroyed the faith in competition as a regulatory mechanism. Countervailing power is also a self-generating force, and this is a matter of great importance. Something, although not very much, could be claimed for the regulatory role of the strong buyer in relation to the market power of sellers, did it happen that, as an accident of economic development, such strong buyers were frequently juxtaposed to strong sellers. However, the tendency of power to be organized in response to a given position of power is the vital characteristic of the phenomenon I am here identifying. As noted, power on one side of a market creates both the need for, and the prospect of reward to, the exercise of countervailing power from the other side.[2] This means that, as a common rule, we can rely on countervailing power to appear as a curb on economic power. There are also, it should be added, circumstances in which it does not appear or is effectively prevented from appearing. To these I shall return. For some reason, critics of the theory have seized with particular avidity on these exceptions to deny the existence of the phenomenon itself. It is plain that by a similar line of argument one could deny the existence of competition by finding one monopoly.

In the market of small numbers or oligopoly, the practical barriers to entry and the convention against price competition have eliminated the self-generating capacity of competition. The self-generating tendency of countervailing power, by contrast, is readily assimilated to the common sense of the situation, and its existence, once we have learned to look for it, is readily subject to empirical observation.

Market power can be exercised by strong buyers against weak sellers as well as by strong sellers against weak buyers. In the competitive model, competition acted as a restraint on both kinds of exercise of power. This is also the case with countervailing power. In turning to its practical manifestations, it will be convenient, in fact, to begin with a case where it is exercised by weak sellers against strong buyers.

III

The operation of countervailing power is to be seen with the greatest clarity in the labor market where it is also most fully developed. Because of his comparative immobility, the individual worker has long been highly vulnerable to private economic power. The customer of any particular steel mill, at the turn of the century, could always take himself elsewhere if he felt he (there were few women) was being overcharged. Or he could exercise his sovereign privilege of not buying steel at all. The worker had no comparable freedom if he felt he was being underpaid. Normally he could not move and he had to have work. Not often has the power of one man over another been used more callously than in the American labor market after the rise of the large corporation. As late as the early twenties, the steel industry worked a twelve-hour day and seventy-two-hour week with an incredible twenty-four-hour stint every fortnight when the shift changed.

No such power is exercised today and for the reason that its earlier exercise stimulated the counteraction that brought it to an end. In the ultimate sense it was the power of the steel industry, not the organizing abilities of John L. Lewis and Philip Murray, that in years long past brought the United Steel Workers into being. The economic power that the worker faced in the sale of his labor — the competition of many sellers dealing with few buyers — made it necessary that he organize for his own protection. There were rewards to the power of the steel companies in which, when he had successfully developed countervailing power, he could share.

As a general though not invariable rule one finds the strongest unions in the United States where markets are served by strong corporations, those in the automobile, steel, electrical, rubber, farm-machinery and nonferrous-metal-mining and smelting industries. Not only has the strength of the corporations in these industries made it necessary for workers to develop the protection of countervailing power; it has provided unions with the opportunity for getting something more as well. If successful, they could share in the fruits of the corporation's market power. By contrast, there has not been a single union of any consequence in American agriculture, the country's closest approach to the competitive model. The reason lies not in the difficulties in organization; these are considerable, but greater difficulties in organization have been overcome. The reason is that the farmer has not possessed any power over his labor force and has not had any rewards from market power which it was worth the while of a union to seek. As an interesting verification of the point, in California the large farmers have had considerable power vis-à-vis their labor force. Almost uniquely in the United States, that state has been marked by persistent attempts at organization by farm workers.

Elsewhere in industries which approach the competition of the model one typically finds weaker or less comprehensive unions. The textile industry,[3] boot and shoe manufacture, lumbering and other forest industries in most parts of the country, and smaller wholesale and retail enterprises, are all cases in point. I do not, of course, advance the theory of countervailing power as a monolithic explanation of trade-union organization. No such complex social phenomenon is likely to have any single, simple explanation. American trade unions developed in the face of the implacable hostility, not alone of employers, but often of the community as well. In this environment organization of the skilled crafts was much easier than the average, which undoubtedly explains the earlier appearance of durable unions here. In the modern bituminous-coal-mining and more clearly in the clothing industries, unions have another explanation. They have emerged as a supplement to the weak market position of the operators and manufacturers. They have assumed price- and market-regulating functions that are the normal functions of managements, and on which the latter, because of the competitive character of the industry, have been forced to default. Nevertheless, as an explanation of the incidence of trade-union strength in the American economy, the theory of countervailing power clearly fits the broad contours of experience. There is, I venture, no other so satisfactory explanation of labor organization in the modern capitalist community and none which so sensibly integrates the union into the theory of that society.

IV

As observed, the labor market serves admirably to illustrate the incentives to the development of countervailing power, and it is of great importance in this market. However, such development in response to positions of market power is pervasive in the economy. As a regulatory device, one of its most important manifestations is in the relation of the large retailer to the firms from which it buys. The way in which countervailing power operates in these markets is worth examining in some detail.

One of the seemingly harmless simplifications of formal economic theory has been the assumption that producers of consumers' goods sell their products directly to consumers. All business units are held, for this reason, to have broadly parallel interests. Each buys labor and materials, combines them and passes the resulting product along to the public at prices that, over some period of time, maximize returns. It is recognized that this is, indeed, a simplification; courses in marketing in the universities deal with what is excluded by this assumption. Yet it has long been supposed that the assumption does no appreciable violence to reality.

Did the real world correspond to the assumed one, the lot of the consumer would be an unhappy one. In fact, goods pass to consumers by way of retailers and other intermediaries, and this is a circumstance of first importance. Retailers are required by their situation to develop countervailing power on the consumer's behalf.

As has been frequently noted, retailing remains one of the industries to which entry is characteristically free. It takes small capital and no very rare talent to set up as a seller of goods. Through history there has always been an ample supply of men with both money and ability and with access to something to sell. The small man can provide convenience and intimacy of service and can give an attention to detail, all of which allow him to coexist with larger competitors.

The advantage of the larger competitor ordinarily lies in its lower prices. It lives constantly under the threat of an erosion of its business by the more rapid growth of rivals and by the appearance of new firms. This loss of volume, in turn, destroys the chance for the lower costs and lower prices on which the firm depends. This means that the larger retailer is extraordinarily sensitive to higher prices charged by its suppliers. It means also that it is strongly rewarded if it can develop the market power which permits it to force lower prices.

The opportunity to exercise such power exists only when the suppliers are enjoying something that can be taken away, i.e., when they are enjoying the fruits of market power from which they can be separated. Thus, as in the labor market, we find the mass retailer, from a position across the market, with both a protective and a profit incentive to develop countervailing power when the firm with which it is doing business is in possession of market power. Critics have suggested that these are possibly important but certainly disparate phenomena. This may be so, but only if all similarity between social phenomena be denied. In the present instance the market context is the same. The motivating incentives are identical. The fact that there are characteristics in common has been what has caused people to call competition competition when they encountered it, say, in agriculture and then again in the laundry business.

Countervailing power in the retail business is identified with the large and powerful retail enterprises. Its practical manifestation over the last half-century has been the rise of the food chains, the variety chains, the mail-order houses (now graduated into chain stores), the department-store chains and the cooperative buying organizations of the surviving independent department and food stores.

The buyers of all the great retail firms deal directly with the manufacturer, and there are few of the latter who, in setting prices, do not have to reckon with the attitude and reaction of their powerful customers. The retail buyers have a variety of weapons at their disposal to use against the market power of their suppliers. Their ultimate sanction is to develop their own source of supply as the food chains, Sears and many others have extensively done. They can also concentrate their entire patronage on a single supplier and, in return for a lower price, give him security in his volume and relieve him of selling and advertising costs. This policy has been widely followed, and there have also been numerous complaints of the leverage it gives the retailer on his source of supply.

The more commonplace but more important tactic in the exercise of countervailing power consists merely in keeping the seller in a state of uncertainty as to the intentions of a buyer who is indispensable to him. The larger of the retail buying organizations place orders around which the production schedules and occasionally the investment of even the largest manufacturers become organized. A shift in this custom imposes prompt and heavy loss. The threat or even the fear of this sanction is enough to cause the supplier to surrender some or all of the rewards of its market power. It must frequently, in addition, make a partial surrender to less potent buyers if it is not to be more than ever in the power of its large customers. It will be clear that in this operation there are rare opportunities for playing one supplier off against another.

A measure of the importance which large retailing organizations attach to the deployment of their countervailing power is the prestige they accord to their buyers. These men (and some women) are the key employees of the modern large retail organization; they are highly paid and they are among the most intelligent and resourceful people to be found anywhere in business. In the everyday course of business, they may be considerably better known and command rather more respect than the salesmen from whom they buy. This is a not unimportant index of the power they wield.

There are producers of consumers' goods who have protected themselves from the exercise of countervailing power. Some, like those in the automobile and the oil industries, have done so by integrating their distribution through to the consumer — a strategy which attests to the importance of the use of countervailing power by retailers. Others have found it possible to maintain dominance over an organization of small and dependent and therefore fairly powerless dealers.

v

There is an old saying, or should be, that it is a wise economist who recognizes the scope of his own generalizations. It is now time to consider the limits in place and time on the operations of countervailing power. A study of the instances where countervailing power fails to function is not without advantage in showing its achievements in the decisively important areas where it does operate. Some industries, because they are integrated through to the consumer or because their product passes through a dependent dealer organization, have not been faced with countervailing power. There are a few cases where a very strong market position has proven impregnable even against the attacks of strong buyers. And there are cases where the dangers from countervailing power have apparently been recognized and where it has been successfully resisted.

An example of successful resistance to countervailing power is the residential-building industry. No segment of American capitalism evokes less pride. Yet anyone approaching the industry with the preconceptions of competition in mind is unlikely to see very accurately the reasons for its shortcomings. There are many thousands of individual firms in the business of building houses. Nearly all are small. The members of the industry oppose little market power to the would-be house owner. Except in times of extremely high building activity there is aggressive competition for business.

The industry does show many detailed manifestations of guild restraint. Builders are frequently in alliance with each other, unions and local politicians to protect prices and wages and to maintain established building traditions. These derelictions have been seized upon avidly by the critics of the industry. Since they represent its major departure from the competitive model, they have been assumed to be the cause of the poor performance of the housing industry. It has long been an article of faith with liberals that if competition could be brought to the housing business, all would be well.

In fact, were all restraint and collusion swept away — were there full and free competition in bidding, no restrictive building codes, no collusion with union leaders or local politicians to enhance prices — it seems improbable that the price of new houses would be much changed and the satisfaction of customers with what they get for what they pay much enhanced. The reason is that the typical builder would still be a small and powerless figure buying his building materials in small quantities at high cost from suppliers with effective market power and facing in this case essentially the same problem vis-à-vis the unions as sellers of labor. It is these factors which, very largely, determine the cost of the house.

VI

The development of countervailing power requires a certain minimum opportunity and capacity for organization, corporate or otherwise. If the large retail buying organizations had not developed the countervailing power which they have used by proxy on behalf of the individual consumer, consumers would have been faced with the need to organize the equivalent of the retailer's power. This would have been a formidable task, but it has been accomplished in

Scandinavia where the consumers' cooperative, instead of the chain store, is the dominant instrument of countervailing power in consumers' goods markets. There has been a similar though less comprehensive development in England and Scotland. In the Scandinavian countries the cooperatives have long been regarded explicitly as instruments for bringing power to bear on the cartels; i.e., for exercise of countervailing power. This is readily conceded by many who have the greatest difficulty in seeing private mass buyers in the same role. But the fact that consumer cooperatives are not of any great importance in the United States is to be explained, not by any inherent incapacity of Americans for such organization, but because the chain stores pre-empted the gains of countervailing power first. The counterpart of the Swedish Kooperative Forbundet or the British Co-operative Wholesale Societies has not appeared in the United States simply because it could not compete with the large food chains. The meaning of this, which incidentally has been lost on devotees of the theology of cooperation, is that the chain stores are approximately as efficient in the exercise of countervailing power as a cooperative would be. In parts of the American economy where proprietary mass buyers have not made their appearance, notably in the purchase of farm supplies, individuals (who are also individualists) have shown as much capacity to organize as the Scandinavians and the British and have similarly obtained the protection and rewards of countervailing power.

VII

I come now to a major limitation on the operation of countervailing power — a matter of much importance in our time. Countervailing power is not exercised uniformly under all conditions of demand. It does not function at all as a restraint on market power when there is inflation or inflationary pressure on markets.

Because the competitive model, in association with Say's Law, was assumed to find its equilibrium at or near full employment levels, economists for a long time were little inclined to inquire whether markets in general, or competition in particular, might behave differently at different levels of economic activity, i.e., whether they might behave differently in prosperity and in depression. In any case, the conventional division of labor in economics has assigned to one group of scholars the task of examining markets and competitive behavior, to another a consideration of the causes of fluctuations in the economy. The two fields of exploration are even today separated by watertight bulkheads or, less metaphorically, by professorial division of labor and course requirements. Those who have taught and written on market behavior have assumed a condition of general stability in the economy in which sellers were eager for buyers. To the extent, as on occasion in recent years, that they have had to do their teaching or thinking in a time of inflation — in a time when, as the result of strong demand, eager buyers were besieging reluctant sellers — they have dismissed the circumstance as abnormal. They have drawn their classroom and textbook illustrations from the last period of deflation, severe or mild.

So long as competition was assumed to be the basic regulatory force in the economy, these simplifications, although they led to some error, were not too serious. There is a broad continuity in competitive behavior from conditions of weak demand to conditions of strong. At any given moment there is a going price in competitive markets that reflects the current equilibrium of supply-and-demand relationships. Even though demand is strong and prices are high and rising, the seller who prices above the going or equilibrium level is punished by the loss of his customers. The buyer still has an incentive to look for the lowest price he can find. Thus market behavior is not fundamentally different from the way it is when demand is low and prices are falling.

There are, by contrast, differences of considerable importance in market behavior between conditions of insufficient and excessive demand when there is oligopoly, i.e., when the market has only a small number of sellers. The convention against price competition, when small numbers of sellers share a market, is obviously not very difficult to maintain if all can sell all they produce and none is subject to the temptation to cut prices. Devices like price leadership, open book pricing and the basing-point system which facilitate observance of the convention all work well because they are under little strain. Thus the basing-point system, by making known or easily calculable the approved prices at every possible point of delivery in the country, provided protection against accidental or surreptitious price-cutting. Such protection is not necessary when there is no temptation to cut prices. By an interesting paradox, when the basing-point system was attacked by the government in the late depression years it was of great consequence to the steel, cement and other industries that employed it. When, after the deliberate processes of the law, the system was finally abolished by the courts in April 1948, the consequences for the industries in question were rather slight. The steel and cement companies were then straining to meet demand that was in excess of their capacity. They were under no temptation to cut prices and thus had no current reason to regret the passing of the basing-point system.

These differences in market behavior under conditions of strong and of weak demand are important, and there are serious grounds for criticizing their neglect — or rather the assumption that there is normally a shortage of buyers — in the conventional market analysis. However, the effect of changes in demand on market behavior becomes of really profound significance only when the role of countervailing power is recognized.

Countervailing power, as noted earlier, is organized either by buyers or by sellers in response to a stronger position across the market. But strength, i.e., relative strength, obviously depends on the state of aggregate demand. When demand is strong, especially when it is at inflationary levels, the bargaining position of poorly organized or even of unorganized workers is favorable. When demand is weak, the bargaining position of the strongest union deteriorates to some extent. The situation is similar where countervailing power is exercised by a buyer. A scarcity of demand is a prerequisite to his bringing power to bear on suppliers. If buyers are plentiful — if supply is small in relation to current demand — sellers are under no compulsion to surrender to the bargaining power of any particular customer. They have alternatives.[4]

NOTES

1. I have been tempted to coin a new word for this which would have the same convenience as the term "competition," and had I done so, my choice would have been "countervailence." However, the phrase "countervailing power" is more descriptive and does not have the raw sound of a newly fabricated word.

2. This has been one of the reasons I have rejected the terminology of bilateral monopoly in characterizing this phenomenon. As bilateral monopoly is treated in economic literature, it is an adventitious occurrence. This, obviously, misses the point, and it is one of the reasons that the investigations of bilateral monopoly, which one would have thought might have been an avenue to the regulatory mechanisms here isolated, have, in fact, been a blind alley. However, this line of investigation has also been sterilized by the confining formality of the assumptions of monopolistic and (more rarely) oligopolistic motivation and behavior with which it has been approached. (Cf. for example, William H. Nicholls, *Imperfect Competition within Agricultural Industries,* Ames, Iowa: 1941, pp. 58 ff.) As noted later, oligopoly facilitates the exercise of countervailing market power by enabling the strong buyer to play one seller off against another.

3. It is important, as I have been reminded by the objections of English friends, to bear in mind that market power must always be viewed in relative terms. In the last century unions developed in the British textile industry, and this industry, in turn, conformed broadly to the competition of the model. However, as buyers of labor the mill proprietors enjoyed a far stronger market position, the result of their greater resources and respect for their group interest, than did the individual workers.

4. The everyday business distinction between a "buyers'" and a "sellers'" market and the frequency of its use reflect the importance which participants in actual markets attach to the ebb and flow of countervailing power. That this distinction has no standing in formal economics follows from the fact that countervailing power has not been recognized by economists. As frequently happens, practical men have devised a terminology to denote a phenomenon of great significance to themselves but which, since it has not been assimilated to economic theory, has never appeared in the textbooks. The concept of the "break-even point," generally employed by businessmen but largely ignored in economic theory, is another case in point.

The Concept of the
Conventional Wisdom

[*from* The Affluent Society]

This article originally appeared in The Affluent Society, *by many considered my most influential book, and certainly the one with the widest audience. It was published in 1958 in the United States and thereafter in a large number of other countries. For many months it was high on the American bestseller list.*

There were occasional mishaps in its reception. In the spring of 1958, just after publication, Catherine Galbraith and I set out on a long journey to Latin America; this took us down the west coast to Ecuador, Peru and Chile, across to Argentina and back up along the east. When we reached Montevideo, where I was giving a major lecture, word had come of the intense discussion of my work back home. Since the Montevideo paper was to put my photograph on the front page, the editors had telephoned to get some details on my new distinction, but unfortunately two words with a similar sound got confused: I was billed not as a leading economist but as a leading American Communist. For better or for worse, my lecture was well attended.

In the following weeks, months, even years, the book received much attention in the United States and variously around the world. This early chapter was designed to set the groundwork for a challenge to the accepted belief. Economics and social thought generally could pursue the truth, but there was no question that the latter could be heavily influenced by what it was convenient or simply traditional to believe. It was my purpose or, in any case, my hope to bring discussion, academic discussion in particular, closer to the reality. The resistance came from what I called the Conventional Wisdom. To my surprise and, no one should doubt, my pleasure, the term entered the language. It has acquired a negative, slightly insulting connotation and is sometimes used by people with views deeply adverse to mine who are unaware of its origin. Few matters give me more satisfaction.

What follows is my characterization of the Conventional Wisdom. I should add that the selection of that name owes more than a little to Harvard colleagues on whom I tried out several possibilities.

*   *   *   *

THE FIRST REQUIREMENT for an understanding of contemporary economic and social life is a clear view of the relation between events and the ideas which interpret them, for each of the latter has an existence of its own and, much as it may seem a contradiction in terms, each is capable for a considerable period of pursuing an independent course.

The reason is not difficult to discover. Economic, like other social, life does not conform to a simple and coherent pattern. On the contrary, it often seems incoherent, inchoate and intellectually frustrating. But one must have an explanation or interpretation of economic behavior. Neither man's curiosity nor his inherent ego allows him to remain contentedly oblivious to anything that is so close to his life.

Because economic and social phenomena are so forbidding, or at least so seem, and because they yield few hard tests of what exists and what does not, they afford to the individual a luxury not given by physical phenomena. Within a considerable range, he is permitted to believe what he pleases. He may hold whatever view of this world he finds most agreeable or otherwise to his taste.

As a consequence, in the interpretation of all social life, there is a persistent and never-ending competition between what is right and what is merely acceptable. In this competition, while a strategic advantage lies with what exists, all tactical advantage is with the acceptable. Audiences of all kinds most applaud what they like best. And in social comment, the test of audience approval, far more than the test of truth, comes to influence comment. The speaker or writer who addresses his audience with the proclaimed intent of telling the hard, shocking facts invariably goes on to expound what the audience most wants to hear.

Just as truth ultimately serves to create a consensus, so in the short run does acceptability. Ideas come to be organized around what the community as a whole or particular audiences find acceptable. And as the laboratory worker devotes himself to discovering scientific verities, so the ghost writer and the public relations man concern themselves with identifying the acceptable. If their clients are rewarded with applause, these artisans are deemed qualified in their craft. If not, they have failed. By sampling audience reaction in advance, or by pretesting speeches, articles and other communications, the risk of failure can now be greatly minimized.

Numerous factors contribute to the acceptability of ideas. To a very large extent, of course, we associate truth with convenience — with what most closely accords with self-interest and personal well-being or promises best to avoid awkward effort or unwelcome dislocation of life. We also find highly acceptable what contributes most to self-esteem. Speakers before the United States Chamber of Commerce rarely denigrate the businessman as an economic force. Those who appear before the AFL-CIO are prone to identify social progress with a strong trade union movement. But perhaps most important of all, people most approve of what they best understand. As just noted, economic and social behavior are complex, and to comprehend their character is mentally tiring. Therefore we adhere, as though to a raft, to those ideas which represent our understanding. This is a prime manifestation of vested interest. For a vested interest in understanding is more preciously guarded than any other treasure. It is why men react, not infrequently with something akin to religious passion, to the defense of what they have so laboriously learned. Familiarity may breed contempt in some areas of human behavior, but in the field of social ideas it is the touchstone of acceptability.

Because familiarity is such an important test of acceptability, the acceptable ideas have great stability. They are highly predictable. It will be convenient to have a name for the ideas which are esteemed at any time for their acceptability, and it should be a term that emphasizes this predictability. I shall refer to these ideas henceforth as the Conventional Wisdom.

II

The conventional wisdom is not the property of any political group. On a great many modern social issues, as we shall see in the course of this essay, the consensus is exceedingly broad. Nothing much divides those who are liberals by common political designation from those who are conservatives. The test of what is acceptable is much the same for both. On some questions, however, ideas must be accommodated to the political preferences of the particular audience. The tendency to make this adjustment, either deliberately or more often unconsciously, is not greatly different for different political groups. The conservative is led by disposition, not unmixed with pecuniary self-interest, to adhere to the familiar and the established. These underlie his test of acceptability. But the liberal brings moral fervor and passion, even a sense of righteousness, to the ideas with which *he* is most familiar. While the ideas he cherishes are different from those of the conservative, he will be no less emphatic in making familiarity a test of acceptability. Deviation in the form of originality is condemned as faithlessness or backsliding. A "good" liberal or a "tried and true" liberal or a "true blue" liberal is one who is adequately predictable. This means that he forswears any serious striving toward originality. In both the United States and Britain, in recent times, American liberals and their British counterparts on the left have proclaimed themselves in search of new ideas. To proclaim the need for new ideas has served, in some measure, as a substitute for them. The politician who unwisely takes this proclaimed need seriously and urges something new will often find himself in serious trouble.

We may, as necessary, speak of the conventional wisdom of conservatives or the conventional wisdom of liberals.

The conventional wisdom is also articulated on all levels of sophistication. At the highest levels of social science scholarship, some novelty of formulation or statement is not resisted. On the contrary, considerable store is set by the device of putting an old truth in a new form, and minor heresies are much cherished. The very vigor of minor debate makes it possible to exclude as irrelevant, and without seeming to be unscientific or parochial, any challenge to the framework itself. Moreover, with time and aided by the debate, the accepted ideas become increasingly elaborate. They have a large literature, even a mystique. The defenders are able to say that the challengers of the conventional wisdom have not mastered their intricacies. Indeed, these ideas can be appreciated only by a stable, orthodox and patient man — in brief, by someone who closely resembles the man of conventional wisdom. The conventional wisdom having been made more or less identical with sound scholarship, its position is virtually impregnable. The skeptic is disqualified by his very tendency to go brashly from the old to the new. Were he a sound scholar, he would remain with the conventional wisdom.

At the same time, in the higher levels of the conventional wisdom, originality remains highly acceptable in the abstract. Here again the conventional wisdom makes vigorous advocacy of originality a substitute for originality itself.

III

As noted, the hallmark of the conventional wisdom is acceptability. It has the approval of those to whom it is addressed. There are many reasons why people like to hear articulated that which they approve. It serves the ego: the individual has the satisfaction of knowing that other and more famous people share his conclusions. To hear what he believes is also a source of reassurance. The individual knows that he is supported in his thoughts — that he has not been left behind and alone. Further, to hear what one approves serves the evangelizing instinct. It means that others are also hearing and are thereby in the process of being persuaded.

In some measure, the articulation of the conventional wisdom is a religious rite. It is an act of affirmation like reading aloud from the Scriptures or going to church. The business executive listening to a luncheon address on the immutable virtues of free enterprise is already persuaded, and so are his fellow listeners, and all are secure in their convictions. Indeed, although a display of rapt attention is required, the executive may not feel it necessary to listen. But he does placate the gods by participating in the ritual. Having been present, maintained attention and having applauded, he can depart feeling that the economic system is a little more secure. Scholars gather in scholarly assemblages to hear in elegant statement what all have heard before. Again, it is not a negligible rite, for its purpose is not to convey knowledge but to beatify learning and the learned.

With so extensive a demand, it follows that a very large part of our social comment — and nearly all that is well regarded — is devoted at any time to articulating the conventional wisdom. To some extent, this has been professionalized. Individuals, most notably the great television and radio commentators, make a profession of knowing and saying with elegance and unction what their audience will find most acceptable. But, in general, the articulation of the conventional wisdom is a prerogative of academic, public or business position. Thus any individual, on being elected president of a college or university, automatically wins the right to enunciate the conventional wisdom. It is one of the rewards of high academic rank, although such rank itself is a reward for expounding the conventional wisdom at a properly sophisticated level.

The high public official is expected, and indeed is to some extent required, to expound the conventional wisdom. His, in many respects, is the purest case. Before assuming office, he ordinarily commands little attention. But on taking up his position, he is immediately assumed to be gifted with deep insights. He does not, except in the rarest instances, write his own speeches or articles, and these are

planned, drafted and scrupulously examined to ensure their acceptability. The application of any other test, e.g., their effectiveness as a
simple description of the economic or political reality, would be regarded as eccentric in the extreme.

Finally, the expounding of the conventional wisdom is the prerogative of business success. The head of almost any large corporation — General Motors, General Electric, IBM — is entitled to do so.
And he is privileged to speak not only on business policy and economics but also on the role of government in the society, the foundations of foreign policy and the nature of a liberal education. In recent years, it has been urged that to expound the conventional
wisdom is not only the privilege but also the obligation of the businessman. "I am convinced that businessmen must write as well as
speak, in order that we may bring to people everywhere the exciting
and confident message of our faith in the free enterprise way of
life . . . What a change would come in this struggle for men's minds
if suddenly there could pour out from the world of American business a torrent of intelligent, forward-looking thinking."[1]

IV

The enemy of the conventional wisdom is not ideas but the march
of events. As I have noted, the conventional wisdom accommodates
itself not to the world that it is meant to interpret but to the audience's view of the world. Since the latter remains with the comfortable and the familiar while the world moves on, the conventional
wisdom is always in danger of obsolescence. This is not immediately
fatal. The fatal blow to the conventional wisdom comes when the
conventional ideas fail signally to deal with some contingency to
which obsolescence has made them palpably inapplicable. This,
sooner or later, must be the fate of ideas which have lost their relation to the world. At this stage, the irrelevance will often be drama-
tized by some individual. To him will accrue the credit for over-
throwing the conventional wisdom and for installing the new ideas.
In fact, he will have only crystallized in words what the events have
made clear, although this function is not a minor one. Meanwhile,

like the Old Guard, the conventional wisdom dies but does not surrender. Society with intransigent cruelty may transfer its exponents from the category of wise man to that of old fogy or even stuffed shirt.

This sequence can be illustrated from scores of examples, ancient and modern. For decades prior to 1776, men had been catching the vision of the liberal state. Traders and merchants in England, in the adjacent Low Countries and in the American colonies had already learned that they were served best by a minimum of government restriction rather than, as in the conventional wisdom, by a maximum of government guidance and protection. It had become plain, in turn, that liberal trade and commerce, not the accumulation of bullion, as the conventional wisdom held, was the modern source of national power. Men of irresponsible originality had made the point. Voltaire had observed that "it is only because the English have become merchants and traders that London has surpassed Paris in extent and in the number of its citizens; that the English can place 200 warships on the sea and subsidize allies."[2] These views were finally crystallized by Adam Smith in the year of American independence. *The Wealth of Nations,* however, continued to be viewed with discontent and alarm by the men of the older wisdom. In the funeral elegy for Alexander Hamilton in 1804, James Kent complimented his deceased friend on having resisted the "fuzzy philosophy" of Smith. For another generation or more, or in all western countries, there would be solemn warnings that the notion of a liberal society was a reckless idea.

Through the nineteenth century, liberalism in its classical meaning having become the conventional wisdom, there were solemn warnings of the irreparable damage that would be done by the Factory Acts, trade unions, social insurance and other social legislation. Liberalism was a fabric which could not be raveled without being rent. Yet the desire for protection and security and some measure of equality in bargaining power would not down. In the end, it became a fact with which the conventional wisdom could not deal. The Webbs, Lloyd George, La Follette, Roosevelt, Beveridge and others crystallized the acceptance of the new fact. The result is what we call the welfare state. The conventional wisdom now holds that these measures softened and civilized capitalism and made it tenable. There have never ceased to be warnings that the break with classical liberalism was fatal.

Another interesting instance of the impact of circumstance on the conventional wisdom was that of the balanced budget in times of depression. Almost from the beginning of organized government, the balanced budget or its equivalent has been the *sine qua non* of sound and sensible management of the public purse. The spendthrift tendencies of princes and republics alike were curbed by the rule that they must unfailingly take in as much money as they paid out. The consequences of violating this rule had always been unhappy in the long run and not infrequently in the short. Anciently it was the practice of princes to cover the deficit by clipping or debasing the coins and spending the metal so saved. The result invariably was to raise prices and lower national self-esteem. In modern times, the issuance of paper money or government borrowing from the banks had led to the same results. In consequence, the conventional wisdom had emphasized strongly the importance of an annually balanced budget.

But meanwhile the underlying reality had gradually changed. The rule requiring a balanced budget was designed for governments that were inherently or recurrently irresponsible on fiscal matters. Until the last century, there had been no other. Then in the United States, England and the British Commonwealth and Europe, governments began to calculate the fiscal consequences of their actions. Safety no longer depended on confining them within arbitrary rules.

At about the same time, there appeared the phenomenon of the truly devastating depression. In such a depression, men, plant and materials were unemployed en masse; the extra demand from the extra spending induced by a deficit — the counterpart of the extra metal made available from the clipped coinage — did not raise prices uniquely. Rather, it mostly returned idle men and plant to work. The effect, as it were, was horizontally on production rather than vertically on prices. And such price increases as did occur were far from being an unmitigated misfortune; on the contrary, they retrieved a previous, painful decline.

The conventional wisdom continued to emphasize the balanced budget. Audiences continued to respond to the warnings of the disaster which would befall were this rule not respected. The shattering circumstance was the Great Depression. This led in the United States to a severe reduction in the revenues of the federal government; it also brought pressure for a variety of relief and welfare expenditures. A balanced budget meant increasing tax rates and reducing public expenditure. Viewed in retrospect, it would be hard to imagine a better design for reducing both the private and the public demand for goods, aggravating deflation, increasing unemployment and adding to the general suffering. In the conventional wisdom, nonetheless, the balanced budget remained of paramount importance. President Hoover in the early thirties called it an "absolute necessity," "the most essential factor to economic recovery," "the imperative and immediate step," "indispensable," "the first necessity of the Nation," and "the foundation of all public and private financial stability."[3] Economists and professional observers of public affairs agreed almost without exception. Almost everyone called upon for advice in the early years of the depression was impelled by the conventional wisdom to offer proposals designed to make things worse. The consensus embraced both liberals and conservatives. Franklin D. Roosevelt was elected in 1932 with a strong commitment to reduced expenditures and a balanced budget. In his speech accepting the Democratic nomination he said, "Revenue must cover expenditures by one means or another. Any government, like any family, can for a year spend a little more than it earns. But you and I know that a continuation of that habit means the poorhouse." One of the early acts of his administration was an economy drive which included a horizontal slash in public pay. Mr. Lewis W. Douglas, through a distinguished life a notable exemplar of the conventional wisdom, made the quest for a balanced budget into a personal crusade and ultimately broke with the administration on the issue.

In fact, circumstances had already triumphed over the conventional wisdom. By the second year of the Hoover administration, the budget was irretrievably out of balance. In the fiscal year ending in 1932, receipts were much less than half of spending. The budget was never balanced during the depression. But not until 1936 did both the necessities and advantages of this course begin to triumph in the field of ideas. In that year, John Maynard Keynes launched his formal assault in *The General Theory of Employment Interest and Money.* Thereafter, the conventional insistence on the balanced budget under all circumstances and at all levels of economic activity was in retreat, and Keynes was on his way to being the new fountainhead of conventional wisdom. By the very late sixties a Republican President would proclaim himself a Keynesian. It would be an article of conventional faith that the Keynesian remedies, when put in reverse, would be a cure for inflation, a faith that circumstances would soon undermine.

v

I will find frequent occasion to advert to the conventional wisdom — to the structure of ideas that is based on acceptability — and to those who articulate it. These references must not be thought to have a wholly invidious connotation. (The warning is necessary because, as noted, we set great ostensible store by intellectual innovation, though in fact we resist it. Hence, though we value the rigorous adherence to conventional ideas, we never acclaim it.) Few men are unuseful and the man of conventional wisdom is not. Every society must be protected from a too facile flow of thought. In the field of social comment, a great stream of intellectual novelties, if all were taken seriously, would be disastrous. Men would be swayed to this action or that; economic and political life would be erratic and rudderless. In the Communist countries, stability of ideas and social purpose is achieved by formal adherence to an officially proclaimed doctrine. Deviation is stigmatized as "incorrect." In our society, a similar stability is enforced far more informally by the conventional wisdom. Ideas need to be tested by their ability in combination with events to overcome inertia and resistance. This inertia and resistance the conventional wisdom provides.

Nor is it to be supposed that the man of conventional wisdom is an object of pity. Apart from his socially useful role, he has come to good terms with life. He can think of himself with justice as socially elect, for society, in fact, accords him the applause which his ideas are so arranged as to evoke. Secure in this applause, he is well armed against the annoyance of dissent. His bargain is to exchange a strong and even lofty position in the present for a weak one in the future. In the present, he is questioned with respect, if not at great length, by congressional committees; he walks near the head of the academic processions; he appears on symposia; he is a respected figure at the Council on Foreign Relations; he is hailed at testimonial banquets. He does risk being devastated by future hostile events, but by then he may be dead. Only posterity is unkind to the man of conventional wisdom, and all posterity does is bury him in a blanket of neglect. However, somewhat more serious issues are at stake.

VI

No society seems ever to have succumbed to boredom. Man has developed an obvious capacity for surviving the pompous reiteration of the commonplace. The conventional wisdom protects the community in social thought and action, but there are also grave drawbacks and even dangers in a system of thought which, by its very nature and design, avoids accommodation to circumstances until change is dramatically forced upon it. In large areas of economic affairs, the march of events — above all, the increase in our wealth and popular well-being — has again left the conventional wisdom sadly obsolete. It may have become inimical to our happiness. It has come to have a bearing on the larger questions of civilized survival. So while it would be much more pleasant (and also vastly more profitable) to articulate the conventional wisdom, I am here involved in the normally unfruitful effort of an attack upon it. I am not wholly barren of hope, for circumstances have been dealing the conventional wisdom a new series of heavy blows. It is only after such damage has been done, as we have seen, that ideas have their opportunity.

Keynes, in his most famous observation, noted that we are ruled by ideas and by very little else. In the immediate sense, this is true. And he was right in attributing importance to ideas as opposed to the simple influence of pecuniary vested interest. But the rule of ideas is only powerful in a world that does not change. Ideas are inherently conservative. They yield not to the attack of other ideas but, as I may note once more, to the massive onslaught of circumstance with which they cannot contend.

NOTES

1. Clarence B. Randall, *A Creed for Free Enterprise* (Boston: Atlantic–Little, Brown, 1952), pp. 3, 5.
2. "Tenth Philosophical Letter." Quoted by Henry Sée, *Modern Capitalism* (New York: Adelphi, 1928), p. 87.
3. Arthur M. Schlesinger, Jr., *The Crisis of the Old Order* (Boston: Houghton Mifflin, 1956), p. 232.

The Myth of Consumer Sovereignty

[*from* The Affluent Society]

My argument in this chapter of The Affluent Society *was one of the more controversial exercises of my life, for it challenged consumer sovereignty, a major professional truth of economics. Nothing had been more important in accepted economic belief than the notion that economic life is ultimately guided by the sovereign consumer. It is consumer choice that governs what is produced, that and changing technology; and in some measure technological change itself occurs in response to consumer need and in service to consumer satisfaction. I argue here that a determining factor in production — perhaps the determining factor — is, in fact, not consumer choice but, in substantial measure, producer manipulation of consumer response. Salesmanship, design and innovation are all utilized to attract and capture the consumer.*

In orthodox economic circles my thesis attracted a nearly universal objection. It was enthusiastically pointed out that the Ford Motor Company had at great expense developed the Edsel, which then didn't sell. I was called to a discussion in New York City attended overwhelmingly by advertising men who were given to unanimous denunciation of my views. In the end, however, circumstance, fact, had their effect: the established belief was undermined; perhaps it could even be said that consumer sovereignty was set aside as a dominant factor in the economic system. From my reading of the literature, including the textbooks, it no longer enjoys its old role as the center of truth in shaping the economy.

Some authors regret controversy; on a few occasions so have I. This was one of the instances where I much enjoyed it.

*   *   *   *

THE NOTION that wants do not become less urgent the more amply the individual is supplied is broadly repugnant to common sense. It is something to be believed only by those who wish to believe. Yet the conventional wisdom must be tackled on its own terrain. Intertemporal comparisons of an individual's state of mind do rest on technically vulnerable ground. Who can say for sure that the deprivation which afflicts him with hunger is more painful than the deprivation which afflicts him with envy of his neighbor's new car? In the time that has passed since he was poor, his soul may have become subject to a new and deeper searing. And where a society is concerned, comparisons between marginal satisfactions when it is poor and those when it is affluent will involve not only the same individual at different times but different individuals at different times. The scholar who wishes to believe that with increasing affluence there is no reduction in the urgency of desires and goods is not without points for debate. However plausible the case against him, it cannot be proven. In the defense of the conventional economic wisdom, this amounts almost to invulnerability.

However, there is a flaw in the case. If the individual's wants are to be urgent, they must be original with him. They cannot be urgent if they must be contrived for him. And, above all, they must not be contrived by the process of production by which they are satisfied. For this means that the whole case for the urgency of production, based on the urgency of wants, falls to the ground. One cannot defend production as satisfying wants if that production creates the wants.

Were it so that a man on arising each morning was assailed by demons which instilled in him a passion sometimes for silk shirts, sometimes for kitchenware, sometimes for chamber pots and sometimes for orange squash, there would be every reason to applaud the effort to find the goods, however odd, that quenched this flame. But should it be that his passion was the result of his first having cultivated the demons, and should it also be that his effort to allay it stirred the demons to ever greater and greater effort, there would be question as to how rational was his solution. Unless restrained by conventional attitudes, he might wonder if the solution lay with more goods or fewer demons.

So it is that if production creates the wants it seeks to satisfy, or if the wants emerge *pari passu* with the production, then the urgency of the wants can no longer be used to defend the urgency of the production. Production only fills a void that it has itself created.

II

The point is so central that it must be pressed. Consumer wants can have bizarre, frivolous or even immoral origins, and an admirable case can still be made for a society that seeks to satisfy them. But the case cannot stand if it is the process of satisfying wants that creates the wants. For then the individual who urges the importance of production to satisfy these wants is precisely in the position of the onlooker who applauds the efforts of the squirrel to keep abreast of the wheel that is propelled by its own efforts.

That wants are, in fact, the fruit of production will now be denied by few serious scholars. And a considerable number of economists, though not always in full knowledge of the implications, have conceded the point. Lord Keynes once observed that needs of "the second class," i.e., those that are the result of efforts to keep abreast or ahead of one's fellow being, "may indeed be insatiable; for the higher the general level, the higher still are they."[1] And emulation has always played a considerable role in the views of want creation of other economists. One man's consumption becomes his neighbor's wish. This already means that the process by which wants are satisfied is also the process by which wants are created. The more wants that are satisfied, the more new ones are born.

However, the argument has been carried farther. A leading modern theorist of consumer behavior, Professor James Duesenberry, has stated explicitly that "ours is a society in which one of the principal social goals is a higher standard of living . . . [This] has great significance for the theory of consumption . . . the desire to get superior goods takes on a life of its own. It provides a drive to higher expenditure which may even be stronger than that arising out of the needs which are supposed to be satisfied by that expenditure."[2] The implications of this view are impressive. The notion of independently established need now sinks into the background. Because the society sets great store by its ability to produce a high living standard, it evaluates people by the products they possess. The urge to consume is fathered by the value system which emphasizes the ability of the society to produce. The more that is produced, the more that must be owned in order to maintain the appropriate prestige. The latter is an important point, for, without going as far as Duesenberry in reducing goods to the role of symbols of prestige in the affluent society, it is plain that his argument fully implies that the production of goods creates the wants that the goods are presumed to satisfy.[3]

III

The even more direct link between production and wants is provided by the institutions of modern advertising and salesmanship. These cannot be reconciled with the notion of independently determined desires, for their central function is to create desires — to bring into being wants that previously did not exist.[4] This is accomplished by the producer of the goods or at his behest. A broad empirical relationship exists between what is spent on the production of consumer goods and what is spent in synthesizing the desires for that production. A new consumer product must be introduced with a suitable advertising campaign to arouse an interest in it. The path for an expansion of output must be paved by a suitable expansion in the advertising budget. Outlays for the manufacturing of a product are not more important in the strategy of modern business enterprise than outlays for the manufacturing of demand for the product. None of this is novel. All would be regarded as elementary by the most retarded student in the nation's most primitive school of business administration. The cost of this want formation is formidable. As early as 1987, total advertising expenditure in the United States — though, as noted, not all of it may be assigned to the synthesis of wants — amounted to approximately one hundred and ten billion dollars. The increase in previous years was by an estimated six billion dollars a year. Obviously, such outlays must be integrated with the theory of consumer demand. They are too big to be ignored.

But such integration means recognizing that wants are dependent on production. It accords to the producer the function both of making the goods and of making the desire for them. It recognizes that production, not only passively through emulation, but actively through advertising and related activities, creates the wants it seeks to satisfy.

The businessman and the lay reader will be puzzled over the emphasis which I give to a seemingly obvious point. The point is indeed obvious. But it is one which, to a singular degree, economists have resisted. They have sensed, as the layman does not, the damage to established ideas which lurks in these relationships. As a result, incredibly, they have closed their eyes (and ears) to the most obtrusive of all economic phenomena, namely, modern want creation.

This is not to say that the evidence affirming the dependence of wants on advertising has been entirely ignored. It is one reason why advertising has so long been regarded with such uneasiness by economists. Here is something which cannot be accommodated easily to existing theory. More pervious scholars have speculated on the urgency of desires which are so obviously the fruit of such expensively contrived campaigns for popular attention. Is a new breakfast cereal or detergent so much wanted if so much must be spent to compel in the consumer the sense of want? But there has been little tendency to go on to examine the implications of this for the theory of consumer demand and even less for the importance of production and productive efficiency. These have remained sacrosanct. More often, the uneasiness has been manifested in a general disapproval of advertising and advertising men, leading to the occasional suggestion that they shouldn't exist. Such suggestions have usually been ill received in the advertising business.

And so the notion of independently determined wants still survives. In the face of all the forces of modern salesmanship, it still rules, almost undefiled, in the textbooks. And it still remains the economist's mission — and on few matters is the pedagogy so firm — to seek the means for filling these wants. This being so, production remains of prime urgency. We have here, perhaps, the ultimate triumph of the conventional wisdom in its resistance to the evidence of the eyes. To equal it, one must imagine a humanitarian who was long ago persuaded of the grievous shortage of hospital facilities in the town. He continues to importune the passersby for money for more beds and refuses to notice that the town doctor is deftly knocking over pedestrians with his car to keep up the occupancy.

In unraveling the complex, we should always be careful not to overlook the obvious. The fact that wants can be synthesized by advertising, catalyzed by salesmanship and shaped by the discreet manipulations of the persuaders shows that they are not very urgent. A man who is hungry need never be told of his need for food. If he is inspired by his appetite, he is immune to the influence of the advertising agency. The latter is effective only with those who are so far removed from physical want that they do not already know what they want. Only in this state are men open to persuasion.

IV

The general conclusion of these pages is of such importance that it had perhaps best be put with some formality. As a society becomes increasingly affluent, wants are increasingly created by the process by which they are satisfied. This may operate passively. Increases in consumption, the counterpart of increases in production, act by suggestion or emulation to create wants. Expectation rises with attainment. Or producers may proceed actively to create wants through advertising and salesmanship. Wants thus come to depend on output. In technical terms, it can no longer be assumed that welfare is greater at an all-round higher level of production than at a lower one. It may be the same. The higher level of production has, merely, a higher level of want creation necessitating a higher level of want satisfaction. There will be frequent occasion to refer to the way wants depend on the process by which they are satisfied. It will be convenient to call it the Dependence Effect.

We may now contemplate briefly the conclusions to which this analysis has brought us.

Plainly, the theory of consumer demand is a peculiarly treacherous friend of the present goals of economics. At first glance, it seems to defend the continuing urgency of production and our preoccupation with it as a goal. The economist does not enter into the dubious moral arguments about the importance or virtue of the wants to be satisfied. He doesn't pretend to compare mental states of the same or different people at different times and to suggest that one is less urgent than another. The desire is there. That for him is sufficient. He sets about in a workmanlike way to satisfy desire, and accordingly, he sets the proper store by the production that does. Like woman's, his work is never done.

But this rationalization, handsomely though it seems to serve, turns destructively on those who advance it once it is conceded that wants are themselves both passively and deliberately the fruits of the process by which they are satisfied. Then the production of goods satisfies the wants that the consumption of these goods creates or that the producers of goods synthesize. Production induces more wants and the need for more production. So far, in a major tour de force, the implications have been ignored. But this obviously is a perilous solution. It cannot long survive discussion.

Among the many models of the good society, no one has urged the squirrel wheel. Moreover, the wheel is not one that revolves with perfect smoothness. Aside from its dubious cultural charm, there are serious structural weaknesses which may one day embarrass us. For the moment, however, it is sufficient to reflect on the difficult terrain we are traversing. Not the goods but the employment provided by their production is something by which we set major store. Now we find our concern for goods further undermined. It does not arise in spontaneous consumer need. Rather, the dependence effect means that it grows out of the process of production itself. If production is to increase, the wants must be effectively contrived. In the absence of the contrivance, the increase would not occur. This is not true of all goods, but that it is true of a substantial part is sufficient. It means that since the demand for this part would not exist were it not contrived, its utility or urgency, *ex* contrivance, is zero. If we regard this production as marginal, we may say that the marginal utility of present aggregate output, *ex* advertising and salesmanship, is zero. Clearly the attitudes and values which make production the central achievement of our society have some exceptionally twisted roots.

Perhaps the thing most evident of all is how new and varied become the problems we must ponder when we break the nexus with the work of Ricardo and face the economics of affluence of the world in which we live. It is easy to see why the conventional wisdom resists so stoutly such change. It is far, far better and much safer to have a firm anchor in nonsense than to put out on the troubled seas of thought.

NOTES

1. J. M. Keynes, "Economic Possibilities for Our Grandchildren," *Essays in Persuasion* (London: Macmillan, 1931), p. 365.
2. James S. Duesenberry, *Income, Saving and the Theory of Consumer Behavior* (Cambridge, Mass.: Harvard University Press, 1949), p. 28.
3. A more recent and definitive study of consumer demand has added even more support. Professors Houthakker and Taylor, in a statistical study of the determinants of demand, found that for most products price and income, the accepted determinants, were less important than past consumption of the product. This "psychological stock," as they called it, concedes the weakness of traditional theory; current demand cannot be explained without recourse to past consumption. Such demand nurtures the need for its own increase. H. S. Houthakker and L. D. Taylor, *Consumer Demand in the United States,* 2nd ed., enlarged (Cambridge, Mass.: Harvard University Press, 1970).
4. Advertising is not a simple phenomenon. It is also important in competitive strategy, and want creation is, ordinarily, a complementary re-

sult of efforts to shift the demand curve of the individual firm at the expense of others or (less importantly, I think) to change its shape by increasing the degree of product differentiation. Some of the failure of economists to identify advertising with want creation may be attributed to the undue attention that its use in purely competitive strategy has attracted. It should be noted, however, that the competitive manipulation of consumer desire is only possible, at least on any appreciable scale, when such need is not strongly felt.

The Case for Social Balance

[*from* The Affluent Society]

When this was first published in The Affluent Society, I called it "The Theory of Social Balance" and thereafter, in slightly stronger terms, "The Nature of Social Balance." The subject is one with which I have been closely associated over the years: the contrast between our wonderful affluence in private goods and the poverty-ridden character of much of our public economy. I later made reference to one more-than-adequate addition to public expenditure: that for defense. This, none should doubt, is also the result of the superior power of private industry, the great weapons producers in particular. They have joined with the Pentagon to take over this part of the budget, and with the acquiescence or positive support of both the major political parties. The private economy here clearly dominates public expenditure.

This chapter follows in all major detail its first presentation, and the material, in turn, has had a prominent part in my speech and writing ever since. When social balance is extended to embrace nuclear weaponry, I regard the problem it poses as perhaps the most urgent of our time.

My argument has not been without effect. When I had finished writing the book, I was in grave doubt about using the description of the car and its occupants as they travel out through the streets of the city to the surrounding countryside and rural park and see in dramatic form the difference between the public and the private estates. I thought this passage might make my point too dramatically or too blatantly. In the end, I included it, and it was, by a wide margin, the most

quoted part of the chapter and perhaps, indeed, of the whole Affluent
Society. *As an engaging consequence, I was appointed to a small governmental commission on the problem of the roadsides in Vermont, a
state where our family has lived many of our summers. With little disagreement, the commission urged that the roads be protected, including, among other things, abolishing billboards outside the cities. The
result has been a substantial improvement of the countryside and a
considerable encouragement to tourism; people now motor to Vermont
to see the unobstructed meadows, forests and mountains. Environmental control can actually be good for business, something I did not originally suspect.*

*   *   *   *

> It is not till it is discovered that high individual incomes will
> not purchase the mass of mankind immunity from cholera,
> typhus, and ignorance, still less secure them the positive ad-
> vantages of educational opportunity and economic security,
> that slowly and reluctantly, amid prophecies of moral degen-
> eration and economic disaster, society begins to make collec-
> tive provision for needs no ordinary individual, even if he
> works overtime all his life, can provide himself.
>
> — R. H. TAWNEY[1]

A CENTRAL PROBLEM of the productive society is what it
produces. This manifests itself in an implacable tendency to
provide an opulent supply of some things and a niggardly
yield of others. This disparity carries to the point where it is a cause
of social discomfort and social unhealth. The line which divides the
area of wealth from the area of poverty is roughly that which divides
privately produced and marketed goods and services from publicly
rendered services. Our wealth in the former is not only in startling
contrast with the meagerness of the latter, but our wealth in privately produced goods is, to a marked degree, the cause of crisis in
the supply of public services. For we have failed to see the impor-

tance, indeed the urgent need, of maintaining a balance between the two.

This disparity between our private and public goods and services (expenditures for defense and a few other favored items apart) is no matter of subjective judgment. On the contrary, it is the source of the most extensive comment, which only stops short of the direct contrast being made here. In recent years, the newspapers of any major city — those of New York are an excellent example — have told daily of the shortages and shortcomings in the elementary municipal and metropolitan services. Schools are old and overcrowded. The police force is inadequate. The parks and playgrounds are insufficient. Streets and empty lots are filthy, and the sanitation department is underequipped and in need of staff. Access to the city by those who work there is uncertain and painful and becoming more so. Internal transportation is overcrowded, unhealthful and dirty. So is the air. Parking on the streets should be prohibited, but there is no space elsewhere. These deficiencies are not in new and novel services but in old and established ones. Cities have long swept their streets, helped their people move around, educated them, kept order and provided horse rails for equipages which sought to pause. That their residents should have a nontoxic supply of air suggests no revolutionary dalliance with socialism.

In most of the last many years, the discussion of this public poverty was matched by the stories of ever-increasing opulence in privately produced goods. The Gross Domestic Product was rising. So were retail sales. So was personal income. Labor productivity also advanced. The automobiles that could not be parked were being produced at an expanded rate. The children, though subject in the playgrounds to the affectionate interest of adults with odd tastes and disposed to increasingly imaginative forms of delinquency, were admirably equipped with television sets. The care and refreshment of the mind was principally in the public domain. Schools, in consequence, were often severely overcrowded and usually underprovided, and the same was even more often true of the mental hospitals.

The contrast was and remains evident not alone to those who read. The family which takes its mauve and cerise, air-conditioned, power-steered and power-braked automobile out for a tour passes through cities that are badly paved, made hideous by litter, blighted buildings, billboards and posts for wires that should long since have been put underground. They pass on into a countryside that has been rendered largely invisible by commercial art. (The goods which the latter advertise have an absolute priority in our value system. Such aesthetic considerations as a view of the countryside accordingly come second. On such matters, we are consistent.) They picnic on exquisitely packaged food from a portable icebox by a polluted stream and go on to spend the night at a park which is a menace to public health and morals. Just before dozing off on an air mattress, beneath a nylon tent, amid the stench of decaying refuse, they may reflect vaguely on the curious unevenness of their blessings. Is this, indeed, the American genius?

II

In the production of goods within the private economy, it has long been recognized that a tolerably close relationship must be maintained between the production of various kinds of products. The output of steel and oil and machine tools is related to the production of automobiles. Investment in transportation must keep abreast of the output of goods to be transported. The supply of power must be abreast of the growth of industries requiring it. The existence of these relationships — coefficients to the economist — has made possible the construction of the input-output table which shows how changes in the production in one industry will increase or diminish the demands on other industries. To this table, and more especially to its ingenious author, Professor Wassily Leontief, the world is indebted for one of its most important modern insights into economic relationships. If expansion in one part of the economy were not matched by the requisite expansion in other parts — were the need for balance not respected — then bottlenecks and shortages, speculative hoarding of scarce supplies and sharply in-creasing costs would ensue. Fortunately in peacetime the market system, combined with considerable planning, serves to maintain this balance, and this, together with the existence of stocks and some flexibility in the coefficients as a result of substitution, ensures that no serious difficulties will arise. We are reminded of the prob-lem only by noticing how serious it was for those countries which sought to solve it by a more inflexible planning.

Just as there must be balance in what a community produces, so there must also be balance in what the community consumes. An increase in the use of one product creates, ineluctably, a require-ment for others. If we are to consume more automobiles, we must have more gasoline. There must be more insurance as well as more space in which to operate them. Beyond a certain point, more and better food appears to mean increased need for medical services. This is the certain result of increased consumption of tobacco and alcohol. More vacations require more hotels and more fishing rods. And so forth.

However, the relationships we are here discussing are not con-fined to the private economy. They operate comprehensively over the whole span of private and public services. As surely as an in-crease in the output of automobiles puts new demands on the steel industry so, also, it places new demands on public services. Simi-larly, every increase in the consumption of private goods will nor-mally mean some facilitating or protective step by the state. In all cases if these services are not forthcoming, the consequences will be in some degree ill. It will be convenient to have a term which sug-gests a satisfactory relationship between the supply of privately pro-duced goods and services and those of the state, and we may call it Social Balance.

The problem of social balance is ubiquitous, and frequently it is obtrusive. As noted, an increase in the consumption of automobiles requires a facilitating supply of streets, highways, traffic control and parking space. The protective services of the police and the highway patrols must also be available, as must those of the hospitals. Al-though the need for balance here is extraordinarily clear, our use of privately produced vehicles has, on occasion, got far out of line with the supply of the related public services. The result has been hideous road congestion, a human massacre of impressive proportions and chronic urban colitis. As on the ground, so also in the air. Planes are delayed or collide over airports with disquieting consequences for passengers when the public provision for air traffic control fails to keep pace with the private use of the airways.

But the auto and the airplane, versus the space to use them, are merely an exceptionally visible example of a requirement that is pervasive. The more goods people procure, the more packages they discard and the more trash that must be carried away. If the appropriate sanitation services are not provided, the counterpart of increasing opulence will be deepening filth. The greater the wealth, the thicker will be the dirt. This indubitably describes a tendency of our time. As more goods are produced and owned, the greater are the opportunities for fraud and the more property that must be protected. If the provision of public law enforcement services does not keep pace, the counterpart of increased well-being will, we may be certain, be increased crime.

The city of Los Angeles in modern times was the near-classic study in the problem of social balance. Magnificently efficient factories and oil refineries, a lavish supply of automobiles, a vast consumption of handsomely packaged products, coupled for many years with the absence of a municipal trash collection service which forced the use of home incinerators, made the air nearly unbreathable for an appreciable part of each year. Air pollution could be controlled only by a complex and highly developed set of public services — by better knowledge of causes stemming from more public research, public requirement of pollution control devices on cars, a municipal trash collection service and possibly the assertion of the priority of clean air over the production of goods. These were long in coming. The agony of a city without usable air was the result.

The issue of social balance can be identified in many other current problems. Thus an aspect of increasing private production is the appearance of an extraordinary number of things which lay claim to the interest of the young. Motion pictures, television, automobiles and the vast opportunities which go with the mobility they provide, together with such less enchanting merchandise as narcotics, comic books and pornographia, are all included in an advancing Gross Domestic Product. The child of a less opulent as well as a technologically more primitive age had far fewer such diversions. The red schoolhouse is remembered mainly because it had a paramount position in the lives of those who attended it that no modern school can hope to attain.

In a well-run and well-regulated community, with a sound school system, good recreational opportunities and a good police force — in short, a community where public services have kept pace with private production — the diversionary forces operating on the modern juvenile may do no great damage. Television and the violent mores of Hollywood must contend with the intellectual discipline of the school. The social, athletic, dramatic and like attractions of the school also claim the attention of the child. These, together with the other recreational opportunities of the community, minimize the tendency to delinquency. Experiments with violence and immorality are checked by an effective law enforcement system before they become epidemic.

In a community where public services have failed to keep abreast of private consumption, things are very different. Here, in an atmosphere of private opulence and public squalor, the private goods have full sway. Schools do not compete with television and the movies. The dubious heroes of the latter, not Ms. Jones, become the idols of the young. Violence replaces the more sedentary recreation for which there are inadequate facilities or provision. Comic books, alcohol, drugs and switchblade knives are, as noted, part of the increased flow of goods, and there is nothing to dispute their enjoyment. There is an ample supply of private wealth to be appropriated and not much to be feared from the police. An austere community is free from temptation. It can also be austere in its public services. Not so a rich one.

Moreover, in a society which sets large store by production, and which has highly effective machinery for synthesizing private wants, there are strong pressures to have as many wage earners in the family as possible. As always, all social behavior is of a piece. If both parents are engaged in private production, the burden on the public services is further increased. Children, in effect, become the charge of the community for an appreciable part of the time. If the services of the community do not keep pace, this will be another source of disorder.

Residential housing also illustrates the problem of the social balance, although in a somewhat complex form. Few would wish to contend that, in the lower or even the middle income brackets, Americans are munificently supplied with housing. A great many families would like better located or merely more houseroom, and no advertising is necessary to persuade them of their wish. And the provision of housing is in the private domain. At first glance at least, the line we draw between private and public seems not to be preventing a satisfactory allocation of resources to housing.

On closer examination, however, the problem turns out to be not greatly different from that of education. It is improbable that the housing industry is significantly more incompetent or inefficient in the United States than in those countries — Scandinavia, Holland or (for the most part) England — where slums have been largely eliminated and where *minimum* standards of cleanliness and comfort are well above our own. As the experience of these countries shows, and as we have also been learning, the housing industry functions well only in combination with a large, complex and costly array of public services. These include land purchase and clearance for redevelopment; good neighborhood and city planning and effective and well-enforced zoning; a variety of financing and other aids to the housebuilder and owner; publicly supported research and architectural services for an industry which, by its nature, is equipped to do little on its own; and a considerable amount of direct or assisted public construction and good maintenance for families in the lowest income brackets. The quality of the housing depends not on the industry, which is given, but on what is invested in these supplements and supports.[2]

The case for social balance has, so far, been put negatively. Failure to keep public services in minimal relation to private production and use of goods is a cause of social disorder or impairs economic performance. The matter may now be put affirmatively. By failing to exploit the opportunity to expand public production, we are missing opportunities for enjoyment which otherwise we might have. Presumably a community can be as well rewarded by buying better schools or better parks as by buying more expensive automobiles. By concentrating on the latter rather than the former, it is failing to maximize its satisfactions. As with schools in the community, so with public services over the country at large. It is scarcely sensible that we should satisfy our wants in private goods with reckless abundance, while in the case of public goods, on the evidence of the eye, we practice extreme self-denial. So far from systematically exploiting the opportunities to derive use and pleasure from these services, we do not supply what would keep us out of trouble.

The conventional wisdom holds that the community, large or small, makes a decision as to how much it will devote to its public services. This decision is arrived at by democratic process. Subject to the imperfections and uncertainties of democracy, people decide how much of their private income and goods they will surrender in order to have public services of which they are in greater need. Thus there is a balance, however rough, in the enjoyments to be had from private goods and services and those rendered by public authority.

It will be obvious, however, that this view depends on the notion of independently determined consumer wants. In such a world, one could with some reason defend the doctrine that the consumer, as a voter, makes an independent choice between public and private goods. But given the dependence effect — given that consumer wants are created by the process by which they are satisfied — the consumer makes no such choice. He or she is subject to the forces of advertising and emulation by which production creates its own demand. Advertising operates exclusively, and emulation mainly, on behalf of privately produced goods and services.[3] Since management of demand and emulative effects operate on behalf of private production, public services will have an inherent tendency to lag behind. Automobile demand, which is expensively synthesized, will inevitably have a much larger claim on income than parks or public health or even roads, where no such influence operates. The engines of mass communication, in their highest state of development, assail the eyes and ears of the community on behalf of more beverages but not of more schools. Even in the conventional wisdom it will scarcely be contended that this leads to an equal choice between the two.

The competition is especially unequal for new products and services. Every corner of the public psyche is canvassed by some of the nation's most talented citizens to see if the desire for some merchantable product can be cultivated. No similar process operates on behalf of the nonmerchantable services of the state. Indeed, while we take the cultivation of new private wants for granted, we would be measurably shocked to see such cultivation applied to public services. The scientist or engineer or advertising man who devotes himself to developing a new carburetor, cleanser or depilatory for which the public recognizes no need and will feel none until an advertising campaign arouses it, is one of the valued members of our society. A politician or a public servant who sees need for a new public service may be called a wastrel. Few public offenses are more reprehensible.

So much for the influences that operate on the decision between public and private production. The calm decision between public and private consumption pictured by the conventional wisdom is, in fact, a remarkable example of the error which arises from viewing social behavior out of context. The inherent tendency will always be for public services to fall behind private production. We have here the first of the causes of social imbalance.

IV

Social balance is also the victim of two further features of our society — the truce on inequality and the tendency to inflation. Since these are now part of our context, their effect comes quickly into view.

With rare exceptions such as the postal service, public services do not carry a price ticket to be paid for by the individual user. By their nature, they must, ordinarily, be available to all. As a result, when they are improved or new services are initiated, there is the ancient and troublesome question of who is to pay. This, in turn, provokes to life the collateral but irrelevant debate over inequality. As with the use of taxation as an instrument of fiscal policy, the truce on inequality is broken. Liberals are obliged to argue that the services be paid for by progressive taxation which will reduce inequality. Committed as they are to the urgency of goods (and also to a somewhat mechanical view of the way in which the level of output can be kept most secure), they must oppose sales and excise taxes. Conservatives rally to the defense of inequality — although without ever quite committing themselves in such uncouth terms — and oppose the use of income taxes. They, in effect, oppose the expenditure not on the merits of the service but on the demerits of the tax system. Since the debate over inequality cannot be resolved, the money is frequently not appropriated and the service not performed. It is a casualty of the economic goals of both liberals and conservatives, for both of whom the questions of social balance are subordinate to those of production and, when it is evoked, of inequality.

In practice, matters are better as well as worse than this description of the basic forces suggests. Given the tax structure, the revenues of all levels of government grow with the growth of the economy. Services can be maintained and sometimes even improved out of this automatic accretion.

However, this effect is highly unequal. The revenues of the federal government, because of its heavy reliance on progressive income taxes, increase more than proportionately with private economic growth. In addition, although the conventional wisdom greatly deplores the fact, federal appropriations have only an indirect bearing on taxation. Public services are considered and voted on in accordance with their seeming urgency. Initiation or improvement of a particular service is rarely, except for purposes of oratory, set against the specific effect on taxes. Tax policy, in turn, is decided on the basis of the level of economic activity, the resulting revenues, expediency and other considerations. Among these, the total of the thousands of individually considered appropriations is but one factor. In this process, the ultimate tax consequence of any individual appropriation is *de minimus*, and the tendency to ignore it reflects the simple mathematics of the situation. Thus it is possible for the Congress to make decisions affecting the social balance without invoking the question of inequality.

Things are made worse, however, by the fact that a large proportion of the federal revenues are pre-empted by defense. The increase in defense costs has also tended to absorb a large share of the normal increase in tax revenues. The position of the federal government in improving the social balance has also been weakened since World War II by the strong, although receding, conviction that its taxes are at artificial levels and that a tacit commitment exists to reduce taxes at the earliest opportunity.

In the states and localities, the problem of social balance is much more severe. Here tax revenues — this is especially true of the general property tax — increase less than proportionately with increased private production. Budgeting too is far more closely circumscribed than in the case of the federal government — only the monetary authority enjoys the pleasant privilege of underwriting its own loans. Because of this, increased services for states and localities regularly pose the question of more revenues and more taxes. And here, with great regularity, the question of social balance is lost in the debate over equality and social equity.

Thus we currently find by far the most serious social imbalance in the services performed by local governments. The F.B.I. comes much more easily by funds than the city police force. The Department of Agriculture can more easily keep its pest control abreast of expanding agricultural output than the average city health service can keep up with the needs of an expanding industrial population. One consequence is that the federal government remains under constant and highly desirable pressure to use its superior revenue position to help redress the balance at the lower levels of government.

V

Finally, social imbalance is the natural offspring of inflation. In the past, inflation had two major effects on public services. Wages in the public service tended to lag well behind those in private industry. There was thus an incentive to desert public for private employment. More important, in the United States the most urgent problems of social balance involve the services of states and localities and, most of all, those of the larger cities. Increasing population, increasing urbanization and increasing affluence all intensify the public tasks of the metropolis. Meanwhile the revenues of these units of government, in contrast with those of the federal government, are relatively inelastic. In consequence of the heavy dependence on the property tax, the revenues of these units of government lag behind when prices rise. The problem of financing services thus becomes increasingly acute as and when inflation continues.

In very recent times in the larger cities, stronger union organization among municipal employees has arrested and in some communities reversed the tendency for wages of public workers to lag. So the competitive position of the public services does not automatically become adverse with inflation. But the inelasticity of the revenues remains. And with high labor costs, the constraints on services — cuts, on occasion, instead of urgent expansion — have become more severe.

VI

A feature of the years immediately following World War II was a remarkable attack on the notion of expanding and improving public services. During the depression years, such services had been elaborated and improved partly in order to fill some small part of the vacuum left by the shrinkage of private production. During the war years, the role of government was vastly expanded. After that came the reaction. Much of it, unquestionably, was motivated by a desire to rehabilitate the prestige of private production and therewith of producers. No doubt some who joined the attack hoped, at least tacitly, that it might be possible to sidestep the truce on taxation vis-à-vis equality by having less taxation of all kinds. For a time, the notion that our public services had somehow become inflated and excessive was all but axiomatic. Even liberal politicians did not seriously protest. They found it necessary to aver that they were in favor of rigid economy in public spending too.

In this discussion, a certain mystique was attributed to the satisfaction of privately supplied wants. A community decision to have a new school means that the individual surrenders the necessary amount, willy-nilly, in his taxes. But if he is left with that income, he is a free man. He can decide between a better car or a television set. The difficulty is that this argument leaves the community with no way of preferring the school. All private wants, where the individual can choose, are thought inherently superior to all public desires which must be paid for by taxation and with an inevitable component of compulsion.

The cost of public services was also held to be a desolating burden on private production, although this was at a time when private production was burgeoning. Urgent warnings were issued of the unfavorable effects of taxation on investment — "I don't know of a surer way of killing off the incentive to invest than by imposing taxes which are regarded by people as punitive."[4] This was at a time when the inflationary effect of a very high level of private investment was causing concern. The same individuals who were warning about the inimical effects of taxes were strongly advocating a monetary policy designed to reduce investment. However, an understanding of our economic discourse requires an appreciation of one of its basic rules: men of high position are allowed, by a special act of grace, to accommodate their reasoning to the answer they need. Logic is only required in those of lesser rank.

Finally, it was argued with no little vigor that expanding government posed a grave threat to individual liberties. "Where distinction and rank is achieved almost exclusively by becoming a civil servant of the state . . . it is too much to expect that many will long prefer freedom to security."[5]

With time, the disorder associated with social imbalance has become visible even if the need for balance between private and public services is still imperfectly appreciated. The onslaught on the public services has left a lasting imprint. To suggest that we canvass our public wants to see where happiness can be improved by more and better services has a sharply radical tone. Even public services that prevent disorder need to be defended. By contrast, the man who devises a nostrum for a nonexistent private need and then successfully promotes both remains one of nature's noblemen.

NOTES

1. *Equality*, 4th ed., rev. (London: Allen & Unwin, 1952), pp. 134–135.
2. In *Economics and the Public Purpose* (Boston: Houghton Mifflin, 1973), I have related the performance of public functions much more closely to the power of the part of the private sector being served. Thus the comparatively ample supply of highways, the more than ample supply of weapons and the poor supply of municipal services and public health care.
3. Emulation does operate between communities. A new school in one community does exert pressure on others to remain abreast. However, as compared with the pervasive effects of emulation in extending the demand for privately produced consumers' goods, there will be agreement, I think, that this intercommunity effect is probably small.
4. Arthur F. Burns, Chairman of the President's Council of Economic Advisers, *U.S. News and World Report*, May 6, 1955.
5. F. A. von Hayek, *The Road to Serfdom* (London: George Routledge & Sons, 1944), p. 98.

The Imperatives of Technology

[*from* The New Industrial State]

This essay, it will be evident, was written before the computer revolution. It was one of the first to be devoted to the deep and dramatic change that technology brought to the task and nature of the industrial enterprise, but its substance was drawn from the automobile, not the computer, industry. My special gratitude for their help goes to a number of automobile executives, particularly those at the Ford Motor Company. Thus it is that I deal with Ford here and not with Microsoft.

However, the essence of this essay, the bearing of technology on modern industrial structure, is still stoutly valid. Power in the modern enterprise has, indeed, passed from the sometimes nominal executive to those in command of technology and its initiatives, once called "invention." To this major change, still far from fully recognized in standard economic textbook literature, I later come.

Were I now writing this piece, I would give more attention to the masters of the microchip world, for they and the organizations they control have increasing influence and authority in the industrial world today — what is known as the computer ascendancy. It is not the individual entrepreneur once beloved by economics but the larger structure, embracing technological innovation and its authors, that is the modern upward dynamic, and the computer industry is its most obvious exponent.

*   *   *   *

O N JUNE 16, 1903, after some months of preparation which included the negotiation of contracts for various components, the Ford Motor Company was formed for the manufacture of automobiles. Production was to be whatever number could be sold. The first car reached the market that October. The firm had an authorized capital of $150,000. However, only $100,000 worth of stock was issued, and only $28,000 of this was for cash. Although it does not bear on the present discussion, the company made a handsome profit that year and did not fail to do so for many years thereafter. Employment in 1903 averaged 125 men.[1]

Sixty-one years later, in the spring of 1964, the Ford Motor Company introduced what is now called a new automobile. In accordance with current fashion in automobile nomenclature, it was called, one assumes inappropriately, a Mustang. The public was well prepared for the new vehicle. Plans carefully specified prospective output and sales; they erred, as plans do, and in this case by being too modest. These preparations required three and a half years. From late in the autumn of 1962, when the design was settled, until the spring of 1964, there was a fairly firm commitment to the particular car that eventually emerged. Engineering and "styling" costs were $9 million; the cost of tooling up for the production of the Mustang was $50 million.[2] In 1964, employment in the Ford Motor Company averaged 317,000. Assets at that time were approximately $6 billion.[3] In the autumn of 1977, Ford brought out two new models — the Zephyr and the Fairmont. For these the cost was roughly $600 million, although part of the increase reflected the diminution of the dollar. By then Ford's assets were approximately $16 billion, and employment worldwide was around 445,000.

Virtually all of the effects of the increased use of technology are revealed by these comparisons. We may pass them in preliminary review.

II

Technology means the application of scientific or other organized knowledge to practical tasks. Its most important consequence, at least for the purposes of economics, is in forcing the division and subdivision of any such task into its component parts. Thus, and only thus, can organized knowledge be brought to bear on performance.

Specifically, there is no way that organized knowledge can be brought to bear on the production of an automobile as a whole or even on the manufacture of a body or chassis. It can only be applied if the task is so subdivided that it begins to be coterminous with some established area of scientific or engineering knowledge. Though metallurgical knowledge cannot be applied to the manufacture of the whole vehicle, it can be used in the design of the cooling system or the engine block. While knowledge of mechanical engineering cannot be brought to bear on the manufacture of the entire automobile, it can be applied to the machining of the crankshaft. While chemistry cannot be applied to the construction of the car as a whole, it can be used to decide on the composition of the finish or trim.

Nor do matters stop here. Metallurgical knowledge is brought to bear not on steel but on the characteristics of special steels for particular functions, and chemistry not on paints or plastics but on particular molecular structures and their rearrangement as required.[4]

Nearly all of the consequences of technology and much of the shape of modern industry derive from this need to divide and subdivide tasks, from the further need to bring knowledge to bear on these fractions and from the final need to combine the finished elements of the task into the finished product as a whole. Six consequences are of immediate importance.

First. An increasing span of time separates the beginning from the completion of any task. Knowledge is brought to bear on the ultimate microfraction of the task; then on that in combination with some other fraction; then on some further combination and thus on to final completion. The process stretches back in time as the root system of a plant goes down into the ground. The longest of the filaments determines the total time required in production. The more thoroughgoing the application of technology — in common or at least frequent language, the more sophisticated the production process — the farther back the application of knowledge will be carried. The longer, accordingly, will be the time between the initiation and the completion of the task.

The manufacture of the first Ford was not an exacting process. Metallurgy was an academic concept. Ordinary steels were used that could be obtained from the warehouse in the morning and shaped that afternoon. Nothing associated with this basic material required that the span of time between initiation and completion of a car be more than a few hours.

The provision of steel for the modern vehicle, in contrast, reaches back to specifications prepared by the designers or the laboratory and proceeds through orders to the steel mill, parallel provision for the appropriate metal-working machinery, delivery, testing and use.

Second. There is an increase in the capital that is committed to production aside from that occasioned by increased output. The increased time, and therewith the increased investment in goods in process, cost money. So does the knowledge which is applied to the various elements of the task. The application of knowledge to an element of a manufacturing problem will also typically involve the development of a machine for performing the function. (The word *technology* brings to mind machines; this is not surprising, for machinery is one of its most visible manifestations.) This too involves capital investment, as does equipment for integrating the various elements of the task into the final product.

The investment in making the original Ford was larger than the $28,000 paid in, for some of it was in the plant, inventory and machinery of those who, like the Dodge Brothers, supplied the components. But investment in the factory itself was minute. Materials and parts were there only briefly; no expensive specialists gave them attention; only elementary machinery was used to assemble them. It helped that the frame of the car could be lifted by two men.

Third. With increasing technology the commitment of time and money tends to be made ever more inflexibly to the performance of a particular task. That task must be precisely defined before it is divided and subdivided into its component parts. Knowledge and equipment are then brought to bear on these fractions, and they are useful only for the task as it was initially defined. If that task is changed, new knowledge and new equipment will have to be found and utilized.

Little thought needed to be given to the Dodge Brothers' machine shop, which made the engine and chassis of the original Ford, as an instrument for automobile manufacture. It was unspecialized as to task. It could have worked as well on bicycles, steam engines or carriage gear and, indeed, had been so employed. Had Ford and his associates decided at any point to shift from gasoline to steam power, the machine shop could have accommodated itself to the change in a few hours.

By contrast, all parts of the Mustang, the tools and equipment that worked on these parts and the steel and other materials going into these parts were designed to serve efficiently their ultimate function. They could serve only that function. Were the car appreciably altered, were it shaped, instead of as a Mustang (or a Zephyr), as a Barracuda or a Serpent, Scorpion or Roach, as one day one will be, much of this work would have to be redone. Thus the firm commitment to this particular vehicle for some eighteen months prior to its appearance.

Fourth. Technology requires specialized manpower. This will be evident. Organized knowledge can be brought to bear, not surprisingly, only by those who possess it. However, technology does not make the only claim on manpower; planning, to be mentioned in a moment, also requires a comparatively high level of specialized talent. To foresee the future in all its dimensions and to design the appropriate action does not necessarily require high scientific qualification. It does require ability to organize and employ information or capacity to react intuitively to relevant experience.

These requirements do not reflect, on some absolute scale, a higher order of talent than was required in a less technically advanced era. The makers of the original Ford were men of talent. The Dodge Brothers had previously invented a bicycle and a steam launch. Their machine shop made a wide variety of products, and Detroit legend also celebrated their exuberance when drunk. Alexander Malcolmson, who was Ford's immediate partner in getting the business under way, was a successful coal merchant. James Couzens, who may well have had more to do with the success of the enterprise than Henry Ford,[5] had a background in railroading and the coal business and went on from Ford to be police commissioner and mayor of Detroit, a notable Republican senator from Michigan and an undeviating supporter of Franklin D. Roosevelt. Not all top members of the present Ford organization would claim as much reach. But they do have a considerably deeper knowledge of the more specialized matters for which they are severally responsible.

Fifth. The inevitable counterpart of specialization is organization. This is what brings the work of specialists to a coherent result. If there are many specialists, this coordination will be a major task. So complex, indeed, will be the job of organizing specialists that there will be specialists on organization and organizations of specialists on organization. More perhaps than machinery, massive and complex business organizations are the tangible manifestation of advanced technology.

Sixth. From the time and capital that must be committed, the inflexibility of this commitment, the needs of large organization and the problems of market performance under conditions of advanced technology comes the necessity for planning. Tasks must be performed so that they are right not for the present but for that time in the future when, companion and related work having also been done, the whole job is completed. And the amount of capital that, meanwhile, will have been committed adds urgency to this need to be right. So conditions at the time of completion of the whole task must be foreseen, as must developments along the way. And steps must be taken to prevent, offset or otherwise neutralize the effect of adverse developments and to ensure that what is ultimately foreseen eventuates in fact.

In the early days of the Ford Motor Company the future was very near at hand. Only days elapsed between the commitment of machinery and materials to production and the appearance of the car.

If the future is near, it can be assumed that it will be very much like the present. If the car did not meet the approval of the customers, it could quickly be changed. The briefness of the time in process allowed this; so did the unspecialized character of manpower, materials and machinery.

Changes were, indeed, needed. The earliest cars, as they came on the market, did not meet with complete customer approval: there were complaints that the cooling system did not cool, the brakes did not brake, the carburetor did not feed fuel to the engine, and a Los Angeles dealer reported the exceptionally disconcerting discovery that, when steered, "front wheels turn wrong."[6] These defects were promptly remedied. They did the reputation of the car no lasting harm.

Such shortcomings in the more recent models would invite reproach. And they would be subject to no such quick, simple and inexpensive remedy; foresight is necessary to ensure, as far as possible, against such misfortune. The machinery, materials, manpower and components of the original Ford, being all unspecialized, could be quickly procured on the open market. Accordingly, there was no need to anticipate possible shortages of these requirements and take steps to prevent them. For the more highly specialized requirements of the Mustang, foresight and associated action were indispensable. In Detroit, when the first Ford was projected, anything on wheels that was connected with a motor was assured of acceptance. Acceptance of the later Mustang could not be so assumed. The prospect had to be carefully studied. And customers had to be carefully conditioned to want this blessing. Thus the need for planning.

III

The more sophisticated the technology, the greater, in general, will be all of the foregoing requirements. This will be true of simple products as they come to be produced by more refined processes or as manufacturers develop imaginative containers or unopenable packaging. With very intricate technology, such as that associated with modern weapons and weapons systems, there will be a quantum change in these requirements. This will be especially so if, as under modern peacetime conditions, cost and time are not decisive considerations.

Thus when Philip II settled on the redemption of England at the end of March 1587, he was not unduly troubled by the seemingly serious circumstance that Spain had no navy. Some men-of-war were available from newly conquered Portugal but, in the main, merchant ships would suffice.[7] A navy, in other words, could then be bought in the market. Nor was the destruction of a large number of the available ships by Drake at Cadiz three weeks later a fatal blow. Despite what historians have usually described as unconscionable inefficiency, the Armada sailed in a strength of 130 ships a little over a year later on May 18, 1588. The cost, though considerable, was well within the resources of the Empire. Matters did not change greatly in the next three hundred years. The *Victory*, from which Nelson called Englishmen to their duty at Trafalgar, though an excellent fighting ship, involved no esoteric and time-consuming problems in design. It was a standard product, a full forty years old at the time. The exiguous flying machines of World War I, built only to carry a man or two and a weapon, were designed and put in combat in a matter of months.

To create a modern fleet of the numerical size of the Armada, with nuclear-powered aircraft carriers and an appropriate complement of aircraft and missiles, together with nuclear submarines, destroyers, supporting craft and bases and communications, would take a first-rate industrial power a minimum of twenty years. Though modern Spain is rich beyond the dreams of its monarchs in its most expansive age, it could not for a moment contemplate such an enterprise. In World War II, no combat plane that had not been substantially designed before the outbreak of hostilities saw major service. Since then the lead time for comparable matériel has become yet greater. In general, individuals in late middle age stand in little danger of weapons now being designed; the latter are a menace only to the unborn and the uncontemplated.

IV

It is a commonplace of modern technology that there is a high measure of certainty that problems have solutions before there is knowledge of how they are to be solved. It was reasonably well known in the early nineteen-sixties that men could land on the moon by the end of the decade. Many, perhaps most, of the details for accomplishing this journey still remained to be worked out.

If methods of performing the specified task are uncertain, the need for bringing organized intelligence to bear will be much greater than if the methods are known. This uncertainty will also lead to increased time and cost, and the increase can be very great. This problem-solving, with its high costs in time and money, is a recognized feature of modern technology. It graces all present-day economic discussion under the cachet of "Research and Development."

The need for planning, it has been said, arises from the long period of time that elapses during the production process, the large investment that is involved and the inflexible commitment of that investment to the particular task. In the case of advanced military equipment, time, cost and inflexibility of commitment are all very great. Time and outlay will be even greater where — a common characteristic of weaponry — design is uncertain and where, accordingly, there must be added expenditure for research and development. In these circumstances planning is both essential and difficult. It is essential because of the time that is involved, the money that is at risk, the number of things that can go wrong and the magnitude of the possible ensuing disaster. It is difficult because of the number and size of the eventualities that must be controlled.

One answer is to have the state absorb the major risks. It can provide or guarantee a market for the product. And it can underwrite the costs of development so that if they increase beyond expectation, the firm will not have to carry them. Or it can pay for and make available the necessary technical knowledge. The drift of this argument will be evident. Technology, under all circumstances, leads to planning; in its higher manifestations it may put the problems and associated cost of planning beyond the resources of the industrial firm. Technological compulsions, not ideology or political wile, will require the firm to seek the help and protection of the state. This is a consequence of advanced technology that is of no small interest.

In examining the intricate complex of economic change, technology, having an initiative of its own, is the logical point at which to break in. But technology not only causes change, it is a response to change. Though it forces specialization, it is also the result of specialization. Though it requires extensive organization, it is also the result of organization. These themes, planning, specialization and organization, like the military symbolism of marching and combat in Protestant hymns and intercollegiate athletics, recur again and again in any discussion of modern technological society.

NOTES

1. Allan Nevins, *Ford: The Times, The Man, The Company* (New York: Scribner, 1954), p. 220 et seq.
2. I am grateful to Mr. Walter T. Murphy of the Ford Motor Company for providing these details and the later ones on the Zephyr and Fairmont. In this essay I also had the earlier help of Robert McNamara, which he gave when he was still an executive of Ford. I wish now, at the outset, not only to concede but to emphasize that one may have planning without precision of result and that there will also be occasional failures. When this was first written, I went on at this point to note that "the more impulsive critic" would cite another Ford creation, the Edsel, to prove that planning of the sort described does not work. He would not notice that the Edsel gained its distinction from being an exception to the common expectation of success. I was not disappointed. Such references to the Edsel were, in fact, compulsive.
3. *Fortune*, July 1964.
4. The notion of division of labor, an old one in economics, is a rudimentary and partial application of the ideas here outlined. As one breaks down a mechanical operation, such as the manufacture of Adam Smith's immortal pins, it resolves itself into simpler and simpler move-

ments, as in putting the head or the point on the pin. This is the same as saying that the problem is susceptible to increasingly homogeneous mechanical knowledge and its use to improve performance.

However, the subdivision of tasks to accord with the area of organized knowledge is not confined to, nor has it any special relevance to, mechanical processes. It occurs in medicine, business management, building design, child and dog rearing and every other enterprise that involves an agglomerate of scientific knowledge.

5. A case I have argued elsewhere. Cf. "Was Ford a Fraud?" in *The Liberal Hour* (Boston: Houghton Mifflin, 1960), p. 141 et seq.

6. Nevins, p. 248.

7. Instructions issued from the Escorial on March 31. Cf. Garrett Mattingly, *The Armada* (Boston: Houghton Mifflin, 1959), p. 80. Philip had, of course, been contemplating the enterprise for some years.

The Technostructure

[*from* The New Industrial State]

As was true of the immediately preceding essay, were this chapter from The New Industrial State *written today, it would duly emphasize the role of technology, Bill Gates and the technicians. Still, it was well ahead of its time, and that is always a good thing.*

*   *   *   *

THE INDIVIDUAL has far more standing in our culture than the group. An individual has a presumption of accomplishment; a committee has a presumption of inaction.[1] We react sympathetically to the individual who seeks to safeguard his personality from engulfment by the mass. We call for proof, at least in principle, before curbing his aggressions. Individuals have souls; corporations are notably soulless. The entrepreneur — individualistic, restless, with vision, guile and courage — has been the economist's hero. The great business organization arouses no similar admiration. Admission to heaven is individually and by families; the top management, even of an enterprise with an excellent corporate image, cannot yet go in as a group. To have, in pursuit of truth, to assert the superiority of the organization over the individual for important social tasks is a taxing prospect.

Yet it is a necessary task. It is not to individuals but to organizations that power in the business enterprise and power in the society have passed. And modern economic society can only be understood as an effort, wholly successful, to synthesize by organization a group personality far superior *for its purposes* to a natural person, and with the added advantage of immortality.

The need for such a group personality begins with the circumstance that in modern industry a large number of decisions, and *all* that are important, draw on information possessed by more than one man.[2] Typically they draw on the specialized scientific and technical knowledge, the accumulated information or experience and the artistic or intuitive sense of many persons. And this is guided by further information which is assembled, analyzed and interpreted by professionals using highly technical equipment. The final decision will be informed only as it draws systematically on all those whose information is relevant. Nor, human beings what they are, can it take at face value all of the information that is offered. There must, additionally, be a mechanism for testing each person's contribution for its relevance and reliability as it is brought to bear on the decision.

II

The need to draw on, and appraise, the information of numerous individuals in modern industrial decision-making has three principal points of origin. It derives, first, from the technological requirements of modern industry. It is not that these are always inordinately sophisticated; a man of moderate genius could, quite conceivably, provide himself with the knowledge of the various branches of metallurgy and chemistry, and of engineering, procurement, production management, quality control, labor relations, styling and merchandising which are involved in the development of a modern motorcar. But even moderate genius is in unpredictable supply, and to keep abreast of all these branches of science, engineering and art would be time-consuming even for a genius. The elementary solution, which allows of the use of far more common talent and with far greater predictability of result, is to have men who are appropriately qualified or experienced in each limited area of specialized knowledge or art. Their information is then combined for carrying out the design and production of the vehicle. It is a common public impression, not discouraged by scientists, engineers and industrialists, that modern scientific, engineering and industrial achievements are the work of a new and quite remarkable race of men. This is pure vanity; were it so, there would be few such achievements. The real accomplishment of modern science and technology consists in taking quite ordinary men, informing them narrowly and deeply and then, through appropriate organization, arranging to have their knowledge combined with that of other specialized but equally ordinary men. This dispenses with the need for genius. The resulting performance, though less inspiring, is far more predictable. No individual genius arranged the flights to the moon. It was the work of organization — bureaucracy. And the men walking on the moon and contemplating their return could be glad it was so. Few things could more reliably cultivate thought than to be on the moon and dependent on some single and perhaps eccentric genius to get you back.

The second factor requiring the combination of specialized talent derives from advanced technology, the associated use of capital and the resulting need for planning with its accompanying control of the external factors bearing on this planning. The market is, in remarkable degree, an intellectually undemanding institution. The Wisconsin farmer need not anticipate his requirements for fertilizers, pesticides or even machine parts; the market stocks and supplies them. The cost of these is substantially the same for the man of intelligence and for his neighbor who, under medical examination, shows daylight in either ear. And the farmer need have no price or selling strategy; the market takes all his milk at the ruling price. Much of the appeal of the market, to economists in particular, has been from the way it seems to simplify life. Better orderly error than complex truth.

For complexity enters with planning and is endemic thereto. The manufacturer of missiles, space vehicles or military aircraft, the extreme cases, must foresee the requirements for specialized plant, specialized manpower, exotic materials and intricate components, and take steps to ensure their availability when they are needed. For procuring such things, we have seen, the market is either unreliable or unavailable. And there is no open market for the finished product. Everything here depends on the care and skill with which contracts are sought and nurtured in Washington or in Whitehall, Paris or Teheran.

The same foresight and responding action are required, in lesser degree, from manufacturers of automobiles, processed foods and detergents. They too must foresee requirements and manage markets. Planning, in short, requires a great variety of information. It requires variously informed individuals who are suitably specialized in obtaining the requisite information. There must be those whose knowledge allows them to foresee need and to ensure a supply of labor, materials and other production requirements; those who have the knowledge to plan price strategies and see that customers are suitably persuaded to buy at these prices; those who, at higher levels of technology, are so informed that they can work effectively with the state to see that it is suitably guided; and those who can organize the flow of information that the above tasks and many others require. Thus to the requirements of technology for specialized technical and scientific talent are added the very large further requirements of planning that technology makes necessary.

Finally, following from the need for this variety of specialized talent, is the need for its coordination. Talent must be brought to bear on the common purpose. More specifically, on large and small matters information must be extracted from the various specialists, tested for its reliability and relevance, and made to yield a decision. This process, which is much misunderstood, requires a special word.

III

The modern business organization, or that part which has to do with guidance and direction, consists of numerous individuals who are engaged, at any given time, in obtaining, digesting or exchanging and testing information. A very large part of the exchange and testing of information is by word of mouth — a discussion in an office, at lunch, with alcohol or over the telephone. But the most typical procedure is through the committee and the committee meeting. One can do worse than think of a business organization as a hierarchy of committees. Coordination, in turn, consists in assigning the appropriate talent to committees, intervening on occasion to force a decision, and, as the case may be, announcing the decision or carrying it as information for a yet further decision by a yet higher committee.

Nor should it be supposed that this is an inefficient procedure. On the contrary, it is, normally, the only efficient procedure. Association in a committee enables each member to come to know the intellectual resources and the reliability of his colleagues. Committee discussion enables members to pool information under circumstances which allow, also, of immediate probing to assess the relevance and reliability of the information offered. Uncertainty about one's information or error is revealed as in no other way. There is also, no doubt, considerable stimulus to mental effort from such association. One may enjoy torpor in private but not so comfortably in public, at least during working hours. Men who believe themselves deeply engaged in private thought are usually thinking of nothing important. Committees are condemned by those who have been captured by the cliché that individual effort is somehow superior to group effort; by those who guiltily suspect that since group effort is more congenial, it must be less productive; by those who do not see that the process of extracting, and especially of testing, information has necessarily a somewhat undirected quality — briskly conducted meetings invariably decide matters previously decided; and by those who fail to realize that (usually) highly paid men, when sitting around a table as a committee, are not necessarily wasting more time than, in the aggregate, they would each waste in a private office by themselves.[3,4] Forthright and determined administrators frequently react to belief in the superior capacity of individuals for decision by abolishing all committees. They then constitute working parties, task forces or executive groups in order to avoid the one truly disastrous consequence of their action, which would be that they would have to make the decisions themselves.

Thus decision in the modern business enterprise is the product not of individuals but of groups. The groups are numerous, as often informal as formal, and subject to constant change in composition. Each contains the men possessed of the information, or with access to the information, that bears on the particular decision, together with those whose skill consists in extracting and testing this information and obtaining a conclusion. This is how men act successfully on matters where no single one, however exalted or intelligent, has more than a fraction of the necessary knowledge. It is what makes modern business possible, and in other contexts it is what makes modern government possible. It is fortunate that men of limited knowledge are so constituted that they can work together in this way. Were it otherwise, business and government, at any given moment, would be at a standstill awaiting the appearance of a man with the requisite breadth of knowledge to resolve the problem presently at hand. Some further characteristics of group decision-making must now be noticed.

IV

Group decision-making extends deeply into the business enterprise. Effective participation is not closely related to rank in the formal hierarchy of the organization. This takes an effort of mind to grasp. Everyone is influenced by the stereotyped organization chart of the business enterprise. At its top is the board of directors and the chairman of the board; next comes the president; next come the executive vice president and other viceregal figures; thereafter come the department or divisional heads — those who preside over the Chevrolet division or the large-generators division. Power is assumed to pass down from the pinnacle. Those at the top give orders; those below relay them on or respond.

This happens, but only in very simple organizations — the peacetime drill of the National Guard or a troop of Boy Scouts moving out on Saturday maneuvers. Elsewhere the decision will require information. Some power will then pass to the person or persons who have this information. If this knowledge is highly particular to themselves, then their power becomes very great. In Los Alamos, during the development of the atomic bomb, Enrico Fermi rode a bicycle up the hill to work; Major General Leslie R. Groves presided in grandeur over the entire atomic effort. In association with his similarly situated co-workers, Fermi could, at various early stages, have brought the whole enterprise to an end.[5] No such power resided with Groves. At any moment he could have been replaced without loss.

When power is exercised by a group, not only does it pass into the organization but it passes irrevocably. If an individual has taken a decision, he can be called before another individual who is his superior in the hierarchy, his information can be examined and his decision reversed by the greater wisdom or experience of the superior. But if the decision required the combined information of a group, it cannot be safely reversed by an individual. He will have to get the judgment of other specialists. This returns the power once more to organization.

No one should insist, in these matters, on pure cases. There will often be instances when an individual has the knowledge to modify or change the finding of a group. But the broad rule holds: if a decision requires the specialized knowledge of a group, it is subject to safe review only by the similar knowledge of a similar group. Group decision, unless acted upon by another group, tends to be absolute.[6]

v

Next, it must not be supposed that group decision is important only in such evident instances as nuclear technology or space mechanics. Simple products are made and packaged by sophisticated processes. And the most massive programs of market control, together with the most specialized marketing talent, are used on behalf of soap, detergents, cigarettes, aspirin, packaged cereals and gasoline. These, beyond others, are the valued advertising accounts. The simplicity and uniformity of these products require the investment of compensatingly elaborate science and art to suppress market influences and make prices and amounts sold subject to the largest possible measure of control. For these products too, decision passes to a group which combines specialized and esoteric knowledge. Here too, power goes deeply and more or less irrevocably into the organization.

For purposes of pedagogy, I for many years illustrated these principles by reference to a technically uncomplicated product, which, unaccountably, General Electric has yet to place on the market.[7] It is a toaster of standard performance, the pop-up kind, except that it etches on the surface of the toast, in darker carbon, one of a selection of standard messages or designs. For the elegant, an attractive monogram would be available or a coat of arms; for the devout at breakfast, there would be an appropriate devotional message from the Reverend Billy Graham; for the patriotic or worried, there would be an aphorism from the late J. Edgar Hoover urging vigilance; for modern painters and economists, there would be a purely abstract design. A restaurant version would sell advertising.

Conceivably this is a vision that could come from the president of General Electric. But the systematic proliferation of such ideas is the designated function of the much more lowly executive who is charged with product development. At an early stage in the development of the toaster the participation of specialists in engineering, production, styling and design and possibly philosophy, art and spelling would have to be sought. No one in a position to authorize the product would do so without a judgment on how the problems of inscription were to be solved and at what cost. Nor, ordinarily, would an adverse finding on technical and economic feasibility be overridden. At some stage further development would become contingent on the findings of market researchers and merchandise experts on whether the toaster could be sold and at what price. Nor would an adverse decision by this group be overruled. In the end there would be a comprehensive finding on the feasibility of the innovation. If unfavorable, this would not be overruled. Nor, given the notoriety that attaches to lost opportunity, would be the more plausible contingency of a favorable recommendation. It will be evident that nearly all powers — initiation, character of development, rejection or acceptance — are exercised deep in the company. It is not the managers who decide. Effective power of decision is lodged deep down in the technical, planning and other specialized staff.[8]

V I

We must notice next that this exercise of group power can be rendered unreliable or ineffective by external interference. Not only does power pass into the organization but the quality of decision can easily be impaired by the efforts of an individual to retain control over the decision-making process.

Specifically, the group reaches a decision by receiving and evaluating the specialized information of its members. If it is to act responsibly, it must be accorded responsibility. It cannot be arbitrarily or capriciously overruled. If it is, it will develop the same tendencies to irresponsibility as an individual similarly treated.

But the tendency will be far more damaging. The efficiency of the group and the quality of its decisions depend on the quality of the information provided and the precision with which it is tested. The last increases greatly as men work together. It comes to be known that some are reliable and that some, though useful, are at a tacit discount. All information offered must be weighed. The sudden intervention of a superior introduces information, often of dubious quality, that is not subject to this testing. The reliability of a newcomer is unknown; the information of a boss may be automatically exempt from the proper discount; or his intervention may take the form of an instruction and thus be outside the process of group decision in a matter where only group decision incorporating the required specialized judgments is reliable. In all cases the intrusion is damaging. All with experience of large-scale business or government know the amount of time that informed juniors spend on considering how to contend with ill-informed superiors.

It follows from both the tendency for decision-making to pass down into organization and the need to protect the autonomy of the group that those who hold high formal rank in an organization — the president of General Motors or General Electric — exercise only modest powers of substantive decision. This power is far less

than conventional obeisance, professional public relations or, on occasion, personal vanity insist. Decision and ratification are often
confused. The first is important; the second is not. There is a further
tendency to associate power with any decision, however routine,
that involves a good deal of money. The most formidable business
protocol requires that money be treated with solemnity and respect,
and therewith the man who passes on its use. The nominal head of a
large corporation, though with slight power and perhaps in the first
stages of retirement, is also visible, tangible and comprehensible. It
is tempting and perhaps valuable for the corporate personality to
attribute to him power of decision that, in fact, belongs to a dull and
not easily comprehended collectivity. Nor is it a valid explanation
that the boss, though impotent on specific questions, acts on broad
issues of policy. Such issues of policy, if genuine, are pre-eminently
the ones that require the specialized information of the group.

Leadership assigns tasks to committees from which decisions
emerge. In doing so, it can break usefully with the routine into
which organization tends to fall. And it selects the men who com-
prise the groups that make the decisions, and it constitutes and re-
constitutes these groups in accordance with changing need. This is,
perhaps, its most important function. In an economy where organized intelligence is the decisive factor of production, the selection
of the intelligence so organized is of central importance. But it cannot be supposed that a boss can replace or even second-guess organized intelligence on substantive decisions.

VII

In the past, leadership in business organization was identified with
the entrepreneur — the individual who united ownership or control
of capital with the capacity for organizing the other factors of production and, in most contexts, with a further capacity for innovation.[9] With the rise of the modern corporation, the emergence of
the organization required by modern technology and planning and
the divorce of the owner of the capital from control of the enterprise, the entrepreneur no longer exists as an individual person in

the mature industrial enterprise.[10] Everyday discourse, except in the economics textbooks, recognizes this change. It replaces the entrepreneur as the directing force of the enterprise with management. This is a collective and imperfectly defined entity; in the large corporation it embraces chairman, president, those vice presidents with important staff or departmental responsibility, occupants of other major staff positions and, perhaps, division or department heads not included above. It includes, however, only a small proportion of those who, as participants, contribute information to group decisions. This latter group is very large; it extends from the most senior officials of the corporation to where it meets, at the outer perimeter, the white- and blue-collar workers whose function it is to conform more or less mechanically to instruction or routine. It embraces all who bring specialized knowledge, talent or experience to group decision-making. This, not the narrow management group, is the guiding intelligence — the brain — of the enterprise. There is no name for all who participate in group decision-making or the organization which they form. I propose we call this organization the Technostructure.

NOTES

1. Writers on management usually feel obliged to apologize before telling of the usefulness of committee action. "Of the various mechanisms of management, none is more controversial than committees . . . Despite their alleged shortcomings, committees are an important device of administration." Paul E. Holden, Lounsbury S. Fish and Hubert L. Smith, *Top Management Organization and Control* (New York: McGraw-Hill, 1951), p. 59.

   "Someone has facetiously suggested that a camel is a horse that was put together by a committee. As the tone of the comment suggests, committees have their critics. In spite of their weaknesses, however, the general consensus among administrators is that committees are essential in managing large organizations and often useful in managing smaller groups." Justin G. Longnecker, *Principles of Management and Organizational Behavior*, 3rd ed. (Columbus: Charles E. Merrill, 1973), p. 263.

2. "The purpose of organizations is to exploit the fact that many (virtu-

ally all) decisions require the participation of many individuals for their effectiveness." Kenneth J. Arrow, "On the Agenda of Organizations" in *The Corporate Society,* Robin Marris, ed. (New York: Wiley, 1974), p. 224. Professor Arrow uses the term "organization" in a larger sense than do I, and here to embrace the exchange of information through the market. Some of the contributors to Professor Marris's excellent volume conclude (p. 239) "that our entire contemporary society is a 'world of organizations.'"

3. Also committees are not, as commonly supposed, alike. Some are constituted not to pool and test information and offer a decision but to accord representation to diverse bureaucratic, pecuniary, political, ideological or other interests. And a particular committee may have some of both purposes. A committee with representational functions will proceed much less expeditiously, for its ability to reach a conclusion depends on the susceptibility of its participants to compromise, attrition and cupidity. The representational committee, in its present form, is engaged in a zero sum game, which is to say what some win, others lose. Pooling and testing information is nonzero sum — all participants end with a larger score.

4. Corporate decision-making is, also, not the expeditious process often imagined. "It is very illuminating to trace the history of an important decision in a major corporation. The length of the process (often a matter of years) and the complexity of its vicissitudes will very likely astonish those who think of the firm as a tightly run autocracy." William J. Baumol and Maco Stewart, "On the Behavioral Theory of the Firm" in *The Corporate Economy,* Robin Marris and Adrian Wood, eds. (Cambridge, Mass.: Harvard University Press, 1971), p. 139.

5. He was head of the Advanced Development Division of the Los Alamos Laboratory. His slightly earlier work was central to the conclusion that a self-sustaining chain reaction was possible. Cf. Henry De Wolf Smyth, *Atomic Energy for Military Purposes* (Princeton: Princeton University Press, 1945).

6. I reached some of these conclusions during World War II when, in the early years, I was in charge of price control. Decisions on prices — to fix, raise, rearrange or, very rarely, to lower them — came to my office after an extensive exercise in group decision-making in which lawyers, economists, accountants, those knowledgeable of the product and industry and specialists in public righteousness had all participated. Alone, one was nearly helpless to alter such decisions; hours or days of investigation would be required and, in the meantime, a dozen other decisions would have been made. Given what is commonly called an "adequate" staff, one could have exercised control. But an adequate

staff would be one that largely duplicated the decision-making group with adverse effect on the good nature and sense of responsibility of the latter and even more on the time required for decision. To have responsibility for all of the prices in the United States was awesome; to discover how slight was one's power in face of group decision-making was sobering. President Kennedy enjoyed responding to proposals for public action by saying, "I agree but I don't know whether the government will agree."

7. Since I first wrote these words, I have been advised by a number of people that they have had the same inspiration. A British engineer informed me that he developed the device while on fire watch in London in World War II.

8. "... the power of the firm's higher officers to enforce a decision is severely restricted by middle management's ability to delay or to act only with limited drive and enthusiasm." Baumol and Stewart.

9. "To act with confidence beyond the range of familiar beacons and to overcome that resistance requires aptitudes that are present in only a small fraction of the population and that define the entrepreneurial type as well as the entrepreneurial function." Joseph A. Schumpeter, *Capitalism, Socialism, and Democracy,* 2nd ed. (New York: Harper, 1947), p. 132.

10. He is still, of course, to be found in smaller firms and in larger ones that have yet to reach full maturity of organization.

The General Theory of Motivation

[*from* The New Industrial State]

The major error of economics has always been that everything is attributed to pecuniary innovation, economic reward. Here is presented what is necessary by way of correction or at least modification — the diverse and important role of other kinds of motivation.

*   *   *   *

OUR NEED IS TO KNOW the real goals of the technostructure and how they are pursued. Then we will know to what purposes and by what means we are governed in that large part of our life which is influenced by the planning system. Men have long thought it important to know how governments determine their taxes. It is rather more important to know the governing processes by which their incomes are determined, their prices set and their purchasing habits shaped.

The problem of goals begins with the relation of the individual to organization, in this case to the technostructure. What an organization will seek from society will be a reflection of what its members seek from the organization. If soldiers serve only for pay, the army is not likely to concern itself deeply in politics — at least so long as the pay is forthcoming. But if, as with Cromwell's men, they serve for the salvation of their souls, they are unlikely long to be politically neutral, at least in a wicked country. Parliaments will do well to keep their doors locked. If, as in Latin America, men join the army less from an excess of martial valor than from an element of political ambition, the danger will be even greater. If men principally want money from a corporation, the corporation will be primarily concerned with extracting money from the society. If they are interested in economic security or personal prestige, the corporation can hardly fail to reflect this in the kind of business it conducts.

What the society can ask from organization will depend, similarly, on the relation of the organization to the individual. When soldiers serve for pay, the state must pay the army that it summons to its call. The southern planter could be summoned by the impressment and made to bring his slaves, for slaves had no choice but to come. A laboratory run by the California Institute of Technology can be asked to work long hours to follow a space probe. That is because those who man it are united with the organization by scientific interest. A textile mill or an auto plant would not be capable of a similar response; its operatives or employees work only for pay.

These matters have not been much studied by economists. Men, it is assumed, act in economic matters solely in response to pecuniary compensation or, as the only alternative, to force. Force in the modern society is largely, although by no means completely, obsolete. So only pecuniary compensation remains of importance. The more of this, broadly speaking, the individual receives, the better and more sustained his effort. Only as to the very poor and those in menial occupations such as domestic service is there occasional concern that excessive pay may prove damaging to character and thus to effort.

Pecuniary compensation as a motivation, in its turn, supports profit maximization as the preclusive goal of the firm. Profit maximization gets the greatest return from the market; this enables the firm to buy the optimum effort from its members.

Though all this notably simplifies the economist's life, it is, unfortunately, at odds with the reality. In addition to pecuniary compensation, two other forces powerfully relate the individual to modern corporate organization. These further motives are inconsistent with a commitment by the firm to profit maximization. This is in keeping. Profit maximization is inconsistent with the behavior of the technostructure in the mature corporation. The other motives repair this inconsistency. What is more, they are essential to a satisfactory explanation of the behavior of the technostructure. As always, reality is in harmony within itself.

II

The most famous definition of an organization holds it to be a "system of consciously coordinated activities or forces of two or more persons."[1] The most important word here is coordinated. It means that the participating individuals are persuaded to set aside their individual purposes or goals and pursue those of the organization. All having done so, all work to the common goals. They are coordinated. Motivation is the means or inducement by which such coordination is effected — the means or inducement by which individuals are led to abandon their own goals and, with greater or lesser vigor, to pursue those of the organization.

The essentials of the matter are evident when a group of men dig a ditch. Ditch-digging is unlikely as an original passion for the average person. A useful completed excavation is a plausible goal of a group or organization. The problem is how to win the surrender of individual preference in favor of the disciplined wielding of a spade. This can be brought about in the following ways:

1. The group may compel the acceptance of its goals. Behind the man with the spade is another with a club. Failure to accept the goals of the group brings the negative reward of punishment. Without extravagant novelty, this motivation may be called *compulsion.*

2. The acceptance of the common goal may be purchased — at the end of the trench is a man with money. Acceptance of the goals of the organization brings not a negative but an affirmative reward. In return for this inducement, the individual "offers the organization . . . undifferentiated time and effort."[2] Such is *pecuniary motivation.*

3. The individual, on becoming associated with the group, may conclude that its goals are superior to his own. In the case of ditch-digging, the likelihood is less than in a chamber music group, a po-

litical conspiracy or the Marine Corps. Yet it exists. If the ditch drains a particularly nauseous and malarial swamp, the individual, on associating himself with the excavators, may then become aware of the utility of their common enterprise. This is to say that he finds the goals of the group superior to his own previous purposes and so he joins. "Humans, in contrast to machines, evaluate their own positions in relation to the value of others and come to accept others' goals as their own."[3] Such an exchange is not compelled. Neither is it purchased, although it is not inconsistent with compensation. Following Professor Herbert Simon, this motivating influence may be called *identification*.[4]

4. Finally, the individual may serve the organization not because he considers its goals superior to his own but because he hopes to make them accord more closely with his own. By being a member of the ditch-digging organization, he can hope for a ditch that, in capacity, depth or direction, conforms more closely to his ideal.

But once again the ditch-digger is not the most powerful example. The cabinet officer or high official who serves and on occasion concurs in action that he finds repugnant in order to advance measures of which he approves is a better case. He came to be part of something approaching a majority of American officialdom as those involved in the Vietnam war came to explain why they went along. Similarly motivated is the politician who would rather influence modestly the policies of a great party than be in full command of a one-man movement. And so is the corporation executive who strings along with much that he thinks unenterprising in the hope of winning support for a few new ideas of his own.

The pursuit of the goals of organization because of the prospect or in the hope of accommodating these goals more closely to the participant's preference is an important motivation. But unlike compulsion, pecuniary compensation or even identification, it has also much less standing in the theory of organization. A name for it must be coined, and I propose to call it *adaptation*. Adaptation, it will be evident, has much to do with the urge for power in a world of organization.

Compulsion, pecuniary compensation, identification and adaptation can motivate an individual either separately or in combination. Their collective influence I shall refer to as the *Motivating System*. The strength of any given motivation or of the motivating system will be measured by the effectiveness with which it aligns the individual with the goals of the organization. The motivating system varies greatly in power depending on the motivations that are combined. Some motivations clash and so neutralize each other. Some combine passively. Some strongly reinforce each other. What is called an effective organization is one which, in substantial measure, has a motivating system that is internally reinforcing. The goals of the organization are thus pursued with the greatest possible effect. I turn now to the relation between the several motivating forces.

III

Compulsion and pecuniary compensation exist in varying degrees of association with each other. Those who are compelled to accept the goals of organization by fear of punishment — of negative reward — always have some affirmative compensation for such acceptance. The slave got the whip when he did not work; he got food and shelter of a sort when he did. The controversy as to which of these motivating forces was strongest in the antebellum South is still intense.[5] As we shall see presently, varying amounts of compulsion are associated with pecuniary compensation.

Compulsion is inconsistent with either identification or adaptation. If a person is compelled to accept the goals of an organization, he is unlikely, at least so long as he is under the sense of compulsion, to find them superior to his own. The conflict is not quite absolute. Household slaves — in contrast with field hands — were believed to accept the goals of their masters. In consequence, they were thought unreliable material for insurrections. The reluctant draftee may come, in time, to relish the barracks and parade ground. But the broad rule holds: what is compelled cannot be a matter of choice. Alienation, not identification, will be the normal result. Bondsmen and serfs have regularly been thought to love their masters — in other words, to have identified themselves deeply with their masters' goals. This has not always prevented them, when the opportunity arose, from asserting their own very different goals, frequently after burning the master's house and its occupants or showing some similar manifestation of distaste.

Nor is compulsion consistent with adaptation. If the individual is obliged to accept the goals of organization, he will not embrace them in the hope of accommodating them more closely to his own. When his acceptance is forced, he will understand that he has no power over the goals to which he is compelled. The serf, slave or prison occupant takes the goals of the organization with which he is associated as given and, eccentric cases apart, is alienated from them all. He does only what avoids punishment. Similarly, the oldest rule of the reluctant soldier is to take life as it comes and never volunteer.

Pecuniary motivation may be associated in greater or lesser measure with compulsion. This will depend on the level of the compensation and the nature of the individual's alternatives. If the element of compulsion is high, it follows that pecuniary motivation will then be inconsistent with identification and adaptation. If it is low, they are readily reconciled. The difference here is of great importance for understanding modern economic behavior.

The worker in a Calcutta jute mill who loses his job — like his American counterpart during the Great Depression — has no high prospect of ever finding another. He has no savings. Nor does he have unemployment insurance. The alternative to his present employment, accordingly, is slow but definitive starvation. So, though nominally a free worker, he is compelled. The fate of a defecting southern slave before the Civil War or a serf before Alexander II was not appreciably more painful. The choice between hunger and flogging may well be a matter of personal taste. The aversion to the organization that compels the acceptance of its goals will be much the same in each instance. This aversion excludes identification. To repeat, the fact that the worker serves because he is compelled sufficiently reveals to him his powerlessness vis-à-vis the organization and its goals. Adaptation is thus also excluded.

The modern industrial employee who loses or abandons his job has, by contrast, every expectation of finding another. In the meantime he has unemployment compensation and perhaps some personal resources, and, if the worst comes to the worst, he can go on welfare. The danger of physical discomfort has been much reduced and therewith, in general, the element of compulsion. In higher income brackets it will be yet lower. As the aspect of compulsion in pecuniary compensation diminishes or disappears, so do the barriers to identification and adaptation.

I V

The diminishing role of compulsion in pecuniary compensation has been a force of no small historical importance. Among other things it goes far to explain the disappearance of slavery itself. Until two centuries ago the motivation of the wage laborer in most parts of the world was not radically different from that of the bondsman. Both got little; both toiled in fear of the alternative.

The slave, accordingly, had no reason to regard the free wage-worker with much envy. He did not press aggressively to change his own position. Nor did society on his behalf. But as the wage-worker improved his material position, the element of compulsion to which he was subject diminished. Then the contrast between free man and slave deepened and slavery became untenable. In the absence of the Civil War, slavery in the United States could have lasted only a few more years. For, in a relatively short time, industrialization and rising living standards in the North together with improving communications would have made it increasingly difficult to keep the slaves in the fields. And the cost of patrols and the machinery for redeeming fugitives, together with the capital loss from those who made good their escape into northern employments, would have been intolerable. Planters would have been forced to pay inducements, i.e., wages, to hold their men. As in other countries at a roughly similar stage in economic development, slavery would have been given up. The reform would have been attributed to the innate humanity of man to man. By 1880 or 1890 at the latest, the more respected philosophers would have been congratulating the nation on having accomplished peacefully what men once feared could only have been done by war.

As it is wrong to deny the role of conscience in human affairs, it is also an error to minimize that of economics. Speaking to the same subject, when bondsmen were still valuable property, Adam Smith observed: "The late resolution of the Quakers in Pennsylvania to set at liberty their negro slaves, may satisfy us that their number cannot be very great."[6]

v

As compulsion and pecuniary compensation are associated in varying mix, so also are identification and adaptation. The two are highly complementary. An individual, on becoming associated with an organization, will be more likely to adopt its goals in place of his own if he has hope of changing those he finds unsatisfactory or repugnant. And if he is strongly identified with the goals of an organization, he will be moved all the more strongly to try to improve it — to alter (i.e., adapt) any unsatisfactory goals so that they accord with his own. A member will identify himself more enthusiastically with a political party if he feels that he has some power to influence its platform. This is why effective political leaders seek to give their rank and file the impression, if not the reality, of participation in the making of the party program.

The relation of identification to adaptation is partly a matter of temperament; the disposition of some on associating themselves with an organization is to accept its goals and of others to improve them. Some college presidents and diplomats, by disposition, accept the goals of their respective institutions; others seek to advance the purposes of education or peace. Adaptation is also partly a matter of position in the hierarchy of the organization. It more strongly motivates a President of the United States than a postman making his rounds, more strongly the general manager than the receptionist, the pastor than the sexton.

Pecuniary motivation cannot be combined with identification and adaptation when the element of compulsion is large — when there is no tolerable alternative to the toil that gets the income. It can be when the element of compulsion is small. This means that the motivational system will be different in the poor country as compared with the rich, and different for the poor as compared with the well-to-do. And what begins as a difference in degree widens, ultimately, into a difference in kind.

In the poor country, and among the poorly paid, labor relations will, in general, be harsh and angry. The compulsion associated with low compensation alienates the worker from the employer. This being so, the employer does not seek to cultivate his employee's loyalty — to encourage his identification with the firm — for this he knows to be impossible. There being nothing to lose, nothing is lost by arrogant or offensive behavior. The worker, not being identified with the employer, will be receptive to the goals of the union. He or she will also be vulnerable to threats from the employer of being fired, for this is precisely the hardship feared and the one that compels effort. The stage is thus set for disagreeable behavior on both sides. Those concerned have rarely failed to conform to expectation.

In the richer country and among the well-to-do, everything is more benign. Compulsion has receded. In consequence, there is little or no alienation; the way is open for the worker to accept the goals of the organization. The worker will have less inducement to join a union but much less to fear in doing so. The employer will seek to encourage the identification of the worker with the firm; the worker having less to fear, the employer will find it less useful to play on his fears. The worker being more identified with the firm, the union has less enmity to arouse. On both sides the motivating system both allows and rewards more agreeable behavior. This mellowing of industrial relations, the result of wealth, will be attributed to humane instincts, greater employer enlightenment, more responsible unions and the spread of industrial statesmanship.

Here is the paradox of pecuniary motivation. In general, the higher the amount, the less its importance in relation to other motivations. With higher income there is, under most circumstances, a lessened dependence on a particular employment. So there is a lessened element of compulsion, and this paves the way for identification and adaptation. These supplement and may transcend pecuniary compensation in their importance in the motivating system.

Pecuniary compensation need not be the sole or even the main motivation of members of the technostructure. Identification and adaptation may be driving forces. Above a certain level these may operate independently of income. Maximization of income by members of the technostructure is not an imperative. The question of what goals members of the technostructure identify themselves with, and to what personal goals they seek adaptation, remains. But it will be clear that there is no absolute conflict with the stockholders as there would be if both were seeking to maximize pecuniary return — if, in short, the conventional economic motivation were accepted.

VII

One test of sound social analysis is that it explains small matters as well as great. One of the most puzzling pleas of the American business executive, regularly echoed in public rituals, is for lower taxes to encourage initiative and effort. The puzzle lies in the fact that few executives would ever admit to putting forth less than their best effort for their present income after taxes. To suggest such malingering would be considered a gross insult.

An explanation is now at hand. The reference to incentives is traditional, a hangover from a more primitive association of income and effort. It accords seeming respectability and social utility to the desire for lower taxes or the natural wish to shift more of the existing burden to the poor. But the reality is that the executive's present level of income allows for identification and adaptation. These are the operative motivations. They are also the only personally reputable ones: the executive cannot afford to have it thought that his commitment to the goals of the corporation is less than complete or that he is at all indifferent to his opportunity to shape these goals. To suggest that he subordinates these latter motives to his response to pay would be to confess that he is an inferior executive.

NOTES

1. Chester I. Barnard, *The Functions of the Executive* (Cambridge, Mass.: Harvard University Press, 1956), p. 73.
2. Herbert A. Simon, *Administrative Behavior,* 2nd ed. (New York: Macmillan, 1957), p. 115.
3. James G. March and Herbert A. Simon, *Organizations* (New York: Wiley, 1958), p. 65.
4. This term, which has overtones of suburban psychology, is not entirely satisfactory. When first working out these ideas, I used the word *conformance* — and this must appear in the long-forgotten lecture notes of my students. Its tone implies, however, that the individual is somehow pressed or forced to conform, and this is not the meaning sought. Identification has no connotation of compulsion and has the claim of prior use. I should like to acknowledge my debt to Professor Simon and his associates. The literature dealing with organization and organization theory is of singular aridity. By far the most distinguished of the exceptions is the work of Herbert A. Simon and his colleagues. The two key volumes are *Administrative Behavior* and *Organizations.* Everyone professionally concerned with organization must know these difficult but rewarding books.
5. In the aftermath of Robert William Fogel's and Stanley L. Engerman's *Time on the Cross* (Boston: Little, Brown, 1974).
6. Adam Smith, *Wealth of Nations,* Book 3 (New York: Modern Library, 1937), Chapter 2, p. 366.

Economics and the Quality of Life[1]

[*from* Economics, Peace and Laughter]

*When this was written, it was a very contentious piece. It was then be-
lieved that an economist does not question economic influence, even
power. All the more need for a contrary view.*

*   *   *   *

IN THIS ARTICLE I suggest the social problems, and therewith
the political tasks, which become most important with a relatively advanced state of economic development. To see these
tasks in proper perspective, one must have in mind the relation of
economic circumstance to social thought and therewith to political
action. In the poor society this relationship is understandably powerful and rigid. For various reasons, the rich society also continues
to assume that economic condition must be the dominant influence
on social thought and action. This assumption becomes, in turn, a
barrier both to rational thought and needed action. It is exploited
by vested intellectual and pecuniary interests. Let me summarize the
matter briefly.

Economic circumstance has a dominant influence on social attitudes in the poor society because for those who are poor, nothing is
so important as their poverty and nothing is so necessary as its miti-
gation. In consequence, among the poor, only religion, with its
promise of a later munificence for those who endure privation with
patience, has been competitive with economic circumstance in

shaping social attitudes. And since for nearly all time nearly all people have lived under the threat of economic privation, men of all temperaments and views have stressed the controlling and permanent influence of economic need. "The mode of production in material life determines the general character of the social, political and spiritual processes of life."[2] "Here and there the ardour of the military or the artistic spirit has been for a while predominant; but religious and economic influences . . . have nearly always been more important than all others put together."[3]

In the poor society not only do economic considerations dominate social attitudes but they rigidly specify the problems that will be accorded priority. Under conditions of scarcity and human privation, there is obvious need to get as much as possible out of the productive resources that are available — to use the labor, capital, natural resources and intelligence of the community with maximum efficiency. Such effort enlarges the supply of goods and thus mitigates the most pressing problem of the society, which is the scarcity of needed things. There is similar concern over who gets the revenues from production and who thus can buy what is produced, for one man's happy advantage will be another man's exploitation. Thus the two classical concerns of normative economics — how to increase productive efficiency and how to reconcile this with distributive equity — are the natural consequences of general poverty.

In the past in poor countries, all whom feudal prerogative, private fortune, exceptional personal accomplishment, imaginative larceny or military or political reward exempted from the common privation quickly became subject to noneconomic preoccupations — military adventure, political ambition, artistic patronage, sexual or other physical achievement, social intercourse or horsemanship. To be accomplished in these matters was to prove economic emancipation.

When people generally experience improved economic well-being, there is a similar and general loosening of the grip of economics on their social attitudes. No longer does increased production mean lessened pain. And no longer does the fact that one person gets more than he needs mean that someone else gets less than enough. Yet economic compulsion continues to have a highly influential bearing on social attitudes and resulting political behavior in the generally affluent community. Although economic goals release their absolute grip, they retain, nonetheless, much of their original prestige.

This is partly for reasons of tradition. Economic goals having been so long considered paramount, they are thought immutable. Economists have also long equated physical with psychic need; for many years, none might pass a Ph.D. qualifying examination who said that the wish of a poor family for adequate shelter was superior in urgency to that of a rich family for a mansion rivaling that of the still richer family next door. To do so was to interpose unscientific judgments and invite immediate discredit. Psychic need being on a parity with physical need and infinitely extensible, the urgency of increased production and thus of the economic problem did not diminish with increased well-being.

Economics also retained its grip on social attitudes because of compassionate appeal to the problem of unemployment and racial disadvantage. As living standards have risen, consumption has pressed less insistently on income. Corporations have had increased freedom to save for their own purposes — notably their expansion, which rewards the corporate bureaucracy. Failure to offset the resulting savings has become a cause of unemployment. Against the well-being of the majority has therefore to be set the misfortune of those whom increasing affluence has left without work and reliable income. And this disadvantage, it has come more recently to be observed, is suffered in special measure by blacks and other minority groups. So even though improvement in living standards might be less urgent, improvement in economic performance to provide jobs for the unemployed and the minorities remains of high importance, and appeals to this purpose have a high moral content. Increasingly, the purpose of the economy has become not the goods it produces but the jobs it provides.

Economic goals are also strongly, if not always visibly, supported by vested interest. The prestige of important groups in the community depends on the priority accorded to their function. If nothing is so important as production, no one is as important as the producer — the businessman. If other goals take precedence, so do other people. The importance of economic goals for the prestige of the economist needs scarcely to be emphasized.

Economic goals also serve vested interest in a very practical way. For if such goals take precedence, public questions will be decided according to economic tests. These are much less complicated than other tests. A road can be cut through a park, the countryside turned over to industry, waste turned into the air or a lake, a welfare measure rejected, a change in work habits commanded, all on a simple showing of beneficial economic effect. This is a great simplification. To validate noneconomic goals is to risk a very different decision with different benefits and beneficiaries.

Finally, economic goals remain important for the vacuum they fill. A society must have a purpose. A highly tangible purpose is to produce goods for private consumption. The annual increase in this production can be measured. The result can be taken as an index of national vigor and success. This measure we now employ.

We are, to be sure, allowed occasional doubts about this index of national achievement. And there are anomalies that are a trifle embarrassing. As more basic requirements are filled, expansion naturally occurs in less urgent items. There is diminished emphasis on steel or bread grains (these or the capacity for producing them may even be redundant) and there is more emphasis on electric golf carts and electric toothbrushes. Questions may arise whether national vigor is to be measured by the ability to have dental hygiene without muscular effort or athletic endeavor while sitting down. However, this is a minor embarrassment. Though economic growth consists increasingly in items of luxury consumption, we have successfully converted the enjoyment of luxury into an index of national virtue. Or almost so.

Some concern is also allowed as to whether all of the important tasks of the society are being equally well performed. The contrast between public penury and private affluence is remarked. The starvation of the public services, notably those of the cities, and the ample consumption of those who live in the adjacent suburbs are increasingly apparent.

But, in general, we remain subject to economic preoccupations. Economic goals are paramount. The guidance of economists on how to achieve them is accepted as a matter of course. There are, I believe, serious dangers in this delegation. This we see if we look more closely at the sociology and the mystique of economics. We then see how this most developed and influential of the social sciences can be influential also in misguidance when the society is subject to change and when the social problem has ceased to be primarily economic.

II

Unlike the natural sciences, which have long been viewed as the behavioral norm by economists, economics is subject to two types of change. The first is in the interpretation of given phenomena. The second is in needed accommodation to change in economic behavior or institutions. The development of the social accounts (national income, gross national product and their components) in the nineteen-thirties, the evolution of the input-output matrix in the forties and the application of computer techniques to economic data in the fifties and sixties are all examples of the first type of change. The accommodation of economic theory to the rise of the trade union, to the development of the large corporation or to the changing behavior resulting from the transition of the average person from comparative privation to, by past standards, comparative well-being are examples of the second type of change.

Economics is progressive as regards the first type of change — conceptual advances or innovations in interpretive apparatus are promptly examined, enthusiastically discussed and, where useful, willingly adopted. From index numbers through the social accounts to modern quantitative methods, these developments have contributed greatly to the guidance of the American economy and also to the conduct of business. Both modern public and business administration are deeply dependent on them.

By contrast, economics is rigorously conservative in accommodating to underlying change. Until quite recently, wage theory did not recognize the unions. Their importance was not denied. But, by an agreeable convention, one was allowed in pedagogy and scientific discourse to assume away their effect. "Let us suppose," the lecture began, "there are no unions or other impediments in the labor market." The modern corporation has not yet been assimilated into economic theory, although the corporate system is all but coterminus with mining, communications, public utilities and manufacturing — in short, the largest part of economic life. The theory of the firm makes little distinction between a Wisconsin dairy farm and the General Motors Corporation except to the extent that the latter may be thought more likely to have some of the technical aspects of monopoly.[4] All economists agree that there has been a revolutionary increase in popular well-being in the past thirty or forty years. Most textbooks have yet to concede that this has altered economic calculation or affected economic motivation. This means that the shape of the economic problem is not assumed to be changed by being solved.

The reasons for this reluctance to admit to the effects of underlying change are three: There is, as always, the tendency to protect vested interest; there is the imitative scientism of the social sciences which is, perhaps, carried farther in economics than in any other discipline; and there is the natural wish of the scholar to avoid controversy.

On vested interest there need be little comment. We all have a deep stake in what we understand. Moreover, much underlying change — this is especially true of the movement to higher levels of well-being — diminishes the urgency and scope of economic judgment. Well-being reduces the importance of economic choice and therewith of economic advice based on economic calculation. Unions and large corporations make the dynamics of organization as important as the authority of the market in telling what will happen. This, in turn, diminishes the authority of economic judgment. So, like cavalry generals, locomotive firemen and fundamentalist preachers, economists deny the existence of what it is professionally disadvantageous to concede.

The natural sciences are not subject to underlying institutional or behavioral change. In consequence, economics seems more scientific if it is deemed to have a similar immutability. This explains, in turn, the considerable scientific self-righteousness with which sophisticated scholars avow the irrelevance of, say, the advent of modern advertising for the theory of demand. It is a libel on the scientific integrity of economics to suppose that its scientific verities are affected by such superficial change. Moreover, the first steps to bring institutional changes within the framework of economic analysis are invariably tentative, oral rather than mathematical and lacking the elegance of a methodological innovation. Hence they are readily dismissed by the men of scientific reputation or pretension as being rather sloppy.[5] Thus does a scientific or pseudoscientific posture direct economics away from accommodation to underlying social and institutional change. And it does so with the blessing of presumptively scientific attitude, method and conscience.

But an instinct to caution also plays a role. Methodological change rarely has implications for public policy; if it does, they are likely to be minor. Adaptation to social and institutional change, by contrast, may have large and radical policy implications.

Economists who have been associated with such change and the related policy — Lord Keynes in Britain, Alvin Hansen and Seymour Harris in the United States — have led a rather controversial existence. This is not to everyone's taste. I do not suggest that economists are peculiarly craven. Other disciplines have far less experience with controversy because they are not under attack at all. But many economists do find harmony agreeable. In the years following World War II, having just come through the Keynesian revolution, which was a major accommodation to major underlying change, and having discovered that the critics who once dissented had become acquiescent and were, indeed, finding a common ground with economists on the conservative consequences of according priority to economic goals, there was a special reluctance among economists to look for new trouble. In the intellectual backwaters, the name of Keynes still struck a radical note. Surely it was possible to bask a bit longer in the reputation for living dangerously that his name thus invoked.[6]

III

This reluctance to accommodate to underlying change is not new. Its consequence is that, in time of social and institutional change, the advice on practical matters which reflects the accepted economic view will often and perhaps usually be in error. The advice will relate to previous and not to present institutions: The needed action, unfortunately, must relate to the reality. If it does not, it will be at best inadequate or useless and at worst damaging.

The danger here can be illustrated by reference to the last great change in underlying behavior and institution and the related watershed in economic decision. In the twentieth century unemployment — the failure to use resources — replaced the problem of efficiency in resource use. In the autumn of 1929, when unemployment began to grow rapidly, President Hoover's first instinct was to cut taxes and to urge corporations to maintain purchasing power by not reducing wages. This was completely in conflict with accepted economic views. The economists continued to respond to the belief that efficient use of productive resources, not full employment, was the central need. This required that there be no interference with the labor market. Or with prices. And since the system was believed to supply itself adequately with its own purchasing power — as in an earlier and simpler day it did — nothing need be done to increase demand by public action. It was sufficient to balance the budget and adhere to the gold standard. This advice was of no value for preventing unemployment; nearly all economists would now agree that if followed, it would only make matters worse. In time, Mr. Hoover himself surrendered to the accepted economic view. The subsequent reversal of the approved policies by Roosevelt in 1933 was viewed with skepticism and even hostility by most economists of acknowledged reputation.[7,8] This outcome was to be expected. There had been extensive underlying change leading to change in the problem to be solved. Accommodation was, as usual, slow. Prescription was, accordingly, for the wrong problem. As a matter of prudence, this tendency of economists must be expected in any time of change.

IV

The preoccupation of economists now continues to be with the volume of output of goods and services both for itself and as the remedy for unemployment. Once again underlying change has made the preoccupation partially obsolete; as a result, the recommendations of economists are again either irrelevant or damaging. I have used the phrase "partially obsolete." The tendency of institutional change is to introduce new preoccupations without entirely dispensing with the old ones. In the nineteen-thirties, though unemployment became the central problem, inefficiency did not become unimportant. A high level of employment remains important now. But the need is to prescribe first for the most important problems. Though production and employment were the central problems of the Great Depression, they have not, by any available standard of measurement, been so serious since. It is logical, accordingly, to ask if underlying circumstances may not have made other goals more urgent. The question is especially in order if there are obvious shortcomings in the lives of those who are employed — if education is deficient, regional development is unequal, slums persist, health care is inadequate, cultural opportunities are unequal, entertainment is meretricious or racial inequality is glaring. And the need for prior concern for education, slum abatement, improved health, regional development or racial equality would be even more clear if these could be shown to be the cause of unemployment and retarded economic growth. In fact, all of the conditions for a shift from the preoccupation with unemployment and growth do exist. The primary prescription must henceforth be for the improvement of what may broadly be called the quality of life. This should now be the foremost goal.

Reference to the quality of life will be thought replete with value judgments; the condemnation of value judgments, in turn, is one of the devices by which scientific pretension enforces adherence to traditional preoccupations.[9] But even economists must agree with a social goal which accords the individual the opportunity of providing for all of his needs, not merely for a part of them. And most must agree that the individual should be the end in himself and not the instrument of the business firm or public bureaucracy which was created to serve him. By both standards, imperfections are easily visible. They are the result of the priority now accorded economic goals and the considerable power of the machinery we have created to pursue these goals.

V

There is, first, the continuing imbalance in the way needs are met. We identify economic performance with the production of goods and services. Such production is, in the main, the task of the private sector of the economy. As a result, privately produced goods and services, even of the most frivolous sort, enjoy a moral sanction not accorded to any public service except defense.

Desire for private goods is subject to active cultivation — a point to which I will return. And the equation of psychic with physical need excludes any notion of satiety. It is a mark of an enfeebled imagination to suggest that two automobiles to a family are sufficient. Public services, by contrast, are the subject of no similar promotion; that there are severe limits to what should be expended for such services is, of course, assumed.

The consequence of this difference in attitude is a sharp discrimination in favor of one and against another class of needs. Meanwhile a series of changes in the society increases the pressure for public services. A growing population, and particularly a growing urban population, increases the friction of person upon person and the outlay that is necessary for social harmony. And it is reasonable to suppose that a growing proportion of the requirements of an increasingly civilized community — schools, colleges, libraries, museums, hospitals, recreational facilities — are by their nature in the public domain.

And increasing private production itself adds to the urgency of public services. The automobile obviously demands streets and highways, traffic control and control of air pollution. From the pressure of mining, fishing, lumbering and other resource industries on the public agencies responsible for regulation and conservation to the needs imposed by the container industry on trash removal, the effect is similar.

It should also be observed that if appropriate attention is not accorded to public needs, the private sector itself will suffer in technical performance. Much of its knowledge and technology is supplied from the public sector. Modern industry has come, in particular, to require its own type of man. One consequence is that a major part of the unemployment is now of people whose place of birth, family characteristics, childhood environment or race denied them access in their youth to normal opportunities for education and training.[10] The same is true of individuals and families that fall below the poverty line.[11] Thus it comes about that the remedy for unemployment and individual privation depends to a very considerable degree on the balance between public and private services — or, more generally, on measures to improve the quality of life.

I have dealt with a number of these concerns before; one must not overdo that particular manifestation of scholarship which consists in repeating one's self and other people. But there is a new danger in this area which is now urgent.

If unemployment is deemed to be the dominant problem, and if, as in the past, expansion of the economy is deemed a complete remedy, it will not matter much how this is achieved. Tax reduction and an acceleration of the expansion in demand for the output of the private sector will be entirely appropriate. Even some reduction in public services, if offset by a larger increase in private outlays, will be sound policy. However, if the problem is the quality of the society, it will matter a great deal how the expansion of demand is managed. Improvement in needed public services, given the tendency to imbalance, improves the quality of the society. Expansion of private services without expansion of public services brings, *prima facie,* no similar improvement. It could lead to distortions that would mean a reduction in the quality of life. And plainly an expansion of the private sector which is won at the expense of the public sector is intolerable. It provides what we least need at the expense of what we most need. And since the ultimate remedy for much unemployment depends on public sector investment in the unemployed (or their children), the policy may fail in even its avowed purpose.

There may be times when tax reduction will be a legitimate measure for securing improved economic performance. Defense expenditures are a large share of all public outlays and also are protected by special attitudes and a powerful constituency. Should it be possible to reduce these, it would be possible and perhaps necessary to reduce taxes — even while improving other services. But tax reduction for the express purpose of expanding production and employment must be regarded with the greatest suspicion.[12] The crude Keynesian case is that any source of spending is acceptable, for it acts equally to expand the economy. But by bringing unbalanced production, tax reduction will ordinarily add to output at the expense of the quality of life. This effect will be increased because the expansion may well be without the added public services that the expansion itself requires. Also, the policy invites a coalition between those who seek tax reduction for purposes of Keynesian policy and those who simply want lower taxes and less government. This could be a formidable and damaging coalition.[13]

VI

The quality of life will also suffer if individuals are not an end in themselves but an instrument of some purpose that is not their own. This too is a danger in our situation. We have developed an economic system of great power. We have reason to be grateful for its achievements. But it has its purposes and it seeks naturally to accommodate people and the society to these purposes. If economic goals are preoccupying, we will accept the accommodation of society to the needs of the great corporations and the supporting apparatus of the state. We will regret our surrender but we will reconcile ourselves to the inevitable. If we have economic goals in proper perspective, we will question the desirability of such subordination.

One part of this subordination is that of the individual to the organization, specifically the corporation, by which he is employed. This has been considerably discussed[14] and none can doubt the tendency. The corporation requires its own type of man; he must be willing to subordinate his own goals to those of the organization. And it is necessary if the organization is to succeed. It is what makes possible group performance of tasks. And by combining experience, knowledge, technical skills and art, such group performance greatly improves on what an individual can accomplish, popular myth to the contrary. This is, of course, regularly combined with vehement protestations of the most muscular individuality on the part of the participants.

We must keep this part of the problem in perspective. The competitive market also has its type. It is not clear that the wary, uncompassionate, self-regarding, wit-matching rug dealer, in whom both deviousness and cupidity may have been as often rewarded as penalized, would have been kept in the Temple while the organization man was expelled. Also the corporation executive commits himself voluntarily to what William Whyte has called the social ethic of the corporation.[15] He can readily escape if he is willing to forgo the compensation which purchases conformity.

The most serious problem is not the discipline imposed by organization on its members but the discipline imposed on society to make the latter accord better with its needs. The behavior and beliefs of society are, in fact, subject to extensive management to accord with economic need and convenience. Not even scientific truth, much as our culture presumes to canonize it, is exempt. The tobacco industry has not yet ceased to reveal its discontent with scientists who, on the basis of rather impressive evidence, aver that cigarettes are a cause not only of lung cancer but of a disconcerting assortment of other fatal or disabling maladies. The economic well-being of the industry requires the active and energetic recruitment of new customers. This need is paramount. So there is no alternative to impeaching the scientists and their evidence.[16]

Similarly, and in conceivably a more dangerous area, we have come to assume that our defense strategy, and even in some degree our foreign policy, will be accommodated to the needs of the industries serving the defense establishment. Before leaving office, President Eisenhower warned of the rise of the military-industrial complex, a concern which had previously been pressed somewhat less influentially by the late C. Wright Mills.[17] The Eisenhower-Mills contention was, in essence, that defense budgets and procurements were being influenced not by national need but by what served the economic interests of suppliers.

However, these are only the extreme cases; they highlight an effort that is pervasive and inherent. No producer, in our present state of economic development, would be so naive as to launch a new product without appropriately attempting to reconstruct the pattern of consumer wants to include the innovation. He cannot be sure of succeeding. But he would never be forgiven if he failed to try. Nor does any commercially viable producer leave the consumer to unpersuaded choice among existing products. The management of consumption in accordance with economic interest has become one of the most complex arts of our time. The participants urge their virtuosity in uninhibited terms save, perhaps, when it becomes a subject for social criticism. At this stage, consumer persuasion ceases to be such and becomes a bland but indispensable exercise in providing the public with greatly needed information.

In a well-to-do community we cannot be much concerned over what people are persuaded to buy. The marginal utility of money is low; were it otherwise, people would not be open to persuasion. The more serious conflict is with truth and aesthetics. There is little that can be said about most economic goods. A toothbrush does little but clean teeth. Alcohol is important mostly for making people more or less drunk. An automobile can take one reliably to a destination and back, and its further features are of small consequence as compared with the traffic encountered. There being so little to be said, much must be invented. Social distinction must be associated with a house or a swimming pool, sexual fulfillment with a particular shape of automobile, social acceptance with a hair oil or mouthwash, improved health with a hand lotion or, at best, a purgative. We live surrounded by a systematic appeal to a dream world which all mature, scientific reality would reject. We, quite literally, advertise our commitment to immaturity, mendacity and profound gullibility. It is the hallmark of the culture. And it is justified as being economically indispensable.

The conflict with aesthetics is even more serious. As the economic problem is resolved, people can be expected to become increasingly concerned about the beauty of their environment. From getting goods, people can be expected to go on to getting the surroundings in which the goods can be enjoyed. But harmony between economic and aesthetic accomplishment cannot be assumed. On the contrary, conflict must be assumed, at least in the short run.

With rare and probably accidental exceptions, an aesthetically attractive environment requires that economic development take place within an overall framework. Thus agreeable urban communities are invariably those in which law or fashion allow of variant treatments within a larger and symmetrical design. Such communities must be related to properly protected open space, for parks and countryside lose their meaning if they are invaded at random by habitation, traffic, industry or advertising. Separation of industry and commerce from living space is essential if the latter is to be agreeable — neither a steel mill nor a service station is an aesthetically rewarding neighbor. Likewise, good theater and good music require the protection of a mood; they cannot be successfully juxtaposed to rhymed jingles on behalf of a laxative.

All of this is in conflict with short-run economic priority.[18] Economic efficiency rightly accords the greatest possible freedom for uninhibited use and uncontrolled dissonance. It is handicapped by the framework that aesthetic goals require. And economic organization strongly affirms its need for freedom. Proposals for control are pictured as subversive; concern for beauty is pictured as effete. Purely as a matter of tactics, this makes sense.

We see, however, that this need not necessarily be accepted. The priority of economic goals will, of course, continue to be defended. The vigor of the defense will increase as people come to see the price that they pay for it. But we can have the social control that establishes the necessary framework for economic development and that erases or segregates industrial squalor and preserves and even enhances beauty. A price in industrial efficiency must be assumed. But economic development enables us to pay the price; it is one of the advantages of development. It cannot be supposed that we have development in order to make our surroundings more hideous and our culture more meretricious.

Nor should scholars and scientists be detained for a moment by the protest that this is a highbrow view and that people must be allowed to have what they want. This is the standard defense of economic priority. It is the argument not of those who want to defend the public choice. It is the argument of those who want no interference in their management of the public choice.

It will be sensed that these are controversial matters — much more controversial than the questions surrounding economic growth and full employment. Important questions of social policy inevitably arouse passion. A consensus is readily reached on things that are unimportant or on their way to solution. That these matters are controversial and that expansion of output and employment is not is very good proof that economics is now concerned with the wrong problem.

Escape from the commitment to economic priority has, it will be clear, a broadly emancipating role. It enables us to consider a range of new tasks from the improvement of our cities to the cleaning up of roadside commerce, to the enlargement of cultural opportunity, to the redemption of mass communications from the hucksters, to the suppression of the influence of weapons makers on foreign policy. The political and social power that is available for these tasks is not negligible. Scientists, humane scholars, teachers, artists and the community that is identified with these preoccupations have been asserting themselves with increasing influence and self-confidence.

Given a clear view of the issue and need and given release from the assumption of economic priority, that influence will surely deepen and expand. Nothing is more to be wished, welcomed and urged.

NOTES

1. This article was originally the AAAS Distinguished Lecture at the annual meeting of the American Association for the Advancement of Science in Cleveland, Ohio, December 27, 1963, and was later changed considerably for publication.
2. Karl Marx, "A Contribution to the *Critique of Political Economy*," Author's Preface to the 1859 German edition of *Capital*.
3. Alfred Marshall, *Principles of Economics*, 5th ed. (London: Macmillan, 1907), p. 1.
4. ". . . the functioning of the modern corporate system has not to date been adequately explained or, if certain explanations are accepted as adequate, it seems difficult to justify." Edward S. Mason, ed., *The Corporation in Modern Society* (Cambridge, Mass.: Harvard University Press, 1959), p. 4.
5. One thinks here of Adolf Berle's efforts to bring the corporation within the framework of economic analysis. Though it had many shortcomings, it had much greater relevance to the behavior of the firm than theoretical models which ignored questions of size and corporate structure. But among the economic cognoscenti his work has enjoyed much lower standing.
6. I should like to stress again that in discussing the reluctance of economists to accommodate to underlying change, my motive is not criticism but to isolate a fact of some contemporary consequence. And while I am identified with the notion that increased well-being has had a profound effect on economic behavior, I am not entering a personal complaint of neglect. On the contrary, it was the view of significant economists that these contentions received too much attention. Thus Professor George Stigler, a past president of the American Economic Association, once expressed "shock" that so many more Americans had read *The Affluent Society* than *Wealth of Nations*. (*The Intellectual and the Market Place;* University of Chicago, Graduate School of Business, *Selected Papers* No. 3, 1963.) I was reluctant to reply to Professor Stigler, for to do so could have seemed to be urging the claims of my book against those of a classic. (And I could have conceivably been missing

the deeper cause of Professor Stigler's sorrow, which might have been not that so many read Galbraith and Smith but that so few read Stigler at all.)

7. The Roosevelt economists were largely without professional prestige. None of them — Rexford G. Tugwell, Gardiner C. Means, Mordecai Ezekiel, Lauchlin Currie — ever fully survived the premature identification with policies that nearly all economists now consider right. All were righteously excluded from professional honors. In 1936 the Harvard Department of Economics dismissed as eccentric a suggestion from its junior members that John Maynard Keynes be numbered among the leading economists of the day who were being endowed with an honorary degree at the Tercentenary celebrations of that year. The honors went to men who, in general, urged wrong but reputable policies.

8. Cf. for example, Douglass V. Brown, Edward Chamberlin, Seymour E. Harris, Wassily Leontief, Edward S. Mason, Joseph A. Schumpeter, Overton H. Taylor, *The Economics of the Recovery Program* (New York: Whittlesey House, McGraw-Hill, 1934).

9. It is held that the provision of an expanding volume of consumer goods, among which the consumer exercises a sovereign choice, involves no value judgments. This might be approximately true if everything the consumer needs were available from the market and if no attempt were made to manage his choice. Conservatives instinctively but wisely insist that almost all important needs can be provided by the market, and that management of the consumer is of negligible importance. This enables them to rest their case on an impersonal manifestation of individual choice. It is also evident that the preconditions for their case are far from being met.

10. In March 1962, 40 percent of the unemployed had eight years of schooling or less. This educational group accounted for only 30 percent of the total labor force. At a time when national unemployment was 6 percent among males aged eighteen and over, it was 10.4 percent of those with four years of schooling or less and 8.5 percent of those with five to seven years of schooling. Unemployment dropped to 4 percent among those with thirteen to fifteen years of schooling and to 1.4 percent of those with college training. (Testimony of Charles Killingsworth, *Automation, Jobs and Manpower,* Subcommittee on Employment and Manpower, United States Senate [The Clark Committee] September 20, 1963.)

11. In 1956, 13 percent of families had incomes of less than $2,000. Of those with eight or fewer years of education, 33.2 percent had incomes of less

than $2,000. Among all unattached individuals 54.1 percent had incomes of under $2,000. Of those with eight or fewer years of education, 80.3 percent had incomes under $2,000. (National Policy Committee on Pockets of Poverty, Washington, D.C., mimeographed, December 6, 1963.)

12. Taxes were reduced on such grounds in 1964 at approximately the time this article was being prepared for original publication.

13. "There is mounting realization of the injury to incentives and economic growth arising out of the magnitude of taxation. From this has come increasing determination to do something about it. This is all to the good. There is also a rising realization that there is something wrong about reducing taxes unless something also is done about curbing expenditures to avoid the need for big deficits in budgets. This also is good. But the general insistence on reducing expenditures falls short of that on reducing taxes. This failure to place equal emphasis on expenditure reduction can mean a danger of continuing big deficits." "Important Trends in Our Economy," United States Steel Corporation, *Annual Report*, 1963, p. 38.

14. Notably in William H. Whyte, Jr., *The Organization Man* (New York: Simon and Schuster, 1956).

15. Ibid.

16. On March 31, 1963, Zach Toms, President of Liggett & Myers Tobacco Company, said of the recent Surgeon General's Report: "We think . . . [it] went beyond the limits of the problem as now understood by other qualified scientists." At the same time the President of the American Tobacco Company, Mr. Robert B. Walker, dismissed the scientific evidence as ". . . first of all the frustrations of those who are unable to explain certain ailments that have accompanied our lengthening span of life on earth and who see in tobacco a convenient scapegoat." On April 14, 1963, Joseph F. Cullman III of Philip Morris, Inc., said that his advisers "do not feel the prime conclusion is justified on the basis of available scientific knowledge and evidence."

17. C. Wright Mills, *The Power Elite* (New York: Oxford University Press, 1956).

18. Given the self-destructive character of much unplanned investment, the longer-run conflict is not so clear.

The Proper Purpose of
Economic Development

[*from* Economics, Peace and Laughter]

This essay shows the effect of my years in India, where I saw at first hand the conflict between entrenched western economic thinking and the problems of the developing countries.

As to our eventual journey to the moon and the scientific, engineering, educational and recreational service it rendered, I do not regret any of it.

*   *   *   *

ONE OF THE generally amiable idiosyncrasies of man is his ability to expend a great deal of effort without much inquiry as to why. Most of the descriptions and pictures of the moon I have seen make it out to be a rather questionable piece of property. The absence of atmosphere would seem to be a real handicap. Likewise of water. The climate is predictable, if poor. In northern Canada and Alaska, agriculture suffers from a very short growing season. The moon presents the confining case of none. Settlement will almost certainly be slow. Yet these and similar shortcomings show no signs of limiting the enthusiasm to get there. Nor can one be completely sorry. Though not an inexpensive adventure, it may be worth pursuing for no particular reason. Evelyn Waugh in *Decline and Fall* tells of a modern churchman who, while reflecting deeply on the sins of the world, came suddenly to wonder why God made it in the first place. Thenceforth he could think of nothing else. He had to give up his church; the only further employment he could find was as chaplain in a progressive penitentiary, where he was soon murdered by another deeply thoughtful man. It is a warning against excessive introspection.

But it may still be useful on occasion to ask about the goals of any costly effort, and such, I am persuaded, is the case with economic development. For some twenty-five years the world — East and West, capitalist and Communist, democratic and more democratic (no significant country since Hitler has described itself as undemocratic or anti-democratic) — has been pursuing such development. Development, semantically if not always practically, is in active voice; it implies movement toward some result. What should be the result? There is always danger that, in the absence of such specification, we will triumphantly achieve some unwanted end. Or we will act less efficiently than we might to get what we really want.

II

One reason for specifying the goals of development for the poor country is that the special circumstances of the economically advanced countries have allowed them, in very considerable measure, to remain unaware of the need for choice. So their economists do not much discuss the matter. In these countries the purpose of the economy is to produce goods. And the particular mix — the distribution of capital and manpower to different products and services — is given or is assumed to be given by the distribution of income, the efficiency of markets and popular political decision. If the distribution of resources between necessaries and luxuries — between products for the masses and the more esoteric delights of the few — seems wrong, the thing to change is the distribution of income. An increase of taxes on the incomes of the well-to-do or the products they consume is an appropriate remedy.

Given the income distribution, the only need is to make production as efficient as possible. Since efficiency is assumed to have its own reward, that too is taken care of. What one gets, accordingly, is the best one can have — or such is the commonly accepted view. At least in peacetime there has been little tendency to think further about the desirability of what is being produced. And there has been a further measure of concurrence from the Soviet-type economies. The Soviet Union has repeatedly proclaimed that its industrial goal is to "catch up" with the United States. This means that it seeks a broadly similar industrial apparatus in the service of similar ends. It has been easy to go to the further and final assumption, which is that the industrial apparatus of the United States, Western Europe and the USSR are the natural and indeed the only model for the newer countries. These newer countries need only re-create in some rough form what the more developed countries already have. Development is and should be the faithful imitation of the developed.

III

In fact, this is not a proper procedure. In the less developed lands the simple goal of an expanding production, the assortment reflecting the demand given by the income pyramid, is not a satisfactory guide. There is, first, a very large population which is very near or below the margin of subsistence. Those who are hungry have a special claim on resources. So do the measures which remedy this privation. For the same reason there is a special case against the luxury consumption of the well-to-do. Certain claims of the state also take on an added or seemingly added urgency in the poor country — a point to which I will return. The question of how much should be consumed now and how much should be invested for larger production and consumption later on is also vastly more urgent in the poor country, for the necessary saving, or some of it, will come from people who are insufficiently supplied. A decision in favor of present starvation in order to secure the consumption of a subsequent generation is one that no rich country has to make. And it has a decided poignancy for the country that does have to make it.

Faced with the special problem of goals that grow out of their poverty, one sees the poor countries coming up with a variety of solutions. Three in particular can be identified. They are as follows:

1. *Symbolic Modernization.* This goal gives development the purpose of according the country the aspect of progress. There are certain things the modern state must have. These include a decently glittering airport, suitably impressive buildings of state, one or more multi-lane highways, an economic plan, a considerable hydroelectric project, at least the intention of creating a steel industry and a balance of payments deficit. No one should be lofty or patronizing about these symbols; leaders have always known the importance of the concrete and visible expressions of national being. Abraham Lincoln insisted during the Civil War that work on the then-unfinished Capitol go on. If that continued, people would feel that the Union would continue. In the last century American settlers had no sooner redeemed some forest or prairie than they bonded themselves to build an impressive courthouse. Perhaps they needed other things more. But nothing else so proved they were civilized people with whom others should reckon.

Yet economic well-being as such is not much advanced by symbolic modernization. More often it is retarded for those who must pay the bill. And much symbolic modernization is a political stratagem for fooling people into believing something is being done. Or it is a form of monument-building by which politicians commemorate their own existence and also their inadequacy at public cost. As it would be unwise to deny a role for symbolic modernization, so it would be unwise to accord it much approval.

2. *Maximized Economic Growth.* I come now to a more respectable formulation of the goal of development and the one which reflects most strongly the influence of Western economic thought. This proclaims it to be, over some period of time, the greatest possible increase in total and per capita product. Import restrictions and duties and domestic taxes may discourage the production of some less essential goods. But the composition of the product is secondary. The goal is to get more. At the extreme, investment outlays are favored in accordance with their capital-output ratios. This means

that the test of an investment is the amount by which it increases total product.

Not only will investment be so tested but there will be emphasis on increasing investment. The more of this over time, the greater the increase in output. This means, in turn, that there will be effort, in principle at least, to increase the savings from which comes the investment. Since voluntary savings are scarce in the poor country, there will be a case for involuntary savings through taxation or inflation.

Questions of priority that cannot be resolved by resort to statistical tests — and these in the poor country tend to be both exiguous and flexible as to outcome — will also be decided in accordance with assumed contribution to expansion of output. The position to be accorded education or other social overhead investment, the balance between industry and agriculture, between light industry and heavy industry, will be so resolved.

As compared with symbolic modernization, this test of increased income and product obviously has much to commend it. The reality of economic advance — the production of goods and services — replaces the mere image. These are solid and objective tests of performance.

Yet this goal too is not without dangers. Considerable extremes of wealth and income continue to exist in nearly all of the less developed lands. These create a strong drag of consumer demand in the direction of higher-priced or luxury products. And this tendency is especially insidious, for many of these products are commonplace in the more advanced countries and equally so in the consumption habits of the upper-income minority of the poorer country. To the extent that the high incomes of the minority draw development resources into privileged consumption, social differences are widened and to the strains associated with poverty may be added those associated with obvious differences in well-being. People soon come to sense that economic development is not for the many but for the few.

There are further dangers. As just noted, in this development goal, taxation — what has come on occasion to be called fiscal savings — plays a considerable role. In the poor country there is a particular likelihood that taxation will be regressive — that it will fall most heavily on the poor who are available in the most abundant supply and have the fewest facilities for escaping the tax collector. And since the underdeveloped country is, *pro tanto*, an agricultural community, there may be a traditional tendency for this taxation to fall upon the farmer or his land. Thus not only does undifferentiated growth tend to support higher-income consumption, it may do so partly as the result of saving from lower-income consumption.

Moreover, the process of development itself both requires and justifies a substantial increase in the number of people earning higher incomes. Administrators, managers, engineers, technicians, accountants, clerks and other civil servants are all required, and all at rates of pay that will seem high to the poorer taxpayer. The political consequences of this may be discomforting in any case. If these jobholders are engaged in forms of development that do not benefit the poor taxpayer, it will obviously be worse. The latter soon comes to think of development as something which rewards not him but some official.

Finally, there are serious dangers in the heavy investment. The saving that this requires can easily reflect the preferences of the planner, not the people. In a number of countries since World War II — Yugoslavia, Poland and China — there have been revolts against rates of saving and investment in excess of what the community could endure.

3. *Selective Growth*. The foregoing problems have not gone unrecognized, although the recognition has been less explicit than might be wished. Much development planning has been based on the belief that benefits must accrue as a matter of priority to the more needy sectors of the population. Resources so painfully conscripted from the people must return benefit to the same people.

Unhappily this politically salutary principle has led to highly contradictory conclusions as to its application. To some, agriculture, agricultural extension, community development and local primary education have seemed the obvious answer. The poor are in the villages. It is to these that the investment should go. But to others this, at best, is only a palliative. People are poor not because of insufficient agricultural investment but because they are in agriculture. The real answer is industrial employment. This argues for investment in manufacturing, power, transportation and the other components of an industrial base. The progressive solution is to rescue people, if not from the idiocy, at least from the inevitable poverty, of rural life.

In some countries, notably in India, there is further disagreement between those who defend modern machine methods and those who contend that, since employment is the goal, labor-intensive enterprises, including rural and cottage industries of various kinds, should be favored.

Thus, although there may be wide agreement on a policy of selective economic growth, there can be very little agreement on what should be selected.

IV

There is a further, and I think preferable, development goal which I believe resolves the foregoing difficulties. It is one, incidentally, that has been implicit in a good deal of past Indian thinking — and in the best planning in other countries. This anchors economic development to the consumption requirements, present and prospective, of the typical citizen — of, statistically speaking, the modal consumer. It organizes development around the protection and increase of the living standard of this consumer. By way of illustration, if, as in India, the annual income of 80 percent of all family units is less than R.1,200 (at the time of writing, about $250), development resources will be concentrated on consumption that is purchasable by people with such income. The number of goods and services is not large. Obviously it means a major emphasis on food, clothing, shelter and education since these are the dominant items in the economy of the low-income family. The same rule operates equally against automobiles, any but the most inexpensive housing, luxury consumer goods and conspicuous public goods. This is not a decision for agriculture or for industry or for light industry as opposed to heavy industry. It is a choice for the industrial structure which supplies the typical or modal citizen. That person wants, perhaps first of all, an abundant supply of inexpensive food. But back of an improved agriculture lie fertilizer plants and a chemical industry and well-designed agricultural implements and an efficient transportation system and hence a source of steel. Back of textiles, bicycles and other low-budget consumer goods is a similar supporting capital investment. To gear investment to the present and prospective requirements of the modal-income family will decisively influence the pattern of development but in a positive and not a negative way.

The goal I am here describing — I have called it the Popular Consumption Criterion — will be seen to resolve the political problems which arise in connection with other criteria. The attention of those who tax, plan or otherwise influence economic resources is kept concentrated on the needs of the typical consumer. The test of development is the reward that accrues to him. The test warns against extracting too much saving from him for a too distant reward. It provides a firm criterion for discouraging luxury imports, production and consumption. It is also a useful barrier to outlays for symbolic modernization. The required taxes for airports and new buildings of state reduce popular consumption or sacrifice investment opportunities that might increase it.

The application of the Popular Consumption Criterion cannot be total. By an odd arrangement of things, poor countries, such as India in the past, have produced luxuries for the affluent lands. Exports are still necessary, and export and domestic markets are never wholly separate. What is supplied to one will leak over to the other. And development that is firmly geared to the income of the modal consumer means higher incomes for some people. Evidently there is no economic arrangement — capitalist, socialist or Communist — which does not give more money to those who manage, invent, devise, instruct or punish. Goods will then be produced to meet this demand — and must be. The Popular Consumption Criterion is a criterion and not a straitjacket.

It is not less important for this reason. For it fixes objectives and establishes the priorities in the distribution of investment. If investment is distributed in accordance with some plan, it guides the plan. If investment is subject to the influence of taxation or import duties, it guides this influence. It provides no final decision. But it does establish the line between what is favored and what is subject to the burden of proof.

The Valid Image of
the Modern Economy

[*from* Annals of an Abiding Liberal]

*This essay is based on the formal acceptance speech I gave on receiving
the Veblen-Commons Award from the Association for Evolutionary
Economics in 1976. A more technical and in some respects more precise
statement of this theme was in my presidential address to the American Economic Association in 1972.[1] The latter, I am not quite alone in
believing, is the best short account of my general economic position.*

*   *   *   *

I AM HERE CONCERNED to see if I can provide a comprehensive
and integrated view of the principal problems of economic
management in our time. In doing so, I shall offer an alternative picture of the structure of modern economic society. This will
compress into brief and, I trust, sharp form without obscuring details of what I have hitherto written about at much greater length.[2]
Finally, I shall attempt to apply this model to some contemporary
problems.

In considering the image of modern industrial society, one must
have clearly in mind two factors that act strongly and persistently to
distort the economist's view of that reality.

The first of these distorting factors is the very great inclination to think of the ultimate subject matter with which we deal in static terms. Physics, chemistry and geology deal with an unchanging subject matter. What is known and taught about them changes only as information is added or interpretation is revised. They are, all agree, sciences. It is the great desire of nearly all economists to see their subject as a science too. Accordingly, and without much thought, they hold that its matter is also fixed. The business firm, the market, the behavior of the consumer, like the oxygen molecule or the geologist's granite, are given. Economists are avid searchers for new information, eager in their discussion of the conclusions to be drawn. But nearly all of this information is then fitted into a fixed, unchanging view of the role of business firms, markets, labor relations, consumer behavior and the economic role of the government. It is not an accident that economists who see their subject in evolutionary terms are a minority in the profession.

This is not a small methodological point. You will not doubt its importance if, in fact, the institutions with which economics deals are not stable, if they are subject to change. In truth, they *are,* and the first step toward a more valid perception of economic society and its problems is an appreciation of the very high rate of movement that has been occurring in basic economic institutions. The business corporation is the greatest of the forces for such change. In consequence of the movement it initiates, there has been a rapid alteration in the nature of the labor market and of trade union organization. Also in the class structure of modern economic society and in the resulting patterns of consumption. Also in the services and responses of the modern state. The ultimate effect of these changes is, in fact, to make the economic knowledge of one generation obsolete in the next. And also the prescription and policy based on that knowledge.

II

The second factor that distorts economic understanding is the very great social and political convenience — or so it seems — of the wrong image of economic society. I can best give substance to this abstraction by proceeding to the structure of the modern industrial economy.

The presently accepted image of this economy is, of course, of numerous entrepreneurial firms distributed as between consumer- and producer-goods industries, all subordinate to their market and thus, ultimately, to the instruction of the consumer. Being numerous, the firms are competitive; any tendency to overprice products by one firm is corrected by the undercutting of a competitor. A similar corrective tendency operates, if less perfectly, in the purchase of materials and labor. Being entrepreneurial, the firm has a simple internal structure. Authority, power within the firm, lies with the entrepreneur, on whom, overwhelmingly, achievement depends. The entrepreneur being the owner, the partial owner or the direct instrument of the owner, the motivation is also simple and straightforward. It is to maximize return.

To say that the firm is subordinate to the market is to say that it submits to prices that it does not control and that it submits, ultimately, to the will of the consumer. Decision originates with the consumer, and this decision, expressed through the market, is sovereign. If the consumer has sovereign power, the firm cannot have any important power at all in the market; there cannot be two possessors of sovereign power. The business firm is also, by assumption rather than by evidence, without organic power in the state.

In one exception, the firm has influence over prices and output; that is the case of monopoly or oligopoly, or their counterparts, in the purchase of materials and components, products for resale or labor. But monopoly — the control of prices and production in an industry by one firm — and oligopoly — control by a few firms — are never the rule in this image; they are always the exception. They are imperfections in the system. The use of the word *imperfection,* which is the standard reference to monopoly and oligopoly, affirms that these are departures from the general competitive rule.

To any economist the broad image of economic society that I have just sketched will not seem replete with novelty. It is also admirable proof of the resistance of the subject to change. In the last hundred years the notion of oligopoly has been added to that of monopoly, and the notion of monopoly has been widened to include partial monopoly in brands, services or the like — monopolistic competition. On occasion, there is now in basic economic instruction some bow to the managerial as distinct from the entrepreneurial character of the modern great corporation. Otherwise the basic structure — competitive entrepreneurial firms, the supremacy of the market, the flawing exception of monopoly — is not very different in the modern textbook from that described in Alfred Marshall's *Principles of Economics,* which was first published in the year 1890. Anyone not deeply conditioned by conventional economic instruction must wonder, as he or she reflects on the extent of economic change in our time, if so static a theory of basic economic arrangements can be valid. It is right to do so.

III

The image is not valid. But it does contribute both to the tranquillity of the economist's existence and to the social and political convenience of modern corporate enterprise.

The service of the accepted image of economic life to the political needs of the business firm — the large corporation in particular — is, in fact, breathtaking. Broadly speaking, it removes from the corporation all power to do wrong and leaves with it only the power to do right.

Are its prices too high? The corporation is blameless. Prices are set by the market. Are profits unseemly? They too are determined by the market. Are products deficient in safety, durability, design, usefulness? They reflect the will of the sovereign consumer. The function of the firm is not to interpose its judgment but to accept that of the consumer. Is there adverse effect on the environment? If so, it reflects (with some minor effect from external diseconomies) the higher preference of people for the goods being produced as opposed to the protection of air, water or landscape.

One sees how great are the political advantages of this image of economic life. It is not easy to think of the accepted economics as the handmaiden of politics. Most economists suppress the thought. None should.

I V

However, self-delusion also has its cost — and this is great. Specifically, this image conceals from us the workings of the modern economic system, the reasons for its successes and its failures and the nature of the needed remedial action. Among the victims of this concealment are those most intimately involved — those with the greatest need to understand the correct image — and they are on occasion businessmen themselves. And there is a damaging public effect. People cannot accept as valid an image of modern society that makes the great corporation the helpless, passive instrument of market forces and itself a force of minimal influence in the state. This is too deeply at odds with commonsense. So they come to believe that there is something intrinsically deceptive about the modern corporation, and perhaps also about the economics that projects the conventional image. Better and safer the truth.

The valid image of the economic system is not, in fact, of a single competitive and entrepreneurial system. It is of a double or bimodal system. The two parts are very different in structure but roughly equal in aggregate product. In the United States, reflecting the force of the corporation for change in the last century, around 1,000 to 2,000[3] firms contribute about half of all private economic product. In 1967, for example, 200 manufacturing corporations (out of 200,000) shipped 42 percent of all manufactured goods by value. Later figures suggest further concentration. Of 13,687 commercial banks in 1971, 50 had 48 percent of all assets; of 1,805 life insurance companies, the 50 largest had 82 percent of all assets.[4] Set against this half of the economy is the dispersed sector; depending on what is called a firm, this consists, in the United States, of between 10 and 12 million small businesses — farms, service and professional enterprises, construction firms, artistic enterprises, small traders. They contribute the other half of product. The division in other advanced industrial countries is roughly similar. Thus the valid image of modern economic society is the division of the productive task between a few large firms that are infinitely large and many small firms that are infinitely numerous.

v

The large corporation differs organically from the small; the burden of proof cannot seem excessive for the individual who asserts that there is a fundamental difference in organization and structure between General Motors, Shell or General Electric and the small farm, neighborhood restaurant, cafe or retail flower shop. The coexistence of these two very different structures and the resulting economic behavior are themselves features of the greatest importance. But first a further word on the corporate sector — what I have elsewhere called the planning system.[5]

The most obvious characteristic of the corporate half of the economy is the great size of the participating units. In the United States a handful of industrial corporations — General Motors, Exxon, Ford, a couple of others at most — have sales equal to all agriculture. Size in turn contributes to the two features of the modern large firm that differentiate it from the entrepreneurial and competitive enterprise and explain its impact on the society. The first of these is its deployment of market and political power. The second — one that is less noticed — is its diffusion of personal power.

The deployment of market and political power is diverse and, except as described in economic instruction, also commonplace. The modern large corporation has extensive influence over its prices and over its costs. It supplies much of its capital from its own earnings. It strongly influences the tastes and behavior of its consumers; even professional economists when looking at television have difficulty concealing from themselves the impact of modern advertising, although many succeed. And it exists in the closest relationship with the modern state.

The government gives the corporation legal existence; establishes the environmental and other parameters within which it functions; monitors the quality and safety of its products and certain of the advertising claims it makes for them; supplies, in the manner of highways to the automobile industry, the services on which sale of its products depends. Also — an increasingly important function — the government is the safety net into which the firm falls in the event of failure. Above a certain size — as the recent history of some large American banks, the eastern railroads in the United States, the Lockheed Corporation, Rolls-Royce, British Leyland, British Chrysler, Krupp and the vast agglomeration of IRI in Italy all show — a very large corporation is no longer allowed to go out of business. The social damage is too great. Modern socialism is extensively the adoption by reluctant governments, socialist and otherwise, of the abandoned offspring of modern capitalism. Being thus so dependent, the corporation must seek power in the state. This power, like that in the market, is not plenary. But its existence can be denied only by those who are trained extensively to ignore it.

VI

As earlier noted, the role of the modern great corporation in diffusing personal power is less celebrated than its deployment of market and public power, but it is not, I believe, less important. In its fully developed form, the corporation, as others have emphasized, removes power from the ownership interest, the traditional locus of capitalist authority. In doing so, it removes it from the representatives of the stockholders — the board of directors. No director of General Motors, Exxon or IBM who is not a member of management — I speak carefully here — has any continuing effective influence on company operations. The ceremony which proclaims that power — usually of aged, occasionally senile men meeting for a couple of hours on complex matters six times a year — is almost wholly implausible except to the participants. Directors do not make decisions; they ratify them. But to remove power from the owners and their alleged representatives — from the capitalists — is only a part of a larger process. That larger process involves extensive diffusion of such power. As power passes from capitalist to management in the large firm, this diffusion occurs in three ways.

First, decisions being numerous and complex, they must be delegated and redelegated, and the decision-making process passes down into the firm. This all recognize to be necessary. Nothing so criticizes an executive as the statement, "He cannot delegate responsibility."

Second, decisions being technically and socially complex, they become the shared responsibility of specialists — engineers, scientists, production men, marketing experts, lawyers, accountants, tax specialists. Power, in other words, passes from individuals to groups — to what I have called the technostructure of the modern corporation.

Finally, where there is no participation in decision, organization takes form to influence it. Thus the trade union. Union power is the natural answer to the power of the corporation. Only in the rarest cases in the developed industrial world is there a large corporation where labor is not organized.

The diffusion of power extends beyond the boundaries of the corporation, for the corporation brings into existence a vast array of supporting professions and services — law firms to advise on, or sometimes bend, the law; accountants to record, and sometimes create, its earnings; universities, colleges and business schools to train its executives and specialists or those who will so pass; dealers to sell its products; repairmen to service the products or advise that they are beyond repair. Marx held that, in its final stages of development, the capitalist firm devoured the small entrepreneur. This may well be true as regards small competitors. But the modern corporation also nurtures and sustains a large penumbra of independent firms. These peripheral groups and firms also assert their right to power. Lawyers and accountants have their special claims on decisions. So do consulting firms and custodians of expert knowledge from the universities. Dealer relations departments exist to consider the rights of those who sell and service the products. All have a claim on power.

We should not test our image of the economic system by its political convenience, or we should not if we are interested in analytically serviceable truths. We should see, instead, whether our image accords with observed circumstance, observed need.

The first test of the system I have just been describing has to do with the foremost problem of our time, the disagreeable and persistent tendency for severe unemployment in the modern industrial society to be combined with severe inflation.

If one accepts the competitive and entrepreneurial image of economic society, this combination does not and cannot occur. There can be inflation. But by conventional macroeconomic monetary and fiscal policy — restricting bank lending and tightening the public budget — the aggregate demand for goods and services in the economy can be reduced. Since, in this image, no firm controls prices, production is affected only as prices fall — that is what brings to the firm the message of declining demand. So, as the first effect, prices will cease to rise, which is to say the inflation will come to an end. Later, as prices and earnings fall, production may be curtailed and there may be unemployment. But unemployment and inflation do not and cannot coexist. One is cured before the other is caused.

Similarly, if there is unemployment, aggregate demand in the economy can be expanded by monetary and fiscal action — more public expenditure, reduced taxes, easier lending and thus more spending from borrowed funds. The initial effect will be more sales, more jobs. Prices may then rise. But, once again, that is because unemployment has been cured or, at a minimum, is by way of being cured.

In the bimodal image of the economy, a combination of inflation and unemployment must be expected at least for so long as fiscal and monetary policy are the sole instruments of economic management. Trade unions, as we have seen, have some power over their wages in the corporate sector of the economy. Corporations, having power in their markets, have the ability to offset concessions to trade unions with higher prices. Modern collective bargaining has lost much of its old-fashioned acerbity for a very simple reason: as an alternative to confrontation, unions and management can reach agreement and pass the resulting cost on to the public. Complaints over the cost of wage settlements now rarely come from employers. Almost invariably they come from the government, which is concerned over the inflationary effect, or from the public, which has to pay the higher price.

When this wage-price inflation is attacked by the traditional methods — monetary and budget restraint to reduce demand — prices do not automatically fall. The firm has the power to maintain its prices. The first industrial effect is, instead, on sales, output and employment. And if unions continue to press for higher wages, prices will continue to increase. Only when unemployment is very severe — so severe as to deter the unions from pressing for wage increases and the corporations from exercising their power to raise prices — do the traditional monetary and fiscal measures begin to bite. Meanwhile unemployment and inflation, as in the world today, do coexist.

Before monetary and fiscal policy act on the corporate sector, however, they work on the competitive and entrepreneurial sector of the economy. Here, as before, prices do respond to monetary and fiscal measures to restrain demand. Also in this half of the economy are industries — housing and construction being the notable cases — that exist on borrowed funds, which makes them uniquely vulnerable to monetary action, to restrictions on bank lending. (This vulnerability is in contrast with the position of the large corporation, which has resort to retained earnings for capital and which, in the event of outside need, is a priority customer at the banks.) So, while inflation continues in the corporate half of the economy, there can be falling farm prices and a painful recession in the entrepreneurial and competitive sector. That too accords fully with recent or present circumstances. Beginning in 1974, monetary restriction was brought sharply to bear on the then-serious inflation. There followed a serious recession, the worst, in fact, since the Great Depression. Farm prices fell. Housing, where output fell by more than a third, was seriously depressed. Unemployment rose to around 10 percent of the labor force. And industrial prices — those of the corporate sector — kept right on rising.

The practical conclusion is that inflation cannot now be arrested by fiscal and monetary policy alone unless there is willingness to accept a very large amount of unemployment. There remains only one alternative; that is to restrain incomes and prices not by unemployment but by direct intervention — by an incomes and prices policy. Such action is not a substitute for orthodox monetary and fiscal management of demand but an essential supplement to it.

There is a further test here of the validity of the revised image, for the policies appropriate to it reflect the direction in which most of the industrial countries of the nonsocialist world are moving — against the advice of all the more clamorous voices of conventional economics. In Germany, Austria, Switzerland and Scandinavia wage negotiation is in accordance with an implicit incomes policy that considers the effect of wage concessions on both domestic inflation rates and external competitive position. Britain, a peculiarly resistant case, has, in the mid-nineteen-seventies, a comprehensive incomes and prices policy. France has a more limited one. And the United States government in its guidelines has conceded the need for such a policy and is reluctant only to bring it to effective reality.

VIII

The bimodal view also explains the increasingly unequal development of the modern economy and the measures that governments find themselves taking to deal with it. The corporate half of the economy combines advanced organization, high technical skills and relatively ample capital with the ability to persuade the consumer and the state as to their need for its products. In consequence, in all industrial countries, automobiles, lethal weapons, household appliances, pharmaceuticals, alcohol, tobacco and cosmetics are amply supplied. The very notion of shortage, inadequacy, in these commodities would strike all as distinctly odd.

In the competitive entrepreneurial sector, where organization, technology, capital and persuasion are less available or absent, inadequacy is assumed. Housing, health care, numerous consumer services and, on occasion, the food supply are a source of complaint or anxiety in all of the developed countries. All governments find themselves seeking ways to compensate for the inadequacies of private enterprise in this half of the bimodal economy. The conventional economics has only one explanation for this unequal development: it reflects consumer choice, which is to say that the consumer is unaware of his — or her — needs. Where housing, health care and food are concerned, this is hard to believe.

I X

The bimodal image of the economy serves also our understanding of inequality of opportunity and reward in the modern economy and its consequences. In the conventional image of the economy, inequality is the result of differences in talent, luck or choice of ancestors. But between occupations it is constantly being remedied by movement from lower- to higher-income jobs. If this remedy is to work, people must, of course, be able to move.

The corporate sector of the economy deserves more approval than it receives for the income it provides. In the United States it is doubtful if any union member with full-time employment in this sector falls below the poverty line. But there are grave barriers to movement into this area. In particular, so long as inflation is the chief problem and monetary and fiscal policy are the remedies, there will be unemployment in this sector — either chronic or recurrent. If there is unemployment, there obviously cannot be easy movement of new workers into its higher-paid employment. The old unemployed have first chance.

In the entrepreneurial part of the economy, by contrast, employment can often be found either by taking a lower self-employment return or possibly low pay in an industry that has no union. There is, accordingly, a continuing source of inequality between the two parts of the economy derived from the occluded movement between them. We have here another reason for forgoing exclusive reliance on monetary and fiscal policy for controlling inflation. The resulting unemployment is also a source of occluded movement and thus of further inequality as between the different sectors of the economy.

X

If fiscal and monetary policy alone are used to control inflation in the modern economy, it will be controlled only by creating unemployment. There must, as noted, be enough unemployment to require unions to forgo added wage claims and to cause consumers (and corporations) to resist price increases. Or there must be an incomes and prices policy. No two countries are likely to resolve this problem with the same choice of measures. In recent years Switzerland, Austria and the German Federal Republic have had low rates of inflation. Something must be attributed to economic wisdom. But more must be attributed to governments that have a history of concern for inflation and trade unions that are cautious about pressing inflationary wage claims. And something must also be attributed to the policy of balancing out the labor force with imported labor. It eases social tension if some of the unemployed, when not needed, are in Italy, Spain, Turkey or Yugoslavia. In Britain and the United States the reserve unemployed are within the country itself.

For the above and yet other reasons different countries solve the unemployment-inflation problem in different ways and with differing degrees of success. The result is widely differing degrees of inflation in the several industrial countries. With different inflation rates there will be, it is certain, compensating movements in exchange rates, and there is no formula for international currency stabilization that will produce stability in the international exchanges in face of these widely varying rates of internal inflation. This is something to remember whenever one hears that central bankers and other monetary experts are meeting on international currency reform. In the absence of broadly coordinate policies to control domestic inflation, there can be no international exchange stabilization that has any hope of being permanent. Promises to the contrary are a fraud.

XI

There are further tests of the image of the economy I am here describing. Let me conclude by combining several into one. In removing power from owners, diffusing it through the technostructure and accepting and even nurturing the organized response of workers, the modern corporation does more than diffuse power. It takes a long step, if not toward a classless society, at least toward one in which class lines are extensively blurred. This, in turn, has a major effect on consumption patterns. Specifically, there is no longer in the corporate sector of the economy full acceptance by any group that it was meant by the nature of its occupation to consume less. And this acceptance will continue to erode. The pressure so exerted both for private goods and services and the requisite wages is one source of inflation. Pressure for such public services as education, health care and public transportation is another source. The thrusts for more private income and consumption and for more public goods and services have, we see, the same sources and can be equally strong. They are associated with the power — the power diffused by the corporation — to make the claim effective. In consequence, to cut consumption of private goods through taxes or for that matter through an incomes policy or to cut the consumption of public goods through reduced public outlays is very difficult. The bimodal image of economic society helps explain the new budget pressures with their inflationary effect as well as the new sources of inflation in the wage-price spiral. And it tells us also why control is politically and socially so difficult.

The business units in the corporate sector of the economy, becoming large, become international. The modern corporation internationalizes its income and wage standards as entrepreneurial industry never did. It also creates an international civil service — men who, like the servants of the Holy Church, are at home in all lands, who differ only in owing their ultimate allegiance not to Rome but to IBM. The international corporation defends relative freedom from tariff barriers and other constraints on trade. That is because competition is rarely cutthroat between large firms; they are restrained by oligopolistic convention. And international competition is never serious if you own the international competitor. It was the growth of the corporate sector of the modern economy that made possible the Common Market — made it necessary, perhaps, because intra-European trade barriers had become only a nuisance for the large corporation. Agriculture and other entrepreneurial enterprises have not changed their attitude on international trade. Their instinct is still protective. Farmers and other small producers would never have brought the EEC into existence. They are the source of at least 90 percent of its problems. Again the bimodal image fits the history.

XII

Finally, the image of the economy here offered explains the new tensions in the relationship between economic institutions and the state. The competitive and entrepreneurial firm seeks services from the state; seeks protection from competition, as just noted; is subject to regulation; pays taxes. This is a familiar and limited relationship. This firm never, by itself, competes with the state in the exercise of power. The modern large corporation, on the other hand, has a far wider range of requirements from the state. It also brings its power directly to bear on the instrumentalities of the state — both the bureaucracy and the legislature. Its needs, since they are put forward by the technostructure — an influential and articulate sector of the population — have a way of becoming public policy. In recent years the aircraft companies have had more success, of a sort, in the making and unmaking of foreign politicians and governments than has the CIA. No one doubts that the oil companies conduct a policy in the Middle East that sometimes supersedes that of the Department of State. A good many people believe that General Motors has had considerably more to do with setting policy on mass transportation in recent times than has the United States government.

These tensions are a great and important fact of life. As with inflation and unemployment, unequal development and inequality, we presently deal with them in the industrial countries by resort to an image of industrial society which holds that they do not exist. Or which holds that they are aberrations *sui generis*. This is unconvincing to the average citizen who, unlike the more acquiescent economist, is untrained in illusion. It precludes effective diagnosis and effective remedial action. It is safer and wiser as well as intellectually more rewarding to accept the reality.

NOTES

1. "Power and the Useful Economist," the next essay in this book.
2. In *Economics and the Public Purpose* (Boston: Houghton Mifflin, 1973).
3. The statistical difference between 1,000 and 2,000 is not, in fact, great, for the contribution of the second thousand is small as compared with that of the first.
4. Jonathan R. T. Hughes, *The Governmental Habit: Economic Controls from Colonial Times to the Present* (New York: Basic Books, 1977), p. 203. William Leonard, adjusting for some underreporting — the tendency to assign some manufacturing activities to mining for tax reasons — puts the share of manufacturing employment of the largest 200 corporations at 60 percent in 1974. "Mergers, Industrial Concentration, and Antitrust Policy," *Journal of Economic Issues*, vol. X, no. 2 (June 1976), pp. 354–381.
5. In *The New Industrial State*, 3rd ed. (Boston: Houghton Mifflin, 1978), and *Economics and the Public Purpose*.

Power and the Useful Economist[1]

[*from* Annals of an Abiding Liberal]

As indicated in the preceding piece, power is central in my thought, and especially since the American election of 2000, when adherents of corporate conservative belief were returned in numbers to positions of authority in Washington.

*   *   *   *

IN THE LAST DOZEN YEARS what before was simply known as economics in the nonsocialist world has come to be called neoclassical economics. Sometimes, in tribute to John Maynard Keynes's design for government intervention to sustain purchasing power and employment, the reference is to Keynesian or neo-Keynesian economics. From being a general and accepted theory of economic behavior, this has become a special and debatable interpretation of such behavior. For a new and notably articulate generation of economists a reference to neoclassical economics has become markedly pejorative. In the world at large the reputation of economists of more mature years is in decline.

However, the established economics has reserves of strength. It sustains much minor refinement which does not raise the question of overall validity or usefulness and which is agreeable employment. It survives especially in the textbooks, although even in this stronghold one senses anxiety among the more progressive or commercially sensitive authors. Perhaps, they are asking, there are limits to what the young will accept.

The arrangements by which orthodoxy is conserved in the modern academy are also still formidable. Economic instruction in the United States is about a hundred years old. In its first half century economists were subject to censoiship by outsiders. Businessmen and their political and ideological acolytes kept watch on departments of economics and reacted promptly to heresy, the latter being anything that seemed to threaten the sanctity of property, profits, a proper tariff policy and a balanced budget, or that suggested sympathy for unions, public ownership, public regulation or, in any organized way, for the poor. The growing power and self-confidence of the educational estate, the formidable and growing complexity of the subject matter of economics and, no doubt, the increasing acceptability to conservatives of our ideas have largely relieved us of this intervention. In leading centers of instruction faculty government is either secure or increasingly so. But in place of the old censorship has come a new despotism. This consists in defining scientific excellence in economics not as what is true but as whatever is closest in belief and method to the scholarly tendency of the people who already have tenure in the subject. This is a pervasive test, not the less oppressive for being, in the frequent case, both self-righteous and unconscious. It helps ensure, needless to say, the perpetuation of the neoclassical orthodoxy.

There are, however, problems even with this control. Neoclassical and neo-Keynesian economics, though providing unlimited opportunity for the demanding niceties of refinement, has a decisive flaw. It offers no useful handle for grasping the economic problems that now beset the modern society. And these problems are obtrusive; they will not lie down and disappear as a favor to our profession. No arrangement for the perpetuation of ideas is secure if the ideas do not make useful contact with the problems they are presumed to illuminate or resolve.

I propose in this essay to mention the failures of neoclassical economics. But I want also to urge the means by which we can reassociate ourselves with reality. Some of this will summarize arguments I have made at greater length on other occasions. Here even conservatives will be reassured. To adumbrate and praise one's own work is in the oldest and most reputable tradition of our profession.

II

The most damaging feature of neoclassical and neo-Keynesian economics is the arrangement by which power — the ability of persons or institutions to bend others to their purposes — is removed from the subject. The business firm is said to be wholly subordinate to the instruction of the market and thereby to the individual or household. The state is similarly subordinate to the instruction of the citizen. There are exceptions, but they are to the general and controlling rules, and it is firmly on these rules that neoclassical theory is positioned. If the business firm is subordinate to the market — if that is its master — then it does not have power to deploy in the economy, save as this is in the service of the market and the consumer. And it cannot bring power to bear on the state, for there the citizen is fully in charge.

The decisive weakness is not in the assumptions by which neoclassical and neo-Keynesian economics elides the problem of power. The capacity even (perhaps especially) of scholars for sophisticated but erroneous belief based on conventionally selected assumptions is very great, particularly where this coincides with convenience. Rather, in eliding power — in making economics a nonpolitical subject — neoclassical theory destroys the relation of economics to the real world. In that world, power is decisive in what happens. And the problems of that world are increasing both in number and in the depth of their social affliction. In consequence, neoclassical and neo-Keynesian economics relegates its players to the social sidelines. They either call no plays or urge the wrong ones. To change the metaphor, they manipulate levers to which no machinery is attached.

Specifically, the exclusion of power and the resulting political content from economics causes it to identify only two intrinsic and important faults in the modern economy. One of these is the problem of market imperfection — more specifically, of monopoly or oligopoly, control of a market by one firm or jointly by a few. This fault leads, in turn, to insufficient investment and output and to unnecessarily high prices. The other fault is a tendency to unemployment or inflation — to a deficiency or excess in the aggregate demand for goods and services in the economic system as a whole. The remedies to which the accepted economics then proceeds are either ridiculous, wrong or partly irrelevant. Neither its microeconomic nor its macroeconomic policy really works.[2] Meanwhile it leaves other urgent economic issues untouched and mostly unmentioned. Let me specify.

III

Beginning with monopoly and oligopoly, it is now the considered sense of the community, even of economists when unhampered by professional doctrine, that the most prominent areas of market concentration — automobiles, rubber, chemicals, plastics, alcohol, tobacco, detergents, cosmetics, computers, bogus and other health remedies, space adventure — are areas not of low but of high development, not of inadequate but, more likely, of excessive resource use. And there is a powerful instinct that in some areas of monopoly or oligopoly, most notably in the production of weapons and weapons systems, resource use is dangerously vast.

In further contradiction of the established conclusions, there is much complaint about the performance of those industries where market concentration is the least — the industries which, in number and size of firms, most closely approach the neoclassical market ideal. Housing, health services and, potentially, food supply are the leading cases. The deprivation and social distress that follow from the poor performance of these industries nearly all economists, when not in the classroom, take for granted.

The well-blinkered defender of established doctrine argues that the ample resource use in the monopolistic industries and the deprivation in the dispersed small-scale industries reflect the overriding fact of consumer preference and choice. And in the areas of deprivation the fault lies with firms that, though small, are local monopolies or reflect the monopoly power of unions. These explanations beg two remarkably obvious questions. Why does the modern consumer increasingly insist on self-abuse and increasingly complain of the discomforts from that self-assault? And why do the little monopolies perform so badly and the big ones so well?

In fact, neoclassical economics has no explanation of the most important microeconomic problem of our time. That is why we have a highly unequal development as between industries of great market power and industries of slight market power, with the development, in defiance of all doctrine, greatly favoring the first.

The failure in respect to unemployment and inflation has been, if anything, more embarrassing. Save in its strictly mystical manifestation in one branch of monetary theory, the accepted policy on these matters depends for its vitality and workability on the existence of the neoclassical market. That market, whether competitive, monopolistic or oligopolistic, must be the ultimate and authoritative instruction to the profit-maximizing firm. When output and accompanying employment are deficient, the accepted policy requires that aggregate demand be increased; this increases market demand, and to this firms, in turn, respond. They increase output, add to their labor force and reduce unemployment.

When output in the economy is at or near the effective capacity of plant and labor force, prices rise and inflation becomes the relevant social discomfort. The remedy is then reversed. Demand is curtailed, and the result is either an initial effect on prices or a delayed one as surplus labor seeks employment, interest rates fall and lower wage and material costs bring stable or lower prices.

Such is the accepted basis of the policy. It follows fully from the neoclassical faith in the market. The market renders its instruction to the producing firm. The latter cannot, because of competition, much raise its prices while there is idle capacity and unemployment. When these disappear, restraints on demand through monetary or fiscal policy or some combination of the two can prevent it from doing so. The practical consequences from pursuing this policy need no elucidation. It has been tried in recent years in every developed country. The result has been either politically unacceptable unemployment or persistent and socially damaging inflation or, normally, a combination of the two. That combination the neoclassical system does not and cannot contemplate. Modern medicine would not be more out of touch with its world if it could not embrace the existence of the common cold.

We should not deny ourselves either the instruction or the amusement that comes from the recent history of the United States in this matter. In 1969, Richard Nixon came to office with a firm commitment to neoclassical orthodoxy. Any direct interference with wages or prices was explicitly condemned. In this position he was supported by some of the most distinguished and devout exponents of neoclassical economics in all the land. His later announcement that he was a Keynesian involved no precipitate or radical departure from this faith; the discovery came nearly thirty-five years after *The General Theory*.[3] But in 1971, facing reelection, Mr. Nixon found that his economists' commitment to neoclassical and neo-Keynesian orthodoxy, however admirable in the abstract, was a luxury he could no longer afford. He apostatized to wage and price controls; so, with exemplary flexibility of mind, did his economists.

There was an effort to reconcile the need for controls with the neoclassical market. This involved an unrewarding combination of economics and archeology with wishful thinking. It held that an inflationary momentum developed during the late nineteen-sixties in connection with the financing — or underfinancing — of the Vietnam war. And inflationary expectation became part of business and trade union calculation. The momentum and expectation survived. The controls would be necessary until the inflationary momentum was dissipated. Then the neoclassical and neo-Keynesian world would return, along with the appropriate policies in all their quiet comfort: no inflation; no serious unemployment. We may be sure that will not happen. Nor will we expect it to happen if we see the role of power and political decision in modern economic behavior.[4]

IV

The assumptions that sustain the neoclassical and neo-Keynesian orthodoxy can no longer themselves be sustained. The growth of the modern great corporation has destroyed their validity. Instead of the widely dispersed, essentially powerless firms of neoclassical orthodoxy, we economists must now come to terms with the world of the modern large corporation. Laymen will be astonished that we have not already done so.

Specifically, we must accept that for around half of all economic output there is no longer a market system but a power or planning system. (Power is used to control what was previously external to the firm and thus unplanned. To stress not the instrument, power, but the process, planning, seems to be more descriptive as well as possibly less pejorative.) The planning system in the United States consists of, at the most, 2,000 large corporations. They do not simply accept the instruction of the market. Instead they have extensive power over prices and also over consumer behavior. They rival, where they do not borrow from, the power of the state. My conclusions on these matters will be somewhat familiar, and I shall spare myself the pleasure of extensive repetition. The power that these ideas ascribe to the modern corporation in relation to both the market and the state, the purposes for which it is used and the associated power of the modern union would not seem implausible or even very novel were they not in conflict with the vested doctrine.

Thus we agree that the modern corporation, either by itself or in conjunction with others, has extensive influence over its prices and often over its major costs. And, accepting the evidence of our eyes and ears, we know that it goes beyond its prices and the market to persuade its customers. We know also that it goes back of its costs to organize supply. And it is commonplace that from its earnings or the possession of financial affiliates it seeks to ensure and control its sources of capital. And likewise that its persuasion of the consumer, joined with the similar effort of other firms — and with the more than incidental blessing of neoclassical pedagogy — helps establish the values of the community, notably the association between well-being and the continuously increased consumption of the products of this part of the economy.

As citizens if not as scholars, we further agree that the modern corporation has a compelling position in the modern state. What it needs in research and development, technically qualified people, public works, emergency financial support when troubles loom, socialism when profit ceases to be probable, becomes public policy. So does the military procurement that sustains the demand for numerous of its products. So, perhaps, does the foreign policy that justifies the military procurement. And the means by which this power is brought to bear on the state is widely accepted. It requires an organization to deal with an organization, and between public and private bureaucracies — between General Dynamics and the Pentagon, General Motors and the Department of Transportation — there is a deeply symbiotic relationship. Each of these organizations can do much for the other. There has been between them a large and continuous interchange of executive personnel.

Finally, over this exercise of power and much enhancing it is the rich gloss of reputability. The men who guide the modern corporation and the outlying financial, legal, legislative, technical, advertising and other sacerdotal services of corporate function are the most respectable, affluent and prestigious members of the national community. They are the Establishment. Their interest tends to become the public interest. It is an interest that numerous economists find it comfortable and rewarding to avow, while denying in instruction and thought the power that produces that reward.

The corporate interest is profoundly concerned with power — with winning the acceptance by others of the collective or corporate purpose. This interest includes the profits of the firm. These are a measure of success. They also ensure the freedom of the management — what I have called the technostructure — from stockholder interference. The ordinary stockholders in the large corporation are aroused, if at all, only by inadequate earnings. And profits are important because they bring the supply of capital within the control of the firm. But of greater importance is the more directly political goal of growth. Growth carries a specific economic reward; it enhances the pay, perquisites and opportunities for promotion of the members of the technostructure, and it rewards most those whose product or service is growing most. But growth also consolidates and enhances authority. It does this for the individual — for the man who now heads a larger organization or a larger part of an organization than before. And it increases the influence of the corporation as a whole.

The unmanaged sovereignty of the consumer, the ultimate sovereignty of the voter and the maximization of profits with the resulting subordination of the firm to the market are the three legs of a tripod on which the accepted neoclassical system stands. These are what exclude the role of power in the system. All three propositions, it will be seen, tax the capacity for belief. That the modern consumer is the object of a massive management effort by the producer is not readily denied. The methods of such management are, as noted, embarrassingly visible. Modern elections are fought extensively on the issue of the subordination of the state to corporate interest. As voters, economists accept the validity of that issue. Only their teaching denies it. But the commitment of the modern corporate bureaucracy to its expansion is, perhaps, the clearest of all. That the modern conglomerate pursues profit over aggrandizement is believed by none. It is a commonplace of these last years, strongly reflected in the price of securities, that agglomeration has been good for growth, bad for earnings.

There does remain in the modern economy — and this I stress — a world of small firms where the instruction of the market is still paramount, where costs are given, where the state is remote and subject through the legislature to the traditional pressures of economic interest groups and where profit maximization alone is consistent with survival. We should not think of this as the classically competitive part of the system, in contrast with the monopolistic or oligopolistic sector from which the planning system has evolved. Rather, in its admixture of competitive and monopolistic structures, it approaches the neoclassical model. The corporation did not take over part of the neoclassical system. It moved in beside what the textbooks teach. In consequence, we have the two systems. In one, the power of the firm is still, as ever, contained by the market. In the second and still evolving system, this power extends incompletely but comprehensively over markets, over the people who patronize them, over the state and thus, ultimately, over resource use. The coexistence of these two systems becomes, in turn, a major clue to economic performance.

v

Power being so comprehensively deployed in a very large part of the total economy, there can no longer, except for reasons of game-playing, busy work or more deliberate intellectual evasion, be any separation between economics and politics. When the modern corporation acquires power over markets, power in the community, power over the state and power over belief, it is a political instrument, different in form and degree but not in kind from the state itself. To hold otherwise — to deny the political character of the modern corporation — is not merely to avoid the reality. It is to disguise the reality. The victims of that disguise are the students we instruct in error. The beneficiaries are the institutions whose power we so disguise. Let there be no question: economics, so long as it is thus taught, becomes, however unconsciously, a part of the arrangement by which the citizen or student is kept from seeing how he or she is, or will be, governed.

This does not mean that economics now becomes a branch of political science. Political science is the captive of the same stereotype — the stereotype that the citizen is in effective control of the state. Political science too must come to terms with corporate enterprise. Also, while economics often cherishes thought, at least in principle, political science regularly accords reverence to the man who knows only what has been done before. Economics does not become a part of political science. But politics does become a part of economics.

There will be fear that once we abandon the present theory with its intellectually demanding refinement and its increasing instinct for measurement, we shall lose the filter by which scholars are separated from charlatans and windbags. The latter are a danger, but there is more danger in remaining with a world that is not real. And we shall be surprised, I think, at the new clarity and intellectual consistency with which we see our world once power is made a part of our system. To such a view let me now turn.

V I

In the neoclassical view of the economy a general identity of interest between the goals of the business firm and those of the community could be assumed. The firm was subject to the instruction of the community through either the market or the ballot box. People could not be fundamentally in conflict with themselves. However, once the firm in the planning system is seen to have comprehensive power to pursue its own interest, this assumption becomes untenable. Perhaps by accident its interests are those of the public, but there is no organic reason why this must be so. In the absence of proof to the contrary, divergence of interest between individual and corporation, not identity of interest, must be assumed.

The nature of the conflict also becomes predictable. Growth being a principal goal of the planning system, it will be the greatest where power is greatest. In the market sector of the economy, growth will, at least by comparison, be deficient. This will not be, as neoclassical doctrine holds, because people have a congenital tendency to misunderstand their needs. It will be because the system is so constructed as to serve their needs badly and then to win greater or lesser acquiescence in the result. That the present system should lead to an excessive output of automobiles, an improbable effort to cover the economically developed sections of the planet with asphalt and a fantastically expensive and potentially suicidal investment in missiles, submarines, bombers and aircraft carriers is as one would expect. These are the industries with power to persuade and to command resources for growth. Thus does the introduction of power as a comprehensive aspect of economic thought correct present error. These, however, are exactly the industries in which the neoclassical view of monopoly and oligopoly (and of associated price enhancement and profit maximization at the expense of resource use and production) would, of all things, suggest a controlled inadequacy of output. How wrong are we allowed to be!

The counterpart of relatively too great a share of manpower, materials and investment in the planning system, where power is comprehensively deployed, is a relatively deficient use of such resources where power is absent. Such will be the flaw in the part of the economy where competition and entrepreneurial monopoly, as distinct from great corporate organization, are the rule. And if the product or service so penalized is closely related to comfort or survival, the resulting discontent will be considerable. That housing, many health services and local transportation are now areas of grave inadequacy is agreed. It is in such industries that all modern governments seek to expand resource use. Here, in desperation, even devout free-enterprisers accept the need for social action, socialism.

Economics serves badly this remedial action. Its instruction not only disguises corporate power but makes remedial action in housing, health care and transportation abnormal — the consequence of *sui generis* error that is never explained. What should be seen as a necessary and legitimate function of government appears, instead, as some kind of accident. This is not the mood that conduces to the imagination, pride and determination which should characterize such important public action.

VII

When power is admitted to our calculus, our professional embarrassment over the coexistence of unemployment with inflation also disappears. Economics makes plausible what governments are forced, in practice, to do. Corporations have power in their markets. So, and partly in protective response, do unions. The competitive claims of unions can most conveniently be resolved by passing the cost of settlement along to the public. Measures to arrest this exercise of power by limiting the aggregate demand for goods must be severe. Only if there is much unemployment, much idle capacity, is the ability to raise prices impaired. Until then, unemployment and inflation coexist. Not surprisingly, the power of the planning system has also been used to favor those restraints on demand that have least effect on its operations. Thus monetary policy is greatly favored. This policy operates by restricting bank lending. Its primary effect, in consequence, is on the neoclassical entrepreneur — the construction firm, for example — which does business on borrowed money. It has little impact on the large established corporation which, as an elementary exercise of power, has ensured itself a supply of capital from earnings or financial affiliates. The power of the planning system in the community has also won immunity for public expenditures important to itself — highways, industrial research, rescue loans, national defense. These have the sanction of a higher public purpose. If demand must be curtailed, these are excepted. There has been similar success with corporate and personal taxes. They are what you now reduce to stimulate employment, support the incentive to invest and ensure against capital shortages. In such fashion, fiscal policy has been accommodated to the interests of the planning system. This has been done with the support of economists in whose defense it must be said that they are not usually aware of the forces by which they are moved.

VIII

In this view of the economy we see also the role of controls. The interaction of corporate and trade union power can be made to yield only to the strongest fiscal and monetary restraints. Those restraints that are available have a comparatively benign effect on those with power, but they weigh adversely on people who vote. When no election is in prospect, such a policy is possible. It will earn applause for its respectability. But it cannot be tolerated by anyone who weighs wisely its popular effect.

As with the need for social action and organization in the market sector, there are many reasons why it would be well were economists to accept the inevitability of wage and price controls. It would help keep politicians, when responding to the resonance of their own past instruction, from supposing controls to be wicked, unnatural and hence temporary and to be abandoned whenever they seem to be working.[5] This is a poor mood in which to develop sound administration. And it would cause economists themselves to consider how controls can be made workable, how the effect on income distribution can be made equitable. With controls this last becomes a serious matter. The market is no longer a device for legitimizing inequality, however egregious, in income distribution. Much inequality is then seen to be, as it is, the result of relative power.

IX

There are differences in development, in performance, as between the planning and market sectors of the economy, and with them goes a difference in income between the two sectors. In the neoclassical system it is assumed that labor and capital will move between industries — from lower to higher — to equalize interindustry return. If there is inequality, it is the result of barriers to such movement. Now we see that, given its comprehensive market power, the planning system can protect itself, as a matter of course, from adverse movements affecting its income. The same power allows it to accept unions, for it need not absorb, even temporarily, their demands. In the market system, limited areas of monopoly or union power apart, there is no similar control. And in this sector of the economy, because of the absence of market power, there can be no similar yielding on wage costs, for there is no similar certainty that they can be passed on. It is because of the market character of the industry he sought to organize, not his original power, that Cesar Chavez was for so many for so long the new Lenin. In chemicals or heavy equipment he would not have been noticed. In the market system the self-employed have the option of reducing their own wages (and sometimes those of their families or immediate employees) in order to survive. That possibility does not exist in the highly organized planning system. This is the source of further inequality.

Thus there is a built-in inequality in income between the two systems. And thus also the case in the market sector for minimum-wage legislation, support to trade unions in agriculture, price-support legislation and, most important perhaps, a floor under family income as antidotes to inequality. All of these measures have their primary impact on the market sector. And again this view of matters fits our present concerns. Minimum-wage legislation, price-support legislation and support to collective bargaining are questions of continuing political moment as they apply to small business and agriculture. They are not issues in highly organized industry — in the planning system. And the question of a floor under family income, a further matter of political interest, has shown some indication of dividing workers in the planning system, who would not be beneficiaries, from those in the market system, who would be. There is surely some reassurance in a view of the economy that prepares us for the political questions of our time.

x

The inclusion of power in our economic calculus also brings into focus the debate over the environment. It is the claim of neoclassical economics that it foresaw possible environmental consequences from economic development. It early embraced the notion of external diseconomies of production and, by inference, of consumption. The price of the product did not include the cost of washing out the soot that descended from the factory chimney on the people of the surrounding city. The owner of the automobile or cigarette did not pay for the damage to other people's air and lungs. Alas, this is a modest claim. The noninclusion of external diseconomies was long viewed as a minor defect of the price system — an afterthought, obtaining at most a paragraph in the textbooks or a comment in classroom discussion. And the notion of external diseconomies does not offer a useful remedy. No one can suppose, or does suppose, that more than a fraction of the damage — especially that to the beauty and tranquillity of our surroundings — could be compensated for in any useful way by including in the cost of the product a provision for remedying the damage from its production or use.

If growth is the central and rewarding purpose of the firm and if power is comprehensively available to impose this goal on the society, conflict between the private interest in that growth and the public interest in the environment is inherent. And also inherent, since this power depends extensively not on force but on persuasion, is the effort to make pollution seem palatable or worth the cost, including the effort to make the advertising of remedial action a substitute for action. And equally inherent is the remedy to which all industrial countries are being forced. This is not to internalize external diseconomies, add them to the price. It is to specify the legal parameters within which growth may proceed. Or, as in the case of automobile use in central cities, airplane use over urban areas or industrial, commercial and residential appropriation of countryside and roadside, to prohibit development that is inconsistent with the public interest. We would have saved ourselves much corruption of our surroundings if our economics had held such result to be the predictable consequence of the pursuit of present economic goals and not the exceptional result of a peculiar aberration of the price system. We see again how the accepted economics supports not the public but the special interest.

XI

Finally, when power becomes part of our system, so does Ralph Nader. If the consumer is the ultimate source of authority, his abuse is an occasional fault. He cannot be fundamentally at odds with an economic system that he commands. But if the producing firm has comprehensive power and purposes of its own, there is every likelihood of conflict. Technology is then subordinate to the strategy of consumer persuasion. Products are changed not to make them better but to take advantage of the belief that what is different is better. There is a high failure rate in engineering because its preoccupation is not with what is good but with what can be sold. So the unpersuaded or disenchanted consumer rebels. This is not a rebellion against minor matters of fraud or misinformation. It is a major reaction against a whole deployment of power by which the consumer is made the instrument of purposes that are not his own.

XII

There are two conclusions to which this exercise — the incorporation of power into our system — compels us. The first is encouraging. It is that economists' work is not yet done. On the contrary, it is just beginning. If we accept the reality of power as part of our system, we have years of useful professional work ahead of us. And since we will be in touch with real issues, and since issues that are real inspire passion, our life will again be pleasantly contentious, perhaps even usefully dangerous. Members of the profession will be saved from the paltry suburban slumber that is the fate of the passive, irrelevant or harmless scholar.

The other conclusion concerns the state. For when we make power and therewith politics a part of our system, we can no longer escape or disguise the contradictory character of the modern state. The state is the prime target in the exercise of economic power. In greater or lesser measure, it is captured by the planning system. Yet on all the matters I have mentioned — organization to offset inadequate performance in such areas as housing and health care, wage and price controls, action to correct systemic inequality, protection of the environment, protection of the consumer — remedial action lies with the state.

Thus perhaps the greatest question of social policy in our time: Is the emancipation of the state from the control of the corporate system possible?

I would be presumptuous to say yes, even more so to suggest that it will be easy. But there is a gleam of encouragement. Elections are now being fought extensively over issues where the purposes of the planning system diverge from those of the public. The question of defense expenditures is such an issue. That of tax reform is another. The deprivation in housing, mass transportation and health services is yet another — one that reflects the relative inability of these industries to organize and command resources. The question of a guaranteed basic income, though quiescent, is another. The environment is such an issue — with its conflict between the technostructure's goal of growth and the public's concern for its surroundings. So is wage and price control. Our politics, forced by circumstance, are coming to accept and deal with this great contradiction between the needs of the planning system and the needs of the public.

It would not be wrong, I believe, to ask that in this effort, economists identify themselves with the public interest, not that of the corporations and the planning system. But if that is too much, I would happily settle for neutrality. Economics now tells the young and susceptible (and also the old and vulnerable) that economic life has no content of power and politics because the firm is safely subordinate to the market and the state and for this reason it is safely at the command of the consumer and citizen. Such an economics is not neutral. It is the influential and invaluable ally of those whose exercise of power depends on an acquiescent public. If the state is the executive committee of the great corporation and the planning system, it is partly because neoclassical economics is its instrument for neutralizing the suspicion that this is so.

NOTES

1. Presidential address at the Eighty-fifth Annual Meeting of the American Economic Association in Toronto, Canada, in December 1972.
2. Neoclassical economics, in modern times, has divided itself into two broad areas of specialization, research and instruction. There is microeconomics, which concerns itself with firms, industries and their response to the market. And there is macroeconomics, which involves itself with aggregative movements in the economy — with gross national product and national income and with employment and general price movements.
3. John Maynard Keynes, *The General Theory of Employment Interest and Money* (New York: Harcourt Brace, 1936).
4. As I've said, this was written in the autumn of 1972 for the Christmas holiday meetings of the American Economic Association. Early in 1973, in accordance with the doctrine just outlined, Mr. Nixon's economists urged and obtained the abandonment of controls. They promised price stability; there followed the worst peacetime inflation so far in our history. This was eventually arrested, though not completely, by the most serious recession and the most severe unemployment since the

Great Depression. There is danger in praising one's foresight, for the gods are not always kind. But the risk on these matters is less than usual.

5. When Secretary of the Treasury George Shultz announced the abandonment of the Nixon controls a few months after this was written, he said, in effect, that it was because they were working.

The Founding Faith:
Adam Smith's *Wealth of Nations*[1]

[*from* Annals of an Abiding Liberal]

More thirty-five years after this was written — years that have included Ronald Reagan, Margaret Thatcher and now George W. Bush
and Dick Cheney — Adam Smith remains undiminished in the scholarly eye and, as here told, is by no means the exclusive possession of
conservatives.

*   *   *   *

> It is not from the benevolence of the butcher, the brewer, or
> the baker, that we expect our dinner but from their regard to
> their own interest. We address ourselves, not to their human-
> ity but to their self-love, and never talk to them of our own
> necessities but of their advantages.
>
> — *Wealth of Nations*

ADAM SMITH, not to put too fine an edge on matters, was
Scotland's greatest son. *Wealth of Nations* is his greatest and
almost his only book. As Karl Marx is much too valuable a
source of social insight to be left as the exclusive property of the
Communists, so Adam Smith is far too wise and amusing to be rele-
gated to conservatives, few of whom have ever read him.

Smith was born in 1723 in what was then the small port town of
Kirkcaldy on the Firth of Forth across from Edinburgh. The endur-

ing exponent of the freedom of trade was the son of the local collector of customs. After study at the evidently excellent local school, he
went on to the University of Glasgow and then to Oxford (Balliol
College) for six years. Returning to Scotland, he became, first, professor of logic and then, in 1752, professor of moral philosophy at
the University of Glasgow. This chair he resigned in 1763 to travel on
the Continent as the well-paid tutor of the young Duke of Buc-
cleuch, a family possessed to this day of a vast acreage of dubious
land on the Border. In Europe Smith made the acquaintance of the
Physiocratic philosophers and economists Quesnay and Turgot, as
well as Voltaire and other notable contemporaries, and used his
time and mind well. He then returned to Kirkcaldy where, for the
next ten years, subject to lengthy sojourns in London and to the despair of some of his friends who feared he would never finish, he engaged himself in the writing of *Wealth of Nations.*

This book was published in 1776, a few weeks before the Declara-
tion of Independence, and there was some relationship between the
two events. Unlike his friend David Hume (who died that August)
and consistent with his economic views, Smith deplored the separation. He had wanted instead full union, full and equal representation of the erstwhile colonies in Parliament, free trade within the
union, equal taxation along with equal representation and the prospect that, as the American part developed in wealth and population,
the capital would be removed from London to some new Constanti-
nople in the West.

Wealth of Nations, at least among the knowledgeable, was an immediate success. Gibbon wrote: "What an excellent work is that
with which our common friend Mr. Adam Smith has enriched the
public . . . most profound ideas expressed in the most perspicuous
language."[2] Hume, in a much quoted letter, was exuberant:

> Euge! Belle! Dear Mr. Smith. — I am much pleased with your
> performance, and the perusal of it has taken me from a state of
> great anxiety. It was a work of so much expectation, by yourself,
> by your friends, and by the public, that I trembled for its ap-

pearance, but am now much relieved . . . it has depth and solid-
ity and acuteness, and is so much illustrated by curious facts
that it must at last attract the public attention.[3]

The public response — to two volumes costing £1 16s., the equivalent of well over forty dollars today — was also good. The first edition was soon sold out, although this intelligence would be more
valuable were the size of the edition known. Smith spent the next
couple of years in London, being, one gathers, much feted by his
contemporaries for his accomplishment, and then, having been appointed Commissioner of Customs in Edinburgh, an admirable si-
necure, he returned to Scotland. He died there in 1790.

By that time, *Wealth of Nations,* though at first ignored by politicians, was having an influence on men of affairs. A year and a
half after Smith's death, Pitt, introducing his budget, said of Smith
that his "extensive knowledge of detail and depth of philosophical research will, I believe, furnish the best solution of every question connected with the history of commerce and with the system
of political economy."[4] Not since, in the nonsocialist world at least,
has a politician committed himself so courageously to an economist.

Smith has not been a popular subject for biographers. He was a
bachelor. His best-remembered personal trait was his absent-mind-
edness. Once, according to legend, he fell into deep thought and
walked fifteen miles in his dressing gown before regaining consciousness. His manuscripts, by his instruction, were destroyed at
his death. He disliked writing letters, and few of these have survived.
The papers of those with whom he did correspond or which reflected his influence were destroyed, mostly because of lack of interest, and some, it appears, as late as 1941 or 1942. Adam Smith's
only other major published work, *The Theory of Moral Sentiments,*
reflects interests that were antecedent to his concern with political
economy. No biography of Adam Smith has superseded that by
John Rae, first published at the end of the nineteenth century.

Although Smith's life has attracted little attention, much has centered on *Inquiry into the Nature and Causes of the Wealth of Nations,* to give the title of his masterpiece its full resonance. With *Das Kapital* and the Bible, *Wealth of Nations* enjoys the distinction of being one of the three books that people may refer to at will without feeling they should have read it. Scholarly dispute over what is Smith's principal contribution has continued ever since publication. This is partly because there is so much in the book that every reader has full opportunity to exercise his own preference.

Exercising that preference, I have always thought that two of Smith's achievements have been neglected. One, mentioned by Gibbon, is his gift for language. Few writers ever, and certainly no economist since, have been as amusing, lucid or resourceful — or on occasion as devastating. Many people rightly remember his conclusion that "People of the same trade seldom meet together, even for merriment and diversion, but the conversation ends in a conspiracy against the public, or in some contrivance to raise prices."[5] There are many more such gems. He noted that "The late resolution of the Quakers in Pennsylvania, to set at liberty all their negro slaves, may satisfy us that their number cannot be very great."[6] And, anticipating Thorstein Veblen, he observed that "With the greater part of rich people, the chief enjoyment of riches consists in the parade of riches . . ."[7] On the function or nonfunction of stockholders, no one in the next two centuries was more penetrating in however many words: "[Stockholders] seldom pretend to understand any thing of the business of the company; and when the spirit of faction happens not to prevail among them, give themselves no trouble about it, but receive contentedly such half-yearly or yearly dividend as the directors think proper to make to them."[8] One of Smith's most useful observations, which should always be kept in mind when alarm substitutes for thought, is not in *Wealth of Nations.* On hearing from Sir John Sinclair in October 1777 that Burgoyne had surrendered at Saratoga and of his friend's fear that the nation was ruined, Smith said, "There is a great deal of ruin in a nation."[9]

Also neglected now are the "curious facts" that enchanted Hume and of which *Wealth of Nations* is a treasure house. Their intrusion has, in fact, been deplored. As a writer Smith was a superb carpenter but a poor architect. The facts appear in lengthy digressions which have been criticized as such. But for any discriminating reader it is worth the interruption to learn that the expenses of the civil government of the Massachusetts Bay Colony "before the commencement of the present disturbances," meaning the Revolution, were only £18,000 a year and that this was a rather sizeable sum compared with the expenses of New York and Pennsylvania at £4500 each and of New Jersey at £1200. (These and numerous other details on the colonies reflect an interest which John Rae believes was stimulated by Benjamin Franklin.)

Also, were it not for Smith, we might not know that after a bad storm, or "inundation," the citizens of the Swiss canton of Underwald (Unterwalden) came together in an assembly where each publicly confessed his wealth to the multitude and was then assessed, *pro rata,* for the repair of the damage. Or that, at least by Smith's exceptionally precise calculation, Isocrates earned £3333, 6s, 8d. for "what we would call one course of lectures, a number which will not appear extraordinary, from so great a city to so famous a teacher, who taught too what was at that time the most fashionable of all sciences, rhetoric."[10] Or that Plutarch was paid the same. Or, continuing with professors, that those who are subject to reward unrelated to their capacity to attract students will perform their duty in "as careless and slovenly a manner as that authority will permit" and that in "the university of Oxford, the greater part of the public professors [those with endowed or salaried chairs] have, for these many years, given up altogether even the pretence of teaching."[11]

So no one should neglect Smith's contribution to expository prose and "curious facts." Now as to economic thought and policy. Here a sharp and obvious distinction must be made between what was important in 1776 and what is important now. The first is very great; the second, save in the imagination of those who misuse Smith as a prophet of reaction, is much less so. The business corporation which Smith deplored and the wealth that accumulated in consequence of his advice combined to reduce the later relevance of that advice. But first we must consider his meaning in 1776.

II

Smith's economic contribution to his own time can be thought of as falling into three categories — method, system and advice. The second, overflowing onto the third, is by far the most important.

As to method, Smith gave to political economy, later to become economics, the basic structure that was to survive almost intact at least for the next hundred and fifty years. This structure begins with the problem of value — how prices are set. Then comes the question of how the proceeds are shared — how the participants in production are rewarded. These latter are the great trinity of labor, capital and land. Along the way is the role of money. Thereafter come banking, international trade, taxation, public works, defense and the other functions of the state. Other writers, notably the Physiocrats, had previously given political economy a fairly systematic frame, although, as Alexander Gray, a later Glasgow professor, observed, they had "embellished it with strange frills." But it was Smith who, for the English-speaking world, provided the enduring structure.

The framework, in turn, was more important than what it enclosed. Although Smith's treatment of value, wages, profits and rents suggested what was to follow, it was, in all respects, a beginning and not an end. Thus, as one example, Smith held that the supply of workers would increase, *pari passu,* with an increase in the sustenance available for their support. David Ricardo translated this thought into the iron law of wages — the rule that wages would tend always to fall to the bare minimum necessary to sustain life. And Thomas Robert Malthus, going a step further, adduced his immortal conclusion that people everywhere would proliferate to the point of starvation. Subsequent scholars — the marginal utility theorists, Alfred Marshall, others — added further modifications to the theory of prices, wages, interest, profits and rent, and yet further transmutations were, of course, to follow. Smith was left far behind.

But the structure he gave to economics and the explanation of economic behavior that it contained were, for Smith, only steps in the creation of his larger system — his complete view of how economic life should be arranged and governed. This was his central achievement. It provided a set of guiding rules for economic policy that were comprehensive and consistent without being arbitrary or dogmatic.

In the Smithian system the individual, suitably educated, is left free to pursue his own interest. In doing so, he serves not perfectly but better than by any alternative arrangement the common public purpose. Self-interest or selfishness guides men, as though by the influence of "an invisible hand," to the exercise of the diligence and intelligence that maximize productive effort and thus the public good. Private vice becomes a public virtue, which has been considered ever since a most convenient thing.

In pursuit of private interest, producers exploit the opportunities inherent in the division of labor — in, broadly speaking, the specialized development of skill for the performance of each small part of a total task of production. Combined with the division of labor is the natural propensity of man "to truck, barter or exchange." The freedom of the individual to do his best both in production and in exchange is inhibited by regulation and taxation. Thus the hand of the state should weigh on him as lightly as possible. The limiting factor on the division of labor — roughly, the scale of specialized productive activity — is the size of the market. Obviously this should be as wide as possible. Thus Smith's case against internal monopolistic or international restrictions on trade.

Smith's precursors, the mercantilists, held that national well-being and national strength derived from and required the accumulation by the country of precious metal. Smith held that — as one would now say and as he in effect did say — that they derived instead from the productivity of the labor force. Given an industrious and productive labor force, in the most majestic of Smith's arguments, there would be no need to worry about the stock of gold. The gold would always come.

Such, in greatest compression, is the Smithian system — the one that Pitt proclaimed as "the best solution of every question connected . . . with the system of political economy."

Smith's third contribution was in the field of practical policy. His advice — on banking, education, colonies, support of the sovereign (including his famous canons of taxation and extending even to recommendations for the reform of taxation in France), public works, joint-stock companies and agriculture — was infinitely abundant. No economist since has offered more. With many exceptions and frequent modifications to fit the circumstances, this advice is in keeping with Smith's system. The bias in favor of freeing or unburdening the individual to pursue his own interest is omnipresent, and so is Smith's belief that men will toil effectively only in the pursuit of pecuniary self-interest. There will be occasion for a further word on this advice; now we must see what of Smith survives.

III

Needless to say, the mordant language and the curious facts remain; it is too bad they are not more read and enjoyed. Also Smith's concept of the economic problem and the division of the subject between value and distribution are still to be found in that part of the textbooks that economists call microeconomics. His particular conclusions as to how prices, wages, rents and return to capital are determined and his views on gold, paper currency, banks and the like are now mostly of antiquarian interest.

Nor does all of the abundant advice just mentioned have modern meaning. It better illuminates life in the eighteenth century than it does any current problems. Until recently the textbooks on taxation included reverent mention of Smith's four great canons. But no one now coming to them without knowledge of their author would think them very remarkable. That taxes should be certain or predictable and arbitrary in their bite; that they should be so levied and collected as to fit the reasonable convenience of the taxpayer; and that the cost of collection should be a modest part of the total take were all important in 1776. They still are, but these things are fairly well accepted now.

Smith's fourth canon, that the "subjects of every state ought to contribute towards the support of the government, as nearly as possible, in proportion to their respective abilities; that is, in proportion to the revenue which they respectively enjoy under the protection of the state,"[12] could be taken as a prescription for a proportional (i.e., fixed percentage) as distinct from a progressive income tax. Some beleaguered rich have so argued. In fact, Smith was speaking only of what seemed possible and sensible in his own day. He would, almost certainly, have moved with the times. It might be added that his modest prescription gives no place to tax shelters, special treatment of state and municipal bonds or the oil depletion allowance and no comfort to those who otherwise believe that they were intended by nature to be untroubled by the IRS. Numerous of the great rich in the United States would find even Adam Smith's proportional prescription rather costly as compared with what they now pay.

The next and more interesting question concerns Smith's system — his rules for guiding economic life. What of that survives? Is economic life still directed in appreciable measure by the invisible hand — in modern language, by the market? What has happened to the notion of the minimal state, and is it forever dead? And what of Smith's plea for the widest possible market both within and between nations?

IV

Nothing so rejoices the conservative soul as the thought that it all survives. It doesn't. Smith was the victim of one major miscalculation. And, as earlier noted, he was damaged by the institution that he deplored, the business corporation. His system was also gravely impaired by the very success of the prescription that he offered.

Smith's miscalculation was of man's capacity, perhaps with some social conditioning, for cooperation. He thought it negligible. Men would work assiduously for their own pecuniary advantage; on shared tasks, even for shared reward, they would continue to do as little as authority allowed. Only in defeating or circumventing that authority — in minimizing physical and intellectual toil and maximizing indolence and sloth — would they bring real effort and ingenuity to bear. But not otherwise. People work only if working for themselves; there is no more persistent theme in *Wealth of Nations.* It is why government tasks are poorly performed. It is why civil servants are an uncivil and feckless crew. It is his case against the British bureaucracy in India. It is why the Oxford professors on a secure salary lapsed into idleness. And especially it is why, in Smith's view, joint-stock companies, except for routine tasks, had little to commend them. Their best chance for survival, one to which the minds of the directors almost invariably turned, was to obtain a monopoly of their industry or trade, a tendency to which Smith devoted some of his finest scorn. Otherwise their officers concerned themselves not with enriching the company but with enriching themselves or not enriching anyone.

In fact, experience since Smith has shown that man's capacity for cooperative effort is very great. Perhaps this was the product of education and social conditioning, something that no one writing in the eighteenth century could have foreseen. Conceivably Smith, handicapped by his environment, judged all races by the Scotch (as we are correctly called) and their much celebrated tendency to self-seeking recalcitrance. Most likely he failed to see the pride people could have in their organization, their desire for the good opinion or esteem of their co-workers and their satisfaction in what Thorstein Veblen would call "the instinct of workmanship."

In any case, governments in the performance of public tasks, some of great technical and military complexity; corporations in pursuit of growth, profit and power; and advanced socialist states in pursuit of national development and power have been able to enlist a great intensity of cooperative effort.

v

The most spectacular example of this cooperative effort — or perhaps, to speak more precisely, of a successful marriage of cooperative and self-serving endeavor — has been the corporation. The way in which the corporation has come to dominate economic life since 1776 need hardly be emphasized. This development Smith did not foresee, an understandable flaw. But he also thought both the form or structure and the cooperative or organized effort inherent in corporate development flatly impossible.

The corporation that Smith did not think possible was then extensively destructive of the minimal state that he prescribed. This destruction it accomplished in several ways. The corporation had needs — franchises, rights-of-way, capital, qualified manpower, support for expensive technological development, highways for its motor cars, airways for its airplanes — which only the state could supply. A state that served its corporations as they required quickly ceased, except in the minds of more romantic conservatives, to be minimal.

Also, a less evident point, the economy of which the great corporation was so prominent a part along with the unions was no longer stable. The corporation retained earnings for investment, as did the individuals it enriched. There was no certainty that all of such savings would be invested. The resulting shortage of demand could be cumulative. And in the reverse circumstances wages and prices might force each other up to produce an enduring and cumulative inflation. The state would be called upon to offset the tendency to recession by offsetting excess savings and stabilizing the demand for goods. This was the message of John Maynard Keynes. And the state would need to intervene to stabilize prices and wages if inflation were to be kept within tolerable limits. Both actions, traceable directly to corporate and counterpart union development, were blows at the Smithian state.

The corporation, as it became very large, also ceased to be subordinate to the market. It fixed prices, sought out supplies, influenced consumers and otherwise exercised power not different in kind from the power of the state itself. As Smith would have foreseen, this power was exercised in the interest of its possessors, and on numerous matters — the use of air, water and land — the corporate interest diverged from the public interest. It also diverged where, as in the case of the weapons firms, the corporation was able to persuade the state to be its customer. Corporate interest did not coincide with public interest as the Smithian system assumed. So there were appeals by the public to the government for redress and further enhancement of the state. All this was not as Smith would have thought.

VI

Finally, Smith's system was destroyed by its own success. In the nineteenth century and with a rather deliberate recognition of their source, Britain was governed by Smith's ideas. So, though more by instinct than by deliberate philosophical commitment, was the United States. And directly or through such great disciples as the French economist J. B. Say, Smith's influence extended to Western Europe. In the context of time and place, the Smithian system worked; there was a vast release of productive energy, a great increase in wealth, a large though highly uneven improvement in living standards. Then came the corporation with its superior access to capital (including that reserved from its own earnings), its great ability to adapt science and technology to its purposes and its strong commitment to its own growth through expanding sales and output. This, and by a new order of magnitude, added to the increase in output, income and consumption.

This increase in well-being was also damaging to the Smithian system. It was not possible to combine a highly productive economy and the resulting affluence with a minimal state. Public regulation had to develop in step with private consumption; public services must bear some reasonable relationship to the supply of private services and goods. Both points are accepted in practice, if not in principle. A country cannot have a high consumption of automobiles, alcohol, transportation, communications or even cosmetics without public rules governing their use and public facilities to rescue people from accidents and exploitation. The greater the wealth, the more men need to protect it, and the more that is required to pick up the discarded containers in which so much of it comes. Also in rough accord with increased private consumption goes an increased demand for public services — for education, health care, parks and public recreation, postal services and the infinity of other things that must be provided or are best provided by the state.

Among numerous conservatives there is still a conviction that the minimal state was deliberately destroyed by socialists, planners, *étatists* and other wicked men who did not know what they were about, or knew all too well. Far more of the responsibility lies with Smith himself. Along with the corporation, his system created the wealth that made his state impossible.

In one last area, it will be insisted, Adam Smith does survive. Men still respect his inspired and inspiring call for the widest possible market, one that will facilitate in the greatest degree the division of labor. After two centuries the dominant body of opinion in industrial nations resists tariffs and quotas. And in Europe the nation-states have created the ultimate monument to Adam Smith, the European Economic Community. In even more specific tribute to Smith, it was called the Common Market.

VII

Even here, however, there is less of Smith than meets the eye. Since the eighteenth century, and especially in the last fifty years, domestic markets have grown enormously. That of insular Britain today is far greater than that of Imperial Britain at the height of empire. The technical opportunities in large-scale production have developed significantly since 1776. But national markets have developed much, much more. Proof lies in the fact that General Motors, IBM, Shell and Nestlé do not produce in ever larger plants as would be the case if they needed to realize the full opportunities inherent in the division of labor. Rather, they regularly produce the same items in many plants all over the world. Except perhaps in the very small industrial countries — Holland, Belgium, Luxembourg — domestic markets have long been large enough so that even were producers confined to the home market, they would realize the full economies of scale and the full technical advantages of the division of labor.

The Common Market and the modern enlightenment on international trade owe much more to the nontechnical needs of the modern multinational corporation than they do to Adam Smith. The multinational corporation stands astride national boundaries. Instead of seeking tariff support from the state against countries that have a comparative advantage, it can move into the advantaged countries to produce what it needs. At the same time modern marketing techniques require that it be able to follow its products into other countries to persuade consumers and governments and, in concert with other producers, to avoid the price competition that would be disastrous for all. So, for the multinational corporation, tariffs, to speak loosely and generally, are both unnecessary and a nuisance. It would not have escaped the attention of Adam Smith, although it has escaped the attention of many in these last few years, that where there are no corporations, as in agriculture, a common market is more contentious and less than popular. The tariff enlightenment following World War II has resulted not from a belated reading of *Wealth of Nations* but from the much more powerful tendency for what serves the needs of large enterprises to become sound public policy.

VIII

But if time and the revolution that he helped set in motion have overtaken Smith's system and Smith's advice, there is one further respect in which he remains wonderfully relevant. That is in the example he sets for professional economists — for what, at the moment, is a troubled, rather saddened discipline. Smith is not a prophet for our time, but, as we have seen, he was magnificently in touch with his own time. He broke with the mercantilist orthodoxy to bring economic ideas abreast of the industrial and agricultural changes that were only then just visible on the horizon. His writing in relation to the Industrial Revolution involved both prophecy and self-fulfilling prophecy. He sensed, even if he did not fully see, what was about to come, and he greatly helped to make it come.

The instinct of the economist, now as never before, is to remain with the past. On that, there is a doctrine, a theory — one that is now elaborately refined. And there are practical advantages. An economist's capital, as I've elsewhere observed, lies in what he knows. To stay with what is accepted is also consistent with the good life — with the fur-lined comfort of the daily routine between suburb, classroom and office. To such blandishments, economists are no more immune than other people. The tragedy lies in their own resulting obsolescence. As the economic world changes, that proceeds relentlessly, and it is a painful thing.

Remarkably, the same institution, the corporation, which helped to take the economic world away from Adam Smith, has taken it away from the mature generation of present-day economists. As even economists in their nonprofessional life concede, the modern corporation controls prices and costs, organizes suppliers, persuades consumers, guides and controls the Pentagon, shapes public opinion, buys politicians and is otherwise a dominant influence in the state. In its contemporary and comprehensively powerful form it also, alas, figures only marginally in the accepted economic theory. That theory still holds the business firm to be solely subordinate to the market, solely subject to the authority of the state and ultimately the passive servant of the sovereign citizen. None of this being so, scholars have lost touch with reality. Older economists and some younger ones are left only with the hope that they can somehow consolidate their forces and live out the threat. It is a fate that calls less for criticism than for compassion.

It is not a fate that Adam Smith would have suffered. Given his avid empiricism, his deep commitment to reality and his profound concern for practical reform, he would have made the modern corporation and its power and the related power of the unions and the state an integral part of his theoretical system. His problem would have been different. With his contempt for theoretical pretense and his intense interest in practical questions, he might have had trouble getting tenure in a first-rate modern university.

NOTES

1. This is a revision of an address given in Kirkcaldy, Scotland, Adam Smith's birthplace, in June of 1973, at a gathering to celebrate the 250th anniversary of his birth.
2. Edward Gibbon, quoted in John Rae, *Life of Adam Smith* (New York: Augustus M. Kelley, 1965), p. 287.
3. David Hume, quoted in Rae, p. 286.
4. William Pitt, before the House of Commons on February 17, 1792, quoted in Rae, pp. 290–291.
5. Adam Smith, *Wealth of Nations* (Edinburgh: Adam and Charles Black, 1863), p. 59.
6. Smith, p. 172.
7. Smith, p. 79.
8. Smith, p. 333.
9. Adam Smith, quoted in Rae, p. 343.
10. Smith, p. 61.
11. Smith, p. 342.
12. Smith, p. 371.

The Massive Dissent of Karl Marx

[*from* The Age of Uncertainty]

Marx was not a central figure in my economic life, but no scholar can ignore him.

*   *   *   *

ADAM SMITH, David Ricardo and their followers affirmed as the natural order an economic society in which men owned the things — factories, machinery, raw materials as well as land — by which goods were produced. Men owned the capital or means of production. Spencer and Sumner gave this the highest social and moral sanction. Thorstein Veblen mused over and was amused by the result. But even Veblen did not dissent. Though a merciless critic of the high capitalist order, Veblen was not a socialist or even a reformer.

The massive dissent originated with Karl Marx. In considerable measure he used the ideas of Ricardo to assail the economic system that Ricardo interpreted and described. I've used the word *massive* to describe his onslaught. If we agree that the Bible is a work of collective authorship, only Mohammed rivals Marx in the number of professed and devoted followers recruited by a single author. And the competition is not really very close. The followers of Marx once far outnumbered the sons of the Prophet.

II

The world celebrates Karl Marx as a revolutionary, and for a century most of the world's revolutions, serious or otherwise, invoked his name. He was also a social scientist, many would say the most original and imaginative economist, one of the most erudite political philosophers of his age. The late Joseph Schumpeter, the famous Austrian (and Harvard) economist, iconoclast and devout conservative, introduced his account of Marx's ideas with the statement that he was a genius, a prophet and, as an economic theorist, "first of all a very learned man."[1]

Marx was also a brilliant journalist, and all American Republicans, including Mr. Gerald Ford and Mr. Ronald Reagan, both highly prominent as I write, may note with suitable pride that, during an exceptionally meager time in his life, he was sustained by the *New York Tribune* and was described by its editor as its most esteemed as well as best-paid correspondent. The *Tribune,* with the *Herald,* the other parent of the *Herald Tribune,* was, for generations, the organ of the highest Republican establishment. Marx had another involvement with Republicans. After the election in 1864, he joined in congratulating Lincoln warmly on the Republican victory — and on the progress of the war: "The working men of Europe," he said, "felt instinctively that the star-spangled banner carried the destiny of their class."[2]

Marx was also an historian, a man for whom history was less a subject to be studied than a reality to be lived and shared. Paul M. Sweezy, the most distinguished of present-day American Marxists, has said that it is this sense of history that gives Marxist economic thought its special claim to intellectual distinction. Other economists have heard of history; Marxists make themselves and their ideas a part of history.

Finally, Marx himself was a major historical event. Often it can be imagined that if someone hadn't lived, someone else would have done his work. The innovating force, to recur to a familiar point, was not the individual but the circumstance. No one will ever suggest that the world would be the same had Marx not lived. Marx, as an historian, would expect one to begin with his history.

III

It begins in Trier, or Trèves, at the head of the Moselle Valley. When Marx was born there in 1818, the surrounding countryside must have been the loveliest in Europe. Many would say that it still is. The valley is filled with towns out of the Brothers Grimm. Above are the vineyards. And beyond the rim of the valley are gently rolling farmlands, much of which is still farmed in the thin, inefficient but vividly contrasting strips that remain a common feature of Rhineland agriculture. Delegations come to Trier as they do to Highgate Cemetery in London where Marx is buried. From the West, travelers come to drink the wine. The local tourist office reports that only the most occasional visitor asks about Marx. A largish store in the town features a variety of merchandise and the family name. The pleasant and spacious house in which Marx was born still survives.

There was much in this small town — it then had a population variously estimated at from 10,000 to 15,000 — to stimulate a feeling for history. Once, as Augusta Trevorum, it was called the Rome of the North. The German tribes regularly erupted southward on the Latins, a habit they did not break until the middle of the twentieth century. Augusta Trevorum was the principal bastion against this aggression. The Porta Negra, the great black gate from the Roman wall, stands to this day as the most impressive Roman relic in what was northern Gaul.

Trier is now, of course, part of Germany; in 1818, it was only recently so. When Marx was born, French occupation had just given way to Prussian rule. The change was a matter of prime importance for the family of Heinrich Marx. The Marx family was Jewish; numerous of Karl Marx's ancestors had been rabbis. The French had been comparatively liberal to the ancient Jewish community of the town. Prussia was not. As an officer of the High Court and the leading lawyer of the town, Heinrich Marx could not be a Jew. So he and later his family were baptized as Protestants. It was, most scholars now agree, a purely practical step, one that did not involve any rejection of the social and intellectual traditions of Jewish life. As to religion, by the time Karl Marx was born, it was no longer thought very important by his family. Their mood was by then strongly secular.

His Jewish antecedents were, nevertheless, to be wonderfully useful to Marx's enemies in later times. Anti-communism could be combined with anti-Semitism. This was a fine start for anyone with an instinct for rabble-rousing, and Hitler and the Nazis found it especially valuable. But many others made use of it.

However, there would also be a lurking suspicion that Marx was himself anti-Semitic. After all, he had been baptized. More important, some of his writing was very hard on Jews. This was partly a literary convention; the word *Jew* in the last century was used extensively as a synonym or metaphor for the avaricious businessman. But it takes effort not to read some racial animus into what he wrote.

Marx was also an atheist. This was an age when most people took religion very seriously, when its active practice was a badge of respectability. And Marx was not a passive but an active atheist. One of his most famous phrases described religion as the opiate of the people, which taught them to acquiesce patiently in hardship and exploitation when they should rise up in angry revolt.

Karl Marx never cultivated popularity but where religion was concerned, he obviously excelled. To be Jewish, open to the charge of anti-Semitism and openly hostile to Christianity as well as all other faiths, was to ensure adequately against religious applause.

IV

Marx was a deeply romantic youth. He wrote poetry, much of it unreadable — or so his family thought — and idealistic essays (some of which have survived) on nature, life and the choice of a career. A career should be where one "can contribute most to humanity . . . and glowing tears of noble men will [then] fall on our ashes."[3] While still in his middle teens, he affirmed his love for Jenny von West-phalen.

Jenny was the daughter of the leading citizen of the town, Baron Ludwig von Westphalen. Baron von Westphalen, obviously a rather remarkable man, was an intellectual and a liberal, and he had taken a great liking to the young Marx. They walked together on the banks of the Moselle, and the Baron introduced his young friend to romantic poetry and also to the notion that the ideal state would be socialist, not capitalist; be based on common property, not private property.[4] This was heady conversation for a German aristocrat to be offering a young lad of the town. It is not suggested that Marx's socialism began with these talks but they do explain how it was possible for him, though not without social strain, to marry into this family.

At seventeen, Marx was sent down the Rhine to Bonn to the University. This was then a small academy of a few hundred students, very aristocratic in tone. Marx was still a romantic; his interests now extended to drinking and duelling. Even by the relaxed academic standards of the time, he was rather idle. His father complained both of his high living costs and his almost complete failure to maintain communications with his family. But after a year he moved on from Bonn to Berlin. This was in 1836, and it was much more than a change in universities. It was a move into the very mainstream of German, even European, even Western intellectual life.

V

The romantic years were now at an end; the years of Hegel began. Not only was Berlin a far more serious place than Bonn but Marx was now surrounded by the disciples of Georg Wilhelm Friedrich Hegel. These young men, the young Hegelians, took themselves and their scholarly mission very seriously indeed. Recurrently in history intellectuals have been so impressed with their unique vision of truth that they have seen themselves fated to change how all men think. This was one of those moments.

What is not so easy to describe is the change the young intellectuals sought. Hegel is not a very accessible figure for the Anglo-Saxon or American mind; certainly I have never found him so. Once, years ago, I was greatly comforted by a story told me by Arthur Goodhart, the Oxford law professor and onetime Master of University College. It concerned a night in 1940 when, as a member of the Home Guard, he was deployed with a fellow professor, a distinguished philosopher at the university, to guard a small private airstrip near Oxford. They may well have been the two most improbable soldiers in the annals of British military history. But they marched back and forth in a light mist, one with a rifle of more or less Crimean vintage, the other with a fowling piece. Occasionally, being professors, they stopped to converse. Toward dawn, during one of these pauses, Goodhart's fellow soldier lit his pipe and said, "I say, Arthur, do you suppose those wretched fellows aren't coming? I did so want a shot at them. I've always detested Hegel."

Marx's lifetime associate and ally was Friedrich Engels. The best short summary of what Hegel meant to both of them comes from him: "The great merit of Hegel's philosophy was that for the first time the totality of the natural, historical and spiritual aspects of the world were conceived and represented as a process of constant transformation and development and an effort was made to show the organic character of this process."[5]

An organic process of transformation and development would become the central feature of Marx's thought. The moving force in this transformation would be the conflict between the social classes. This would keep society in a condition of constant change. Once it had developed a structure that was seemingly secure, the structure would nurture the antagonistic forces that would challenge and then destroy it. A new structure would then emerge, and the process of conflict and destruction would begin anew.

Thus, in the real world at the time, the capitalists — the bourgeoisie — were challenging and destroying the old and seemingly immutable structure of feudalism, the traditional ruling classes of the old aristocratic system. In gaining power, the bourgeoisie would nurture the development of a class-conscious proletariat from the exploited, property-less and denationalized workers. In time, the proletariat would move against the capitalists. The capitalists, including the bourgeois state, would be overthrown. The workers' state would be the next new structure.

By all Hegelian law, the process should continue. Perhaps the workers' state, by the nature of its productive tasks, would be highly organized, bureaucratic, disciplined. It would need scientists, other intellectuals. And it would nurture artists, poets, novelists for whose work the literate masses would now have a large demand. These artists would then begin to assert themselves. Their opposition to the bureaucracy would become acute. Thus the next conflict, one that was far from invisible in the countries of Eastern Europe and the Soviet Union. However, Marx did not allow Hegel to take him so far. Nor do modern Marxists as they look at their dissident scientists, novelists, poets. Rigorously applied to modern Communist society, Hegel could be quite a problem.

Hegel's ideas did not come easily to Marx. Their acceptance, or more likely the experience of serious study itself, involved him in emotional crises, weakened his health and, it appears, brought him to the edge of a physical breakdown. For a time he left the city and went to the small village of Stralau outside Berlin to recover. Each day he walked several miles to attend his lectures — and wrote in surprise at how good it was for his health. It was a lesson he would soon forget. For much of his life he would be in poor health, the result of singularly unwholesome living. Much of the world's work, it has been said, is done by men who do not feel quite well. Marx is a case in point.

In 1841, Marx left Berlin. Henceforth he would be part of the Hegelian process — one of the prime instruments of its transformation. A new factor would also now begin to influence his movements. Hitherto they were relaxed and voluntary. Henceforth, for years, they would be sudden and compelled. Germany, France and Belgium would all unite in the belief that Marx was an excellent resident for some other country. For a man pursued by the police, an insufficiently recognized point, there are two sources of solace and protection: one is to be innocent of the crime. The other is to be righteous in committing it. Marx was always to have this second and greater support.

VI

Marx went to Cologne. Like Trier, Cologne is also in the Rhineland, and, like Trier, it was also then recently redeemed from France and somewhat more liberal for the experience. In France it was said that what wasn't prohibited was permitted. Prussia followed a sterner rule: what wasn't permitted was prohibited. In Cologne Marx became a journalist. The paper was the brand-new *Rheinische Zeitung;* it was well-financed and by, of all people, the burgeoning industrialists and merchants of the Rhineland and the Ruhr. Marx was an immediate success; he was first a highly valued correspondent and very soon the editor. None of this was surprising. He was intelligent, resourceful and extremely diligent and in some ways a force for moderation. He was also the champion of high standards. Revolution was much discussed. The word "communism," though still indistinct as to meaning, was now coming into use. Marx said that numerous of the resulting contributions were:

> . . . scrawls pregnant with world revolutions and empty of thought, written in a slovenly style and flavoured with some atheism and communism (which these gentlemen have never studied) . . . I declared that I considered the smuggling of communist and socialist ideas into casual theatre reviews was unsuitable, indeed immoral . . .[6]

Marx would still be a force for editorial good in dealing with highly motivated writers of the left today.

Under Marx's editorship the *Rheinische Zeitung* grew rapidly in circulation, and its influence extended to the other German states. It became also of increasing interest to the censors who reviewed the proofs each night before it went to press. They reacted adversely to Marx on many things; the most important collision was over dead wood. I must acknowledge my debt on numerous matters to David

McLellan's very lucid biography of Marx, and they include the story of this conflict.[7]

From ancient times, residents of the Rhineland had been accustomed to go into the forests to collect fallen wood for fuel. Like air or most water, it was a free good. Now, with increasing population and prosperity, the wood had become valuable and the collectors a nuisance. So the privilege was withdrawn; wood now became serious private property. The cases seeking to protect it clogged the Prussian courts. Some eighty to ninety percent of all prosecutions were, it is said, for theft of dead wood or what was so described. The law was now to be yet further tightened — the keepers of forests would be given summary power to assess damages for theft. In commenting on this power, Marx asked:

> . . . if every violation of property, without distinction or more precise determination, is theft, would not all private property be theft? Through my private property, do not I deprive another person of this property? Do I not thus violate his right to property?[8]

In these same months of 1842, Marx also came to the support of old neighbors, the winegrowers of the Moselle Valley. They were suffering severely from competition under the *Zollverein*, the common market that the German states had recently adopted. His solution was not radical — more free discussion of their problems — and he came to this also with rather labored caution:

> To resolve the difficulty, the administration and the administered both need a third element, which is political without being official and bureaucratic, an element which at the same time represents the citizen without being directly involved in private interests. This resolving element, composed of a political mind and a civic heart, is a free Press.[9]

Marx also criticized the Czar and urged a more secular approach to divorce. Prussia was Prussia: here was a man supporting wood collection and free discussion and criticizing the Czar. A line had to be drawn. In March 1843, the *Rheinische Zeitung* was suppressed.

Marx went to Paris. First, however, on June 19, he went to Kreuz-
nach, a resort town some fifty miles from Trier. There, in a Protestant and civil ceremony, he married Jenny von Westphalen. It can
be said without exaggeration that for no woman since Mary did
marriage portend so much. A few months earlier Jenny had written
her future husband urging him, come what may, to keep clear of
politics.

VII

For Marx, Paris was the beginning of a new life. The streets of Paris
were then, as so often, the nursery of revolution. Many of the revolutionaries at this time were German, refugees from Prussian censorship and repression. Many, of course, were socialists. Their influence on Marx during his stay in Paris was very great.

The Marx family lived at various addresses on rue Vaneau — for
the longest time at number 38, now a small hotel-boardinghouse. A
sign in the entrance hallway tells of its most famous tenant, as does,
most willingly, the proprietor. André Gide lived in recent times at
one end of the street. One imagines that the neighborhood has
come up a bit since Marx's day.

Once settled in Paris, Marx went ahead with his next journalistic
enterprise, the editing of the *Deutsch-Französische Jahrbücher,* the
German-French Yearbooks. This was really a magazine but by calling it a book, he hoped to avoid censorship. The reference to France
in the title was also a gesture. Though he was in Paris, Marx's
thoughts were on Germany, and it was for Germany that the Yearbooks were written. Rue Vaneau was a convenient location for
Marx's editorial activities, for his co-editor, Arnold Ruge, was a near
neighbor.

A review in the very first issue of the Yearbooks led to another
collision with the censors. Again it sounds rather innocuous — also
complicated, labored, with distinct elements of wishful thinking:

> The emancipation of Germany is the emancipation of man. The
> head of this emancipation is philosophy, its heart is the prole-

tariat. Philosophy cannot realize itself without transcending the proletariat, the proletariat cannot transcend itself without realizing philosophy.[10]

But the Prussian police showed themselves to be very sensitive men. This was dangerous stuff. The first double-issue of the Yearbooks was confiscated at the border. There could now be no German readers, and since there never were any French contributors or readers, the publication was obviously in trouble. Marx, by this time, was also quarreling with his fellow editor, Ruge. So the first issue of the German-French Yearbooks was the last.

In the next weeks, however, something far more important happened. Friedrich Engels was passing through Paris; the two men had met briefly once before; now at the Café de la Régence, once frequented by Benjamin Franklin, Denis Diderot, Sainte-Beuve and Louis Napoleon, they met and talked, met again and formed what was to be one of the world's most famous partnerships. Engels would be Marx's editor, collaborator, admirer, friend — and financial angel. His name would forever, and all but exclusively, appear in association with that of Marx. "Our complete agreement in all theoretical fields became obvious," he later wrote, "and our joint work dates from that time."[11] Engels always considered himself a junior partner, and so, without doubt, he was. But that does not lessen his role. Had he not been the junior partner, much for which his senior partner is known would not have been done.

Like Marx, Engels was a German. And like Marx, he was a member of the upper middle class. All of the early revolutionary leaders (it is hard to think of any exceptions at all) were middle-class intellectuals. Only in hope and oratory did they come from the masses.

However, the Engels family — textile manufacturers in the Ruhr and, in an early way, a multinational enterprise — was much wealthier than that of Marx. Engels would spend most of his life in England, in Manchester, where he combined revolutionary thought with the supervision of the local branch of the family firm.

Relieved of his editorial duties, Marx settled down for a period of serious reading and study, perhaps the most intense of his life. Numerous of the ideas which were to dominate his later years are thought to have taken form in this period. No one should imagine, although some do, that socialism began with Marx. By this time it was under the most intense discussion. Saint-Simon and Charles Fourier had preceded Marx. So had Robert Owen in the United States. Louis Auguste Blanqui (who spent most of his life in prison), Louis Blanc, P. J. Proudhon, all Frenchmen, and the Germans, Ferdinand Lassalle and Ludwig Feuerbach, were contemporaries. All, and especially the Germans, were sources of Marx's thought.

Marx, during these years, was not only gathering ideas but considering the role of ideas themselves. For John Maynard Keynes ideas were the motivating force in historical change. Marx, while not denying the importance of ideas, carried the proposition a step further back. The accepted ideas of any period are singularly those that serve the dominant economic interest:

> . . . intellectual production changes its character in proportion as material production is changed. The ruling ideas of each age have ever been the ideas of the ruling class.[12]

I have never thought Marx wrong on this. Nothing more reliably characterizes great social truth, economic truth in particular, than its tendency to be agreeable to the significant economic interest. What economists believe and teach is rarely hostile to the institutions that reflect the dominant economic power. Not to notice this takes effort, although many succeed.

Taking form, also, in these years were Marx's views on the process by which capitalism itself would be changed. Sir Eric Roll, a remarkably eclectic English student of Marx — he has been a professor, a senior civil servant, an accomplished international negotiator who led the negotiations for both the Marshall Plan and the EEC, a banker, a member of the Court of the Bank of England and a respected writer on the history of economic thought — many years ago gave the most succinct summary of the motivating influence in capitalist change:

It had to be some contradiction in the system which produced conflict, movement and change . . . This basic contradiction of capitalism is the increasingly social, cooperative nature of production made necessary by the new powers of production which mankind possesses and (as opposed to this) the individual ownership of the means of production . . . [From this comes the] inevitable antagonism . . . between the two classes whose interests are incompatible.[13]

The notion of contradiction and inevitable conflict was leading Marx to its consequences. As a result, he was forming his ideas on communism and beginning to identify himself with the ultimate vision of the classless society.

With all else, he continued writing. His preoccupation was still with Germany, and his new outlet was *Vorwärts* (*Forward*), the organ of the German refugee community in Paris. But the censors were still on guard. Once again one must read what he said:

. . . Germany has a vocation to social revolution that is all the more classic in that it is incapable of political revolution. For as the impotence of the German bourgeoisie is the political impotence of Germany, so the situation of the German proletariat . . . is the social situation of Germany. The disproportion between philosophical and political development in Germany is no abnormality. It is a necessary disproportion. It is only in socialism that a philosophical people can find a corresponding activity, thus only in the proletariat that it finds the active element of its freedom.[14]

One yearns for policemen who could be aroused today by such prose. But, reliably, the Prussian police *were* aroused. They complained to the French; to harbor such a writer was not a neighborly act. They asked for a friendly, fraternal gesture of repression. Guizot, the French Minister of the Interior, was obliging in such matters and issued an order for Marx's expulsion. That was on January 25, 1845. On twenty-four hours' notice the Marx family — there was now a baby girl — departed for Brussels. *Vorwärts* was also closed down.

VIII

The Communist Manifesto was composed by Marx with the help of Engels in the next, rather peaceful and happy years in Belgium. The *Manifesto* was an organizing document, a brochure for the League of the Just (soon to become the Communist League) which Marx was now actively promoting. It is, incomparably, the most successful propaganda tract of all time. There was also, in comparison with Marx's early writing, a quantum advance in the impact of the prose. What before had been wordy and labored was now succinct and arresting — a series of hammer blows:

> The history of all hitherto existing society is the history of class struggles. Freeman and slave, patrician and plebeian, lord and serf, guild-master and journeyman, in a word, oppressor and oppressed, stood in constant opposition to one another, carried on an uninterrupted, now hidden, now open fight, a fight that each time ended either in a revolutionary reconstitution of society at large, or in the common ruin of the contending classes.

> . . . The executive of the modern State is but a committee for managing the common affairs of the whole bourgeoisie . . .

> The bourgeoisie, by the rapid improvement of all instruments of production, by the immensely facilitated means of communication, draws all, even the most barbarian nations, into civilisation. The cheap prices of its commodities are the heavy artillery with which it batters down all Chinese walls . . .

> It [the bourgeoisie] has created enormous cities, has greatly increased the urban population as compared with the rural, and has thus rescued a considerable part of the population from the idiocy of rural life . . . during its rule of scarce one hundred years, it has created more massive and more colossal productive forces than have all preceding generations together. . . .

> [Initially] the proletarians do not fight their enemies [the great bourgeoisie or capitalists], but the enemies of their enemies, the remnants of absolute monarchy, the landowners, the nonindustrial bourgeoisie, the petty bourgeoisie.

The Communists disdain to conceal their views and aims. They openly declare that their ends can be attained only by the forcible overthrow of all existing social conditions. Let the ruling classes tremble at a communistic revolution. The proletarians have nothing to lose but their chains. They have a world to win. Working men of all countries, unite![15]

Even more durable than the political impact of *The Communist Manifesto* has been its effect on political style. Its assertive, uncompromising, thrusting mood has become part of the consciousness of all politicians, including those for whom the name of Marx is anathema and those who identify it only with Hart, Schaffner and men's suits. In consequence, when American Democrats or Republicans, British socialists or Tories, Frenchmen of the right or left decide to tell the people of their purposes, the crescendo tones of the *Manifesto* sound in their ears and presently in those of the public. The prose so contrived is, invariably, a terrible thing.

The *Manifesto* is not without its contradictions. There is none, as some might suppose, in Marx's praise of capitalism and its accomplishments and his call for its extinction. These are different stages in the historical process. Nor, as pedants have suggested, is there any real conflict between his call for revolution and his claim that it is inevitable. One can always try to advance the inevitable. But there was a great and intensely practical conflict between his immediate program and his hope of revolution. The program in the *Manifesto* is, by all modern standards, mostly a collation of reformist measures. The demands are for:

Ending of private ownership of land.
A progressive income tax.
Abolition of inheritance.
. . .
A national bank with a monopoly of banking operations.
Public ownership of railroads and communications.
Extension of public ownership in industry; cultivation of
    idle lands.
Better soil management.
Work by all.

Combination of agriculture with industry; decentralization
   of population.
Free education.
Abolition of child labor.
Education along with work.[16]

In one way or another in the advanced capitalist countries quite a
few of these things — ending of the private ownership of land, decentralization of population and a public monopoly of banking are
the major exceptions — have been done. And these reforms have
helped take the raw edge off capitalism. Thus they have had the effect of postponing that "forcible overthrow of all existing social
conditions" for which Marx called. In such fashion did Marx work
against Marx. The internal revolution came in those countries —
Russia, China, Cuba — where the reforms Marx urged were never
known.

IX

A revolution did come on the heels of the *Manifesto*. In the Italian
states, France, Germany and Austria, governments now tottered and
crowned heads fell, some to rise again in a few weeks. This was in
1848, the year of revolutions, a year that is still connected in the
minds of many people with Marx and the *Manifesto*, neither of
which, in fact, had an appreciable influence on events. When the
revolution came, the words of the *Manifesto* were still all but unknown. It was, however, the first revolution that could be identified,
however indistinctly, with the aims and aspirations of the workers
— with the proletariat as a class. So it was watched closely by Marx,
especially as it developed in Paris. And it had a profound effect on
his view of the nature of revolution. For that reason the events in
Paris require a closer look.
   Every great event has its geographical epicenter — that of the
American Revolution was the few city blocks around Carpenters'
and Independence Halls in Philadelphia; that of the great French
Revolution was the Place de la Bastille; that of the Revolution of

1848 was the Luxembourg Gardens. The setting had something to do with causes and participants, neither of which were much to Marx's taste. In the years before 1848 in France there had been a severe depression and much unemployment. Businessmen suffered as well as the workers. The crops had also been bad and bread prices very high. Then, in 1847, crops were very good and prices fell. So now the peasants took a beating. Almost everyone was being punished; the market, which is much loved by conservatives, was playing a very revolutionary role.

In particular, the circumstances greatly encouraged a dangerous line of thought now coming into circulation. It was that private production of goods might not be the only possible form of economic organization. This was the influence of Saint-Simon, Charles Fourier, Louis Blanc and others mentioned above. In circulation, also, was the compelling notion that every man had the right to a job; the reference was to *the right to work*.

In the United States, the phrase, the right to work, now stands for opposition to unions, for the principle that no person should have to join a union to hold a job. It is heard by conservatives with approval, or at least with a pleasant sense of nostalgia, and never by a devout liberal without a distinct shudder. A state with right-to-work laws, even though they are unenforced, is, in trade-union matters, a very retarded place indeed. Time changes everything. In 1848, the right to work was a truly radical thought.

The uprising in February 1848 united highly disparate groups, something that did not encourage Marx. There were the workers who wanted work and income. They were joined by businessmen, mostly smaller entrepreneurs, who wanted freedom of enterprise and a chance to recoup the losses suffered in the preceding years of depression. And, initially, there was support from the peasants who wanted better prices. The leadership was mostly by men who wanted freedom of expression — freedom from censorship and the attentions of the police. By most standards, the leaders were conservative. As the symbol of revolution, the red flag was rejected in favor of the tricolor. The tricolor was thought less damaging to business confidence and the public credit.

The revolt was quickly successful. The Tuileries Palace was occupied. Louis Philippe found it convenient to depart. The Luxembourg Palace was brought into use as the seat of a commission to study means for rescuing the workers from their poverty. This device was not yet a transparent stall.

The concern with the workers brought the focus on the Gardens. The assemblage there was, or has been called, the first congress of workers in history. It was also, more than incidentally, a means for segregating and keeping under control the most troublesome and dangerous participants in the revolt. It was one thing to be liberal, republican, romantic. It was another thing to question private property, be for workers' rights, higher pay, a twelve-hour day. Let there be a revolution but let it not be irresponsible.

The word *revolution* comes easily to the tongue; revolutions are always being threatened. If we knew how hard it is to have one, we might use the word less, and conservatives might fret less about the danger. They are far, far safer than they know.

Three conditions are absolutely essential. There must be determined leaders, men who know exactly what they want and who also know that they have everything to gain and everything to lose. Such men are rare. Revolutions attract men who have an eye on the main chance.

The leaders must have disciplined followers, people who will accept orders, carry them out without too much debate. This too is unlikely; revolutionaries have a disconcerting tendency to believe they should think for themselves, defend their own beliefs. There is opportunity and attraction for windbags. These cannot be allowed. Such men will be crushed while they debate.

And, above all, the other side must be weak. All successful revolutions are the kicking in of a rotten door. The violence of revolutions is the violence of men who charge into a vacuum. So it was in the French Revolution. So it was in the Russian Revolution in 1917. So it was in the Chinese Revolution after World War II. So it was not in 1848.

In the Luxembourg Palace the leadership was weak and the talk was long. It was of government workshops in which men would produce cooperatively for the common good; it didn't matter much what or at what cost. Or it was of public works, a great underground canal across Paris, in which imagination took the place of engineering. Wages were, indeed, raised. But this and associated relief measures had the effect of raising taxes and giving the peasants the impression that they were paying for the revolution. Meanwhile no real thought was given to seizing the instruments of power — guardsmen, police, soldiers. These are extremely important people in the moment of revolutionary truth.

This moment of revolutionary truth came in the early summer days of 1848. On June 23, the workers decided to leave their revolutionary ghetto and assemble at the Pantheon a few hundred yards away. From there they marched to the Place de la Bastille to enforce the much-discussed demands on the provisional government. The government was not without resources, and it had been viewing the workers with increasing alarm.

The workers succeeded in getting to the Place de la Bastille and in building a formidable barricade. The first attack by the National Guard was repelled, and some thirty guardsmen were killed. The romantic tendencies of revolutionaries now asserted themselves. Two handsome prostitutes climbed to the top of the barricade, raised their skirts and asked what Frenchman, however reactionary, would fire on the naked belly of a woman. Frenchmen rose to the challenge with a lethal volley.

Presently the barricades were stormed and the workers overcome. Prisoners were taken, and initially they were shot. Then, it is said, out of consideration for the neighbors who objected to the noise, they were put to the bayonet instead. The massacre extended to the Gardens. In another thoughtful gesture, again according to legend, these were kept closed for several days until the blood was washed or cleaned away. Already by 1848, people were becoming conscious of the environment.

Marx was not greatly surprised by this outcome. The bourgeois leadership of the revolution did not inspire his confidence. And as far as the workers were concerned, the timing and sequence were wrong: first, there had to be the bourgeois revolution, then the socialist triumph. Later in the year Marx noted that the revolution, symbolically at least, had succeeded in the matter of the flag. "The tricolour republic now bears only *one colour,* the colour of the defeated, the *colour of blood.*"[17]

Elsewhere in Europe even the monarchies survived. Concessions were made to the bourgeois power but not to the workers. Before 1848, to speak generally, the old feudal classes and the new capitalist class were in conflict. Thereafter they were united, with the capitalists gaining in real, if not visible, power. This union would be secure for another sixty-five years — until the great ungluing of World War I.

X

The year 1848 did bring great personal changes for Marx. The Belgians were more liberal than their neighbors but just as nervous; they decided that even they could not harbor so dangerous a man. By now Marx was at the head of the police lists, a celebrated name in all the dossiers.

For the moment the revolutionary mood had its effect. On almost the day he was expelled from Brussels, he was invited back to France. And he was able to go from there to Cologne to revive the *Rheinische Zeitung,* now become the *Neue Rheinische Zeitung.* His first loyalty was still to the German workers.

However, the revived paper was, financially speaking, a shoestring operation. And it existed only because of the uncertainty of the conservative and counterrevolutionary forces as to whether they had the power to suppress it. Once they saw the feebleness of the revolutionary threat, they moved in again. Marx was still, in some ways, a voice for moderation. He had warned strongly against reckless, adventurist action by the workers that could only lead to disaster.

Nevertheless he had once more to move. Only two countries were still available, England and the United States. Marx gave thought to going to the United States, and it is interesting to speculate on his future and that of the Republic had he done so. But he didn't have the money. So he went to London. This was his last move; he lived in London for the rest of his life.

Marx crossed the Channel on August 24, 1849. Though he had the experience of several lifetimes behind him, he was, incredibly, only thirty-one. Before him lay three further tasks: the first was to put in final form the ideas that would guide the masses to their salvation; the second was to create the organization that would bring and lead the revolution; the third was to find the means by which he and his family could eat, be housed and survive. Each of these tasks interfered sadly with the others but, in the end, all were accomplished.

The financial help came from Engels and from other friends. There was an occasional inheritance windfall from Trier, and there was the *New York Tribune.* (In 1857, when times were lean, the *Tribune* fired all of its foreign correspondents but two. Marx was one of the two who were kept.) But Marx was always a terrible hand with money. Where before his movements were at the behest of the police, now they were at the behest of landlords and creditors. Thus the migrations — from rooms in Leicester Square to a flat off the King's Road in Chelsea, to 64 Dean Street in Soho, to number 28 further up the street. Children came, six in all, and three of them died in the squalid, crowded rooms in Soho. (There was, additionally, an illegitimate son.) The uncertainty, the sudden moves and the squalor were Jenny Marx's marriage portion. She accepted it, one gathers, with infinite good nature.

The Prussian police maintained their interest in Marx. In 1852, a police spy infiltrated Marx's rooms and sent back a lucid account of the Marx ménage. It is a valuable contribution to history from the files and holds forth hope as to what, one day, the CIA may offer:

> As father and husband, Marx, in spite of his wild and restless character, is the gentlest and mildest of men. Marx lives in one of the worst, therefore one of the cheapest, quarters of London. He occupies two rooms. The one looking out on the street is the salon, and the bedroom is at the back. In the whole apartment there is not one clean and solid piece of furniture. Everything is broken, tattered and torn, with a half inch of dust over everything and the greatest disorder everywhere. In the middle of the

salon there is a large old-fashioned table covered with an oil-
cloth, and on it there lie manuscripts, books and newspapers, as
well as the children's toys, the rags and tatters of his wife's sewing basket, several cups with broken rims, knives, forks, lamps,
an inkpot, tumblers, Dutch clay pipes, tobacco ash — in a word,
everything topsy-turvy, and all on the same table. A seller of
second-hand goods would be ashamed to give away such a remarkable collection of odds and ends.

When you enter Marx's room smoke and tobacco fumes make
your eyes water so much that for a moment you seem to be
groping about in a cavern, but gradually, as you grow accustomed to the fog, you can make out certain objects which dis-
tinguish themselves from the surrounding haze. Everything is
dirty, and covered with dust, so that to sit down becomes a thor-
oughly dangerous business.[18]

In 1856, seven years after coming to London, a small inheritance
enabled the family to escape, as Jenny Marx wrote of them to a
friend, "the evil, frightful rooms which encompassed all our joy and
all our pain."[19] They moved with vast delight to a suburban villa in
Hampstead, a brand-new real estate development. There were more
financial troubles but the worst was over. Although the myth is to
the contrary, in later years in London Marx had a very satisfactory
income by the standards of the time.

In the thirty-odd years that he lived in England, Marx had something more important even than income, although income is rarely
a secondary matter for those who do not have one. This was nearly
complete security in thought and expression. The governments under which Marx had previously lived had the greatest difficulty in
seeing why he should be so favored.

On arriving in London, the practical problems of his life not-
withstanding, Marx plunged immediately into political work. He
attended meetings; highly disreputable characters gathered in his
squalid quarters to consider the strategy and tactics of revolution. In
1850, the Austrian Ambassador made an official protest to the British government. Marx and his fellow members of the Communist
League were engaging in all kinds of dangerous discussions, even

debating the wisdom or unwisdom of regicide. The Ambassador received a superbly insouciant reply: ". . . under our laws, mere discussion of regicide, so long as it does not concern the Queen of England and so long as there is no definite plan, does not constitute sufficient grounds for the arrest of the conspirators."[20] However, as a conciliatory gesture, the British Home Secretary said that he was prepared to give the revolutionaries financial assistance for emigrating to the United States. Regicide could not be practiced there. However, in the following year, when a joint request came from Austria and Prussia for the transportation of Marx and his friends, it was rejected.

In London Marx had one other resource that has been more celebrated. That was the library of the British Museum.

XI

In the British Museum Marx read and wrote. He wrote, in particular, his enduring testament, the three volumes of *Das Kapital*.

No one, least of all the person who attempts it, can be satisfied with a short characterization of the conclusions of this vast work. And no modern Marxist will ever be satisfied even by a much lengthier effort. It has long been the acknowledged right of every Marxist scholar to read into Marx the particular meaning that he himself prefers and to treat all others with indignation. This is especially the case if Marx's words are taken literally, as he may have meant. The decently subtle mind always discerns a deeper, more valid, less vulgar meaning. Still, the effort must be made.

David Ricardo, it will be recalled, gave the world (or gets credit for giving, for there were precursors) the labor theory of value, the proposition that things exchange in accordance with the amount and quality of the labor required in their manufacture. And with the labor theory of value went the iron law of wages, the ineluctable tendency of wages to reduce themselves to the lowest level that still sustained life and perpetuated the race. Given anything more, the workers proliferated. The price of the means of subsistence — food, in the main — was bid up. Wages were bid down. The landlords did well; workers were kept at, or returned to, the level at which they just survived.

Where Ricardo left off, Marx began. It is David Ricardo's unique position in history that he was an innovating force in both capitalist and socialist thought. For Marx the value that labor gave to a product was divided between the worker and the owner of the means of production. What workers did not get was surplus value. This surplus value accrued not as in the case of Ricardo primarily to the landlord but to the bourgeoisie, to the capitalist. Wages were now kept down by unemployment, by an industrial reserve army always waiting and eager for jobs. Should that labor be brought into employment and wages rise, this would reduce profits, precipitate an economic crisis, later variously to be called a panic, a depression, a recession or, in the days of Richard Nixon, a growth correction. The requisite unemployment and wage level would thereby be restored.

From the surplus value accruing to the capitalists would also come investment. This would grow more rapidly than the surplus; thus capitalism would suffer a declining rate of profit. Finally, out of the surplus value would come the wherewithal by which the large capitalists would gobble up the small — the process of capitalist concentration. In consequence of this concentration, individual capitalists would grow stronger but the system as a whole would be ever more attenuated, ever weaker. This weakness, in combination with the falling rate of return and the increasingly severe crises, would make the system progressively more vulnerable to its own destruction. Confronted by the angry proletariat it created, a force fully aware of its exploitation, disciplined by its work, there would come the final attack and collapse:

> Along with the constantly diminishing number of the magnates of capital, who usurp and monopolise all advantages of this process of transformation, grows the mass of misery, oppression, slavery, degradation, exploitation; but with this too grows the revolt of the working class, a class always increasing in numbers, and disciplined, united, organised by the very mechanism of the process of capitalist production itself. The monopoly of capital becomes a fetter upon the mode of production, which

has sprung up and flourished along with, and under it. Centralisation of the means of production and socialisation of labour at last reach a point where they become incompatible with their capitalist integument. This integument is burst asunder. The knell of capitalist private property sounds. The expropriators are expropriated.[21]

So the capitalist world ends. By such words the police might well have been aroused, for by now Marx was endowing his great events with great phrases. His capitalist was given the satisfaction of knowing that his end came not with a whimper but with a bang.

XII

The first volume of *Capital* — in the German original, *Das Kapital: Kritik der Politischen Oekonomie von Karl Marx*, Erster Band, Buch 1: "Der Produktions process des Kapitals" (Hamburg: Verlag von Otto Meissner) — was published in 1867. The second two volumes, with a claimed readership many times the real, were not published in Marx's lifetime. They were prepared for the press from notes and manuscripts by the ever-faithful Engels and could not have been completed by anyone else.

One reason for the delay was the early poverty and struggle. Another was scholarship; as his friends observed, Marx was incapable of writing anything until he had read everything. Yet another was the endless swirl of discussion, debate and polemic in which Marx lived. What he disliked he described with great pleasure and no instinct for understatement. Thus he described a well-known London daily:

> By means of an artificially hidden sewer system all the lavatories of London spew their physical filth into the Thames. By means of the systematic pushing of goose quills the world capital spews out all its social filth into the great papered central sewer called the *Daily Telegraph*.[22]

Thus Adolphe Thiers, President of the French Republic, following the defeat and fall of Napoleon III:

> A master in small state roguery, a virtuoso in perjury and trea-
> son, a craftsman in all the petty stratagems, cunning devices,
> and base perfidies of parliamentary party-warfare; never scru-
> pling, when out of office, to fan a revolution, and to stifle it in
> blood when at the helm of state.[23]

But the most important reason was that in these years Marx was
laying the foundations for the revolution which he hoped and occasionally allowed himself to believe was imminent. The instrument
of revolution would be an organization that would link together
in common purposes and action the workers of all the industrial
countries — those proletarians who, as Marx powerfully averred,
knew no motherland. Now known as the First International, the organization was born in London on September 28, 1864, at a meeting
attended by some 2000 workers, trade unionists and intellectuals
from all over Europe. A governing council was selected, of which
Marx, naturally, became secretary. Its first task was to produce a
statement of principles and purposes; this was done, and Marx was
appalled by the verbosity, illiteracy and general crudity of the result.
So, knowing the subject to be irresistible, he got the members discussing rules. He then attended to the principles. The result, his *Address to the Working Classes,* is another famous document in the history of Marxist thought:

> . . . no improvement of machinery, no application of science to
> production, no contrivance of communication, no new colo-
> nies, no emigration, no opening of markets, no free trade, nor
> all these things put together, will do away with the miseries of
> the industrial masses. . . .

> . . . to conquer political power has therefore become the great
> duty of the working classes.[24]

And, once again, the call: "Proletarians of all countries, unite."
The International had individual members and affiliated trade
unions and other organizations. In the next years it grew in mem-
bership and influence. Notable Congresses were held, especially in
1867 in Lausanne and in the following years in Brussels and Basel.

The resolutions — calling for limitations on working hours, state support for education, nationalization of railways — were not very revolutionary. Reform was again showing itself to be the nemesis of revolution.

Revolution had another nemesis. That was nationalism. In 1870, Bismarck, who had once made overtures to Marx to put his pen at the service of his fatherland, went to war with Napoleon III. In a prelude to the vastly greater drama of August 1914, the proletarians of the two countries showed themselves far from being denationalized; instead they rallied to the defense, as they saw it, of their respective homelands. Then, as later, nothing was so easy as to persuade the people of one country, workers included, of the wicked and aggressive intentions of those of another. The First International, already split by disputes, was outlawed by Bismarck and soon by the Third Republic. Its headquarters was moved to Philadelphia, not a place of seething class consciousness; there, a few years later, it expired. In 1889, as a union of working-class political parties and trade unions, it rose again — the Second International. This Marx did not live to see.

XIII

But if the Franco-Prussian War was the nail in the coffin of the International, it also gave Marx a moment of hope. For where revolution is concerned, war in modern times has worked with double effect. It has been extremely efficient for mobilizing the proletarians of the world into opposing armies, defeating the dream of the internationally unified working class for which Marx (and those to follow) hoped. But it has been equally efficient for discrediting, at least temporarily, the ruling classes that conducted it — a tendency by no means confined to the countries suffering defeat. This now happened in France.

On March 1, 1871, the Assembly of the Third Republic met. The overthrow of Napoleon III was affirmed, and the legislators acquiesced in the peace terms. The Prussian army made its triumphal march down the Champs Élysées. Outrage at the incompetence of the old rulers, knowledge that the wealthy had departed Paris, offended pride, the experience of hunger and hardship, all combined to bring revolt. It began on Montmartre when the troops of the Republic sought to secure guns which were in the hands of the Parisian National Guard whom, rightly, they did not trust. There were echoes, most of them soon suppressed, in Marseilles, Lyons, Toulouse and other cities. Only in Paris was power truly taken — the Paris Commune of 1871.

It lasted but a few weeks. On May 21, the troops of the Republic entered the city, and on May 28, after a week of street fighting, the revolt was over. The rule of the Commune had been confused, purposeless and often bloody. When Thiers had shot prisoners, the Communards had shot hostages, including, in the final days, the Archbishop of Paris. The repression in the aftermath was exceedingly cruel. Such of the leading Communards as were spared execution (or did not escape France) were sent to populate New Caledonia.

The war, the siege of Paris and the Commune were reported with much of the avidity with which all modern disasters are now enjoyed. Again Paris events were followed closely by Marx, and by now such was his fame that when there was bloodletting by the revolutionaries, it was attributed to him. The Red Terrorist Doctor. This time, in contrast with his doubts of a quarter century earlier, he was optimistic as to both leadership and aims. It is not clear why he should have been. Much of the leadership of the Commune was middle-class in both origin and outlook. The aims were incoherent. The opposition had the power that comes out of gun barrels. The requirements for successful revolution were again far from complete.

When it was all over, Marx sent a final reflective and saddened Address to the Council of the dying International — *The Civil War in France*. It is one of the most eloquent of Marxist tracts:

> Working men's Paris, with its Commune, will be for ever celebrated as the glorious harbinger of a new society. The martyrs are enshrined in the great heart of the working class. Its exter-

minators history has already nailed to the eternal pillory from which all the prayers of their priests will not avail to redeem them.[25]

The Commune and the Communards have not been forgotten. But neither have they ever been wholly enshrined in the great heart of the working class. Though now eloquent, Marx was still not above some wishful thinking.

Thus ended the first revolution that was to use, seriously, however inaccurately, the root word of communism. It was the only one Marx was to see.

XIV

After the Paris revolt Marx lived on for another twelve years. He continued his work; he also remained the high, though not the undisputed, judge of what was right and what was error in socialist thought. One of these judgments brought the most enduring of his phrases. In the years following the Franco-Prussian War, the working class in Germany grew rapidly in political strength. Again the aftermath of war. Not one but two working-class parties emerged, and in 1875, they met at Gotha in central Germany to merge and agree on a common program. The result was extremely displeasing to Marx: the program offended deeply against Marxist principles, and once again reform replaced revolution. His *Critique of the Gotha Programme* held, with much else, that after the workers had taken power, the scar tissue remaining from capitalist habits and thought would have first to disappear. Only then would come the great day when society would "inscribe on its banners: from each according to his ability, to each according to his needs!"[26] It is possible that these last twelve words enlisted for Marx more followers than all the hundreds of thousands in the three volumes of *Capital* combined.

His last years were not a happy time for Marx. His health was bad and not improved by the abuse to which he had long subjected himself in matters of food, sleep, tobacco and alcohol. (He was a prodigious consumer of beer.) On frequent occasions he was forced, in the fashion of the time, to retire to a spa for the cure. Several times he went to Carlsbad in what was then Austria and is now Czechoslovakia where the police watched over him along with his doctors and reported principally on the very satisfactory way that he kept to his prescribed regimen. In 1881, his wife, Jenny, was found to have cancer and that December she died. A few months later she was followed by their daughter Jenny, the first and most beloved of Marx's children. Distraught and very lonely, Marx too ceased in any real sense to live. On March 13, 1883, with Engels at his bedside, he died. Not since the Prophet has a man's influence been so little diminished by his death.

NOTES

1. Joseph Schumpeter, *Capitalism, Socialism, Democracy,* 3rd ed. (New York: Harper's Torchbooks, 1967), p. 21.
2. Karl Marx in Karl Marx and Friedrich Engels, *Selected Works,* Vol. II (Moscow, 1962), p. 22.
3. Karl Marx quoted in David McLellan, *Karl Marx: His Life and Thought* (New York: Harper and Row, 1973), p. 14.
4. McLellan, p. 16.
5. Friedrich Engels quoted in McLellan, p. 28.
6. Karl Marx quoted in McLellan, p. 58.
7. McLellan, pp. 56–57.
8. Karl Marx quoted in McLellan, p. 56.
9. Karl Marx quoted in McLellan, p. 60.
10. *Karl Marx, Early Texts,* David McLellan, ed. (Oxford: Blackwell, 1972), p. 129.
11. Friedrich Engels quoted in McLellan, p. 131.
12. Karl Marx in Karl Marx and Friedrich Engels, Vol. I, p. 52.
13. Eric Roll, *A History of Economic Thought* (London: Faber and Faber, 1973), pp. 257–258.
14. *Karl Marx: Early Texts,* p. 217.
15. Karl Marx, *The Communist Manifesto* in Karl Marx and Friedrich Engels, Vol. I, pp. 108–137.
16. Karl Marx, *The Communist Manifesto* in Karl Marx and Friedrich Engels, Vol. I, p. 126.
17. Karl Marx, *The Revolutions of 1848,* Vol. I: Political Writings (London: Allen Lane and New Left Review, 1973), p. 129.

18. A spy for the Prussian government quoted in McLellan, pp. 268–269.

19. Jenny Marx quoted in McLellan, p. 265.

20. Sir George Grey, British Home Secretary, quoted in McLellan, p. 231.

21. Karl Marx, *Capital; A Critique of Political Economy,* Vol. I (Chicago: Charles H. Kerr and Co., 1926), pp. 836–837.

22. Karl Marx quoted in McLellan, p. 315.

23. Karl Marx, *The Civil War in France: Address of the International Working Men's Association,* quoted in Karl Marx and Friedrich Engels, Vol. II, p. 208.

24. Karl Marx, *Address to the Working Classes,* quoted in McLellan, pp. 365–366.

25. Karl Marx, *The Civil War in France,* quoted in McLellan, p. 400.

26. Karl Marx, *Critique of the Gotha Programme,* quoted in McLellan, p. 433.

Who Was Thorstein Veblen?

[*from* Annals of an Abiding Liberal]

In 1931, when I registered as a graduate student at the University of California, the most discussed, most influential figure in the progressive intellectual establishment was Thorstein Veblen, who was claimed, with reservations, by the neighboring Stanford University community or its more courageous members. No one in those bleak years of the Great Depression could reasonably be for the current system. Only Marx was an alternative. I became, partly no doubt from caution, a close student of Veblen. He was the subject of many hours, even days, of discussion among my fellow students at Berkeley, as in academic centers elsewhere.

Sadly, but inevitably, the discussion has moved on. This essay, written with purpose and some knowledge, is to remind of and inform on one of the truly influential figures in American intellectual history. I do not hope to restore Thorstein Veblen to his one-time eminence, although I had a prominent role in seeking the restoration and historic preservation of the Veblen homestead in Minnesota. My purpose is to tell of a man and his work, which is deeply a part of the American economic and academic past and of which, quite frankly, all should be aware.

The highest honor bestowed by economists on their colleagues — or at least what is so regarded — is the presidency of the American Economic Association. In 1971, my name came up at a meeting of the chosen leaders of the profession, who were considering who would be the next president. There was a sharp conservative resistance; I had been, it was believed, too close to the politics of the time. This objection, it is said, came from, among others, Professor Milton Friedman, the distinguished spokesman for what is called the Chicago School. The case against me was made on the grounds that Thorstein Veblen had never been the association's president. It was an ill-advised argument; I promptly won the election.

*   *   *   *

THE NEAREST THING in the United States to an academic legend — the equivalent of that of Scott Fitzgerald in fiction or of the Barrymores in the theater — is the legend of Thorstein Veblen. A legend is reality so enlarged by imagination that, eventually, the image has an existence of its own. This happened to Veblen. He was a man of great and fertile mind and a marvelously resourceful exponent of its product. His life, beginning on the frontier of the upper Middle West in 1857 and continuing, mostly at one university or another, until 1929, was not without romance of a kind. Certainly by the standards of academic life at the time it was nonconformist. There was ample material both in his work and in his life on which to build the legend, and the builders have not failed. There is also a considerable debt to imagination.

What is believed about Veblen's grim, dark boyhood in a poor, immigrant Norwegian family in Wisconsin and Minnesota, his reaction to those oppressive surroundings, his harried life in the American academic world in the closing decades of the nineteenth century and the first three of the twentieth, the fatal way he attracted women and vice versa and its consequences in his tightly corseted surroundings, the indifference of right-thinking men to his work, has only a limited foundation in fact.

Economics can be a dull enough business, and sociology is sometimes worse. So, on occasion, are those who teach these subjects. One reason they are dull is the belief that everything associated with human personality should be made as mechanical as possible. That is science. Perhaps one should, instead, perpetuate any available myth. When, as with Veblen, the man is enlarged by a nimbus, the latter should be brightened, not dissolved.

Still, there is a certain case for truth, and what we know about Veblen is also far from tedious. He is not, as some have suggested, a universal source of insight on American society. Like Smith and Marx, he did not see what had not yet happened. Also, on some things, he was wrong, and faced with a choice between strict accuracy and what would outrage his audience, he rarely hesitated. But no man of his time, or since, looked with such a cool and penetrating eye at pecuniary gain and the way its pursuit makes men and women behave.

This cool and penetrating view is the substance behind the Veblen legend. It is a view that still astonishes the reader with what it reveals. While there may be other deserving candidates, only two books by American economists of the nineteenth century are still read. One of these is Henry George's *Progress and Poverty;* the other is Veblen's *The Theory of the Leisure Class.* Neither of these books, it is interesting to note, came from the sophisticated and derivative world of the eastern seaboard. Both were the candid, clear-headed, untimid reactions of the frontiersman — in the case of Henry George to speculative alienation of land, in the case of Veblen to the pompous social ordinances of the affluent. But the comparison cannot be carried too far. Henry George was the exponent of a notably compelling idea; his book remains important for that idea — for the notion of the high price that society pays for private ownership and the pursuit of capital gains from land. Veblen's great work is a wide-ranging and timeless comment on the behavior of people who possess or are in pursuit of wealth and who, looking beyond their possessions, want the eminence that, or so they believe, wealth was meant to buy. No one has really read very much social science if he hasn't read *The Theory of the Leisure Class* at least once. Not many of more than minimal education and pretense get through life without adverting at some time or other to "conspicuous consumption," "pecuniary emulation" or "conspicuous waste," even though they may not know whence these phrases came.

II

Veblen's parents, Thomas Anderson and Kari Bunde Veblen, emi-
grated from Norway to a farm in rural Wisconsin in 1847, ten years
before Thorstein's birth. There were the usual problems in raising
the money for the passage, the quite terrible hardships on the voy-
age. In all, the Veblens had twelve children, of whom Thorstein was
the sixth. The first farm in Wisconsin was inferior to what later
and better information revealed to be available farther west. They
moved, and, in 1865, they moved a second time. The new and final
holding was on the prairie, now about an hour's drive south from
Minneapolis. It is to this farm that the legend of Veblen's dark and
deprived boyhood belongs. No one who visits this countryside will
believe it. There can be no farming country in the world with, at
least until very recent times, a more generous aspect of opulence.
The prairie is gently rolling. The soil is black and deep, the barns are
huge, the silos numerous and the houses big, square and comfortable, without architectural ambition. The Veblen house, with a long
view of the surrounding farmland, is an ample, pleasant, white
frame structure bespeaking not merely comfort but prosperity.[1]
Families in the modern middle-income suburban tract are not
housed as well.

Since this countryside was originally open, well-vegetated prairie,
it must have looked very promising to the settler in the mid-nine-
teenth century. Thomas Veblen acquired 290 acres of this wealth; it
is hard to imagine that he, his wife or, by their instruction, any of
their children could have thought of themselves as poor. Not a
thousand, perhaps not even a hundred farmers working their own
land were so handsomely provided in the Norway they had left. Nor,
in fact, did the Veblens think themselves poor. Later, in letters,
Thorstein's brothers and sisters were to comment, sometimes with
amusement, on occasion with anger, on the myth of their poverty-
stricken origins.[2]

If this part of the Veblen story is unremarkable and commonplace — the tearing up of roots, departure, hardship, miscalculation,
eventual reward — there were other things that separated the Veb-

lens from the general run of Scandinavian settlers and that help to explain Thorstein. Thomas Veblen, who had been a skilled carpenter and cabinetmaker, soon proved himself a much more than normally intelligent and progressive farmer. And, however he viewed the farm for himself, he almost certainly regarded it as a stepping-stone for his children. Even more exceptional was Kari, his wife. She was an alert, imaginative, self-confident and intelligent woman, lovely in appearance, who, from an early age, identified, protected and encouraged the family genius. In later years, in a family and community where more hands were always needed and virtue was associated, accordingly, with efficient toil — effectiveness as a worker was what distinguished a *good* boy or girl from the rest — Thorstein Veblen was treated with tolerance. Under the cover of a weak constitution he was given leisure for reading. This released time could only have been provided by remarkably perceptive parents. One of Veblen's brothers later wrote that it was from his mother that "Thorstein got his personality and brains," although others thought them decidedly his own property.

III

Thorstein, like his brothers and sisters, went to the local schools, and, on finishing these, to Carleton College (then styled Carleton College Academy) in the nearby town of Northfield. His sister Emily was in attendance at the same time; other members of the family also went to Carleton. In an engaging and characteristic move their father acted to keep down college expenses. He bought a plot of land on the edge of town for the nominal amount charged for such real estate in that time and put up a house to shelter his offspring while they were being educated. The Veblen legend further holds that the winning of an education involved Thorstein in major and even heroic hardship. This can be laid decisively to rest. A letter in the archives of the Minnesota Historical Society from Andrew Veblen, Thorstein's brother, notes that money was available, if not abundant: "Father gave him the strictly necessary assistance through his schooling. Thorstein, like the rest of the family, kept his

expenses down to the minimum . . . all in line with the close economy that the whole family practiced." A sister-in-law, Florence (Mrs.
Orson) Veblen, wrote more indignantly and with a characteristic
view of what was virtue in those times: "There is not the slightest
ground for depriving my father-in-law of the credit of having paid
for the education of his children — *all* of them — he was well able to
do so; he had two good farms in the richest farming district in
America."[3]

It was, nevertheless, an exception to the general community practice that the Veblen children should be sent to college rather than be
put to useful work, as Norwegian farmers would then have called it,
on the farm. Exceptionally too they were sent to an Anglo-Saxon
denominational college — Carleton was Congregationalist — rather
than to one of the Lutheran institutions which responded to the
language, culture and religion of the Scandinavians. The Veblen
myth (as the family has also insisted) has exaggerated somewhat the
alienation of the Norwegians in general and the Veblens in particular in an English-speaking society. It is part of the legend that
Thorstein's father spoke no English and that his son had difficulty
with the language. This is nonsense. But in the local class structure
the Anglo-Saxons were the dominant town and merchant class, the
Scandinavians the hard-working peasantry. The Veblen children
were not intended for their class.

Carleton was one of the denominational colleges which were
established as the frontier moved westward and by which it was
shown that along with economic and civic achievement in America
went also culture and religion. Like the others of its age, it was unquestionably fairly bad. But, like so many small liberal arts colleges
of the time, it was the haven for a few learned men and devoted
teachers — the saving remnant that seemed always to show up when
one was established. Such a teacher at Carleton in Veblen's time was
John Bates Clark, later, when at Columbia University, to be recognized as the dean of American economists of his time. (He was one
of the originators of the concept of marginality — the notion that
decisions concerning consumption are made not in consequence of
the total stock of goods possessed but in consequence of the satis-

factions to be derived from the possession or use of another unit added to the stock already owned.) Veblen became a student of Clark's; Clark thought well of Veblen.

This must have required both imagination and tolerance, for in various of his class exercises Veblen was already giving indication of his later style and method. He prepared a solemn and ostentatiously sincere classification of men according to their noses; one of his exercises in public rhetoric defended the drunkard's view of his own likely death; another argued the case for cannibalism. Clark, who was presiding when Veblen appeared to favor intoxication, felt obliged to demur. In a denominational college in the Midwest at the time, distant cannibalism had a somewhat higher canonical sanction than intoxication. Veblen resorted to the defense that he was to employ with the utmost consistency for the rest of his life: no value judgment was involved; he was not being partial to the drunk; his argument was purely scientific.

IV

Veblen finished his last two years at the college in one and graduated brilliantly. His graduation oration was entitled "Mill's Examination of Hamilton's Philosophy of the Conditioned." It was described by contemporaries as a triumph, but it does not survive. While at Carleton Veblen had formed a close friendship with Ellen Rolfe; she was the daughter of a prominent and prosperous Midwestern family and, like Veblen, was independent and introspective, very much apart from the crowd and also highly intelligent. They were not married for another eleven years, although this absence of haste did not mean that either had any less reason to regret it in later leisure. The legend holds Veblen to have been an indifferent and unfaithful husband who was singularly incapable of resisting the advances of the women whom, however improbably, he attracted. The Veblen family seems to have considered the fault to be at least partly Ellen's. She had a nervous breakdown following an effort at teaching; in a far from reticent and, one supposes, deeply partisan letter in the St. Paul archives,[4] a sister-in-law concludes: "There is not the least doubt that she is insane." Only one thing is certain: it was an unsuccessful and unhappy marriage.

After teaching at a local academy following his graduation from Carleton, Veblen departed for Johns Hopkins University in Baltimore to study philosophy. At this time, 1881, Johns Hopkins was being advertised as the first American university with a specialized postgraduate school following the earlier European design. The billing, as Veblen was later to point out, was considerably in advance of the fact. Money and hence professors were very scarce; the Baltimore context was that of a conservative southern town. Veblen was unhappy and did not complete the term. He began what — with one major interruption — was to be a lifetime of wandering over the American academic landscape.

V

His next stop was Yale. It was an interesting time in New Haven — what scholars inclined to metaphors from the brewing industry call a period of intellectual ferment. One focus of contention was between Noah Porter, a seemingly pretentious divine then believed to be an outstanding philosopher and metaphysician, and William Graham Sumner, the American exponent of Herbert Spencer. The practical thrust of Noah Porter's effort was to prevent Sumner from assigning Spencer's *Principles of Sociology* to his classes. In this he prevailed; Spencer was righteously suppressed. Porter's success, one imagines, proceeded less from the force of his argument against Spencer's acceptance of the Darwinian thesis — natural selection, survival of the fittest — as a social and economic axiom than from the unfortunate fact that he was also the president of the university. In Veblen's later writing there is a strong suggestion of Spencer and Sumner. Natural selection is not the foundation of Veblen's system, but it serves him as an infinitely handy explanation of how some survive and prosper and others do not.

There has been much solemn discussion of the effect on Veblen's later writing of the philosophical discussion at Yale and of his own dissertation on Kant. My instinct is to think it was not too great.

This is affirmed in a general way by the other Veblens. In later years his brother Andrew (a physicist and mathematician) responded repeatedly and stubbornly, though, no doubt with some exaggeration, to efforts to identify the sources of Thorstein Veblen's thought: "I do not think that any person much influenced the formation of his views or opinions."[5]

After two and a half years at Yale — underwritten by a brother and the Minnesota family and farm — Veblen emerged with a Ph.D. He wanted to teach; he also had rather favorable recommendations. But he could not find a job and so he went back to the Minnesota homestead. There, endlessly reading and doing occasional writing, he remained for seven years. As in his childhood, he again professed ill health. Andrew Veblen, later letters show, thought the illness genuine; other members of his family diagnosed his ailment as an allergy to manual toil. He married, and Ellen brought with her a little money. From time to time he was asked to apply for teaching positions; tentative offers were righteously withdrawn when it was discovered that he was not a subscribing Christian. In 1891, he resumed his academic wandering by registering as a graduate student at Cornell.

The senior professor of economics at Cornell at the time was J. Laurence Laughlin, a stalwart exponent of the English classical school, who, until then, had declined to become a member of the American Economic Association in the belief that it had socialist inclinations. (There has been no such suspicion in recent times.) Joseph Dorfman of Columbia University, an eminent student of American economic thought and the preeminent authority on Veblen, tells of Laughlin's meeting with Veblen in *Thorstein Veblen and His America,* a massive book to which everyone who speaks or writes on Veblen is indebted.[6,7] Laughlin "was sitting in his study in Ithaca when an anemic-looking person, wearing a coonskin cap and corduroy trousers, entered and in the mildest possible tone announced: 'I am Thorstein Veblen.' He told Laughlin of his academic history, his enforced idleness, and his desire to go on with his studies. The fellowships had all been filled, but Laughlin was so impressed with the quality of the man that he went to the president and other powers of the university and secured a special grant."[8]

Apart from the impression that Veblen's manner and dress so conveyed, the account is important for another reason. Always in Veblen's life there were individuals — a small but vital few — who strongly sensed his talents. Often, as in the case of Laughlin, they were conservatives — men who, in ideas and habits of life, were a world apart from Veblen. Repeatedly these good men rescued or protected their prodigious but always inconvenient friend.

VI

Veblen was at Cornell rather less than two years, although long enough to begin advancing his career with uncharacteristic orthodoxy by getting articles into the scholarly journals. Then Laughlin was invited to be head of the Department of Economics at the new University of Chicago. He took Veblen with him; Veblen was awarded a fellowship of $520 a year for which he was to prepare a course on the history of socialism and assist in editing the newly founded *Journal of Political Economy.* He was now thirty-five years old. In the next several years he advanced to the rank of tutor and instructor, continued to teach and to edit the *Journal* (known to economists as the J.P.E.), wrote a great many reviews and, among other articles, one on the theory of women's dress, another on the barbarian status of women and a third on the instinct of workmanship and the irksomeness of labor. All these foreshadowed later books.

In these years he also developed his teaching style, if such it could be called. He sat at a table and spoke in a low monotone to the handful of students who were interested and who could get close enough to hear. He also discovered, if he had not previously learned, that something — mind, manner, dress, his sardonic and challenging indifference to approval or disapproval — made him attractive to women. His wife now found that she had more and more competition for his attention. It was something to which neither she nor the academic communities in which Veblen resided ever reconciled themselves.

In 1899, while still at Chicago and while Laughlin was still having trouble getting him small increases in pay or even, on occasion, getting his appointment renewed, Veblen published his first and greatest book. It was *The Theory of the Leisure Class.*

VII

There is little that anyone can be told about *The Theory of the Leisure Class* that he or she cannot learn better by reading the book himself or herself. It is a marvelous thing and, in its particular way, a masterpiece of English prose. But the qualification is important. Veblen's writing cannot be read like that of any other author. Wesley C. Mitchell, regarded, though not with entire accuracy, as Veblen's leading intellectual legatee, once said that "one must be highly sophisticated to enjoy his [Veblen's] books."[9] Those who cherish Veblen would like, I am sure, to believe this. The truth is of a simpler sort. One needs only to realize that, if Veblen is to be enjoyed, he must be read very carefully and very slowly. He enlightens, amuses and delights but only if he is given a good deal of time.

That is because one cannot divorce Veblen's ideas from the language in which they are conveyed. The ideas are pungent, incisive and insulting. But the writing is a weapon as well. Veblen, as Mitchell also noted, writes "with one eye on the scientific merits of his analysis, and his other eye fixed on the squirming reader."[10] And he startles his reader with an exceedingly perverse use of meaning. This never varies from that sanctioned by the most precise and demanding usage, but in the context it is often unexpected. His usage Veblen then attributes to scientific necessity. Thus, in his immortal discussion of conspicuous consumption, he notes that expenditure, if it is to contribute efficiently to the individual's "good fame," must generally be on "superfluities." "In order to be reputable it [the expenditure] must be wasteful."[11] All of this is quite exact. The rich do want fame; reputable expenditure is what adds to their repute or fame; the dress, housing, equipage that serve this purpose and are not essential for existence are superfluous. Nonessential expenditure is wasteful. But only Veblen would have used the words "fame," "reputable" and "waste" in such a way. In the case of "waste," he does decide that some explanation is necessary. This is characteristically airy and matter-of-fact. In everyday speech, "the word carries an undertone of deprecation. It is here used for want of a better term . . . and it is not to be taken in an odious sense . . ."[12]

And in a similar vein: The wives of the rich forswear useful employment because "abstention from labor is not only an honorific or meritorious act, but it presently comes to be a requisite of decency."[13] "Honor," "merit" and "decency" are all used with exactness, but they are not often associated with idleness. A robber baron, Veblen says, has a better chance of escaping the law than a small crook because "a well-bred expenditure of his booty especially appeals . . . to persons of a cultivated sense of the proprieties, and goes far to mitigate the sense of moral turpitude with which his dereliction is viewed by them."[14] Scholars do not ordinarily associate the disposal of ill-gotten wealth with good breeding.

One sees also from this sentence why Veblen must be read slowly and carefully. If one goes rapidly, words will be given their usual contextual meaning — not the precise and perverse sense that Veblen intended. Waste will be wicked and not a source of esteem; the association of idleness with merit, honor and decency will somehow be missed, as well as that of the social position of the crook with the public attitude toward his expenditure. *The Theory of the Leisure Class* yields its meaning, and therewith its full enjoyment, only to those who also have leisure.

When Veblen had finished his manuscript, he sent it to the publisher, and it came back several times for revision. Eventually, it appears, publication required a guarantee from the author. The book could not have been badly written in any technical or grammatical sense. Veblen by then was an experienced editor. Nor was he any novice as a writer. One imagines that the perverse and startling use of words, combined no doubt with the irony and the attack on the icons, was more than the publisher could readily manage. But, on the other side, some very good reader or editor must have seen how much was there.

VIII

The Theory of the Leisure Class is a tract, the most comprehensive ever written, on snobbery and social pretense. Some of it has application only to American society at the end of the nineteenth century — at the height of the gilded age of American capitalism. More is wonderfully relevant to modern affluence.

The rich have often been attacked by the less rich because they have a superior social position that is based on assets and not on moral or intellectual worth. And they have also been accused of using their wealth and position to sustain a profligate consumption of resources of which others are in greater need, and of defending the social structure that accords them their privileged status. And they have been attacked for the base, wicked or immoral behavior that wealth sustains and their social position sanctions. These attacks the rich can endure. That is because the assailants concede them their superior power and position; they only deny their right to that position or to behave as they do therein. The denial involves a good deal of righteous anger and indignation. The rich are thus reminded that they are thought worth such anger and indignation.

Veblen's supreme literary and polemical achievement is that he concedes the rich and the well-to-do nothing; and he would not dream of suggesting that his personal attitudes or passion is in any way involved. The rich are anthropological specimens; the possession of money and property has made their behavior interesting and visibly ridiculous. The effort to establish one's importance and precedence and the yearning for the resulting esteem and applause are matters only of sociological and anthropological interest and are common to all humans. Nothing in the basic tendency differentiates a Whitney, Vanderbilt or Astor from a Papuan chieftain or "for instance, the tribes of the Andamans." The dress, festivals or rituals and artifacts of the Vanderbilts are more complex; the motivation is in no way different from or superior to that of their barbarian counterparts.

That is why the rich are not viewed with indignation. The scientist does not become angry with the primitive tribesman because of the extravagance of his sexual orgies or the vengeance of his self-mutilation. So with the social observances of the rich. Their banquets and other entertainments are equated in commonplace fashion with the orgies; the self-mutilation of the savage is the equivalent of the painfully constricting dress in which, at that time, the women of the well-to-do were corseted.

One must remember that Veblen wrote in the last years of the nineteenth century — before the established order suffered the disintegrating onslaught of World War I, V. I. Lenin and the leveling oratory of modern democratic politics. It was a time when gentlemen still believed they were gentlemen and that it was mostly wealth that made the difference. Veblen calmly identified the manners and behavior of these so-called gentlemen with the manners and behavior of the people of the bush. Speaking of the utility of different observances for the purpose of affirming or enhancing the individual's repute, Veblen notes that "presents and feasts had probably another origin than that of naive ostentation, but they acquired their utility for this purpose very early, and they have retained that character to the present . . . Costly entertainments, such as *the potlatch or the ball,* are peculiarly adapted to serve this end."[15] The italics equating the potlatch and the ball are mine; Veblen would never have dreamed of emphasizing so obvious a point.

IX

While *The Theory of the Leisure Class* is a devastating putdown of the rich, it is also more than that. It brilliantly and truthfully illuminates the effect of wealth on behavior. No one who has read this book ever again sees the consumption of goods in the same light. Above a certain level of affluence the enjoyment of goods — of dress, houses, automobiles, entertainment — can never again be thought intrinsic as, in a naive way, the established or neoclassical economics still holds it to be. Possession and consumption are the banner that advertises achievement, that proclaims, by the accepted standards of the community, that the possessor is a success. In this sense — in revealing what had not hitherto been seen — *The Theory of the Leisure Class* is a major scientific achievement.

Alas, also, much of the process by which this truth is revealed — by which Veblen's insights are vouchsafed — is not science but contrivance. Before writing *The Leisure Class*, Veblen had, it is certain, read widely in anthropology. Thus he had a great many primitive communities and customs at his fingertips. And he refers to these with a casual insouciance which suggests — and was meant to suggest — that he had much more such knowledge in reserve. But the book is devoid of sources; no footnote or reference tells on what Veblen relied for information. On an early page he explains that the book is based on everyday observation and not pedantically on the scholarship of others. This is adequate as far as Fifth Avenue and Newport are concerned. There accurate secondhand knowledge could be assumed. But Veblen had no similar access to everyday knowledge about the Papuans.

In fact, Veblen's anthropology and sociology are weapon and armor which he contrives for his purpose. He needs them to illuminate (and to make ridiculous) the behavior of the most powerful — the all-powerful — class of his time. By doing this in the name of science and with the weapons of science — and with no overt trace of animus or anger — he could act with considerable personal safety. The butterfly does not attack the zoologist for saying it is more decorative than useful. That Marx was an enemy whose venom was to be returned in kind, capitalists did not doubt. But Veblen was not. The American rich never quite understood what he was doing to them. The scientific pretense, the irony and the careful explanations that the most pejorative words were being used in a strictly nonpejorative sense put him well beyond their comprehension.

The protection was necessary at the time. And there is a wealth of evidence that Veblen was conscious of the need for it. During the years when he was working on *The Leisure Class*, liberal professors at the University of Chicago were under frequent attack from the neighboring plutocracy. The latter expected economics and the other social sciences to provide the doctrine that graced its privileges. In the mid-eighteen-nineties Chauncey Depew told the Chicago students (in an address quoted by Joseph Dorfman) that "this institution, which owes its existence to the beneficence of Rockefeller, is in itself a monument of the proper use of wealth accumulated by a man of genius. So is Cornell, so is Vanderbilt, and so are the older colleges, as they have received the benefactions of generous, appreciative, and patriotic wealth."[16] In 1895, Edward W. Bemis, an associate professor of political economy in the extension, i.e., out-patient, department of the university, attacked the traction monopoly in Chicago which, assisted by wholesale bribery, had fastened itself on the backs of Chicago streetcar patrons. There was a great uproar, and his appointment was not renewed. The university authorities, like many godly and scholarly men in academic positions, took for granted that their devotion to truth accorded them a special license to lie. So they compounded their crime in dismissing Bemis by denying that their action was to appease the traction monopoly or that it reflected any abridgment of academic freedom. The local press was not misled; it applauded the action as a concession to sound business interest. In a fine sentence on scholarly responsibility, *The Chicago Journal* said: "The duty of a professor who accepts the money of a university for his work is to teach the established truth, not to engage in the 'pursuit of truth.'"[17] A forthright sentiment.[18]

Veblen did not miss this lesson. The last chapter of *The Leisure Class* is on "The Higher Learning as an Expression of the Pecuniary Culture." It anticipates his later, much longer and much more pungent disquisition on the influence of the pecuniary civilization on the university (*The Higher Learning in America; A Memorandum on the Conduct of Universities by Business men,* published in 1918). In this chapter Veblen stresses the conservative and protective role of the universities in relation to the pecuniary culture. "New views, new departures in scientific theory, especially new departures which touch the theory of human relations at any point, have found a place in the scheme of the university tardily and by a reluctant tolerance, rather than by a cordial welcome; and the men who have occupied themselves with such efforts to widen the scope of human knowledge have not commonly been well received by their learned contemporaries."[19] No one will be in doubt as to whom, in the last clause, Veblen had in mind. Elsewhere, contemplating university administration, he notes that "as further evidence of the close relation between the educational system and the cultural standards of the community, it may be remarked that there is some tendency latterly to substitute the captain of industry in place of the priest, as head of seminaries of the higher learning."[20]

Given such an environment and given also his subject, it will be evident that Veblen needed the protection of his art. On the whole, it served him well. In the course of his academic career he was often in trouble with university administrators — it was they, not the great men of industry and commerce, who kept him moving. His more orthodox and pedestrian, though more fashionable, academic colleagues also disliked him. A man like Veblen creates great problems for such people. They cherish the established view and rejoice in the favor of the Establishment. Anyone who does not share their values is a threat to their position and, worse still, to their self-esteem, for he makes them seem sycophantic and routine, which, of course, they are. Veblen, throughout his life, was such a threat. But the rich, to whom ultimately he addressed himself, rarely penetrated his defenses.

x

Veblen also enjoyed a measure of political immunity in a hostile world because he was not a reformer. His heart did not beat for the proletariat or otherwise for the downtrodden and poor. He was a man of animus but not of revolution.

The source of Veblen's animus has regularly been related to his origins. As the son of immigrant parents, he had experienced the harsh life of the frontier. This was at a time when Scandinavians were, by any social standard, second-class citizens. They were saved only because they could not readily be distinguished by their color. What was more natural than that someone from such a background should turn on his oppressors? *The Theory of the Leisure Class* was thought to be Veblen's revenge for the abuse to which he and his parents were subject.

This misunderstands Veblen. The Veblens, we have seen, were not of the downtrodden. And as one from a similar background perhaps can know, there is danger of mistaking contempt or derision for resentment. Some years ago, to fill in the idle moments of an often undemanding occupation — that of the modern ambassador — I wrote a small book[21] about the clansmen among whom I was reared on the north shore of Lake Erie in Canada. The Scotch, like the Scandinavians, inhabited the farms. The people of the towns were English. They were the favored race. In Upper Canada in earlier times, Englishmen, in conjunction with the Church of England as a kind of holding company for political and economic interest, dominated the economic, political, religious and social life to their own unquestioned pecuniary and social advantage.

Our mood, really that of the more prestigious class, was not, I think, different from that of the Veblens. We felt ourselves superior to the storekeepers, implement salesmen, grain dealers and other entrepreneurs of the adjacent towns. We worked harder, spent less, but usually had more. The leaders among the Scotch took education seriously and, as a matter of course, monopolized the political life of the community. Yet the people of the towns were invariably under the impression that social position resided with them. Being English and Anglican, they were identified, however vicariously, with the old ruling class. Their work did not soil the hands. We were taught to think that claims to social prestige based on such vacuous criteria were silly. We regarded the people of the towns not with envy but with amiable contempt. On the whole, we enjoyed letting them know.

When I published the book, I received a quite unexpected flow of letters from people who had grown up in the German and Scandinavian towns and small cities of the Midwest. They told me that it was their community that I had described. "That was how we felt. You could have been writing about our community." The Veblens regarded themselves, not without reason, as the representatives of a superior culture. The posturing of the local Anglo-Saxon elite they also regarded with contempt. *The Theory of the Leisure Class* is an elongation of what Veblen observed and felt as a youth.

XI

The Theory of the Leisure Class, when it appeared, admirably divided the men of reputable academic position from those who were responsive to ideas or capable of thought. One great man said that it was such books by dilettantes that brought sociology into disrepute among "careful and scientific thinkers." Science, as ever in economics and sociology, was being used to disguise orthodoxy. He went on to say that it was illegitimate to classify within the leisure class such unrelated groups as the barbarians and the modern rich. Another predictable scholar avowed that the rich were rich because they earned the money; the gargantuan reward of the captain of industry and the miserly one of the man with a spade were the proper valuation of their contribution to society as measured by their economic efficiency. The names of these critics are now lost to fame.

Other and more imaginative men were delighted. Lester Ward, one of the first American sociologists of major repute, said that "the book abounds in terse expressions, sharp antitheses, and quaint, but happy phrases. Some of these have been interpreted as irony and satire, but . . . the language is plain and unmistakable . . . the style is the farthest removed possible from either advocacy or vituperation."[22] Ward was admiring but a bit too trusting. William Dean Howells, then at the peak of his reputation, was equally enthusiastic. And he too was taken in by Veblen. "In the passionless calm with which the author pursues his investigation, there is apparently no animus for or against a leisure class. It is his affair simply to find out how and why and what it is."[23] The sales of *The Leisure Class* were modest, although few could have guessed for how long they would continue. Veblen was promoted in 1900 to the rank of assistant professor. His pay remained negligible.

XII

In the years following the publication of *The Theory of the Leisure Class* Veblen turned to an examination of the business enterprise in its social context — an interest that is foreshadowed in *The Leisure Class* in the distinction between "exploit," which is that part of business enterprise that is devoted to making money, and "industry," which is that part that makes things. (In a characteristically matter-of-fact assertion of the shocking, Veblen notes that "employments which are to be classed as exploit are worthy, honorable, noble"; those involving a useful contribution to product being often "unworthy, debasing, ignoble.")[24] In 1904, Veblen developed this point (and much else) in *The Theory of Business Enterprise*. Out of his meager income, he was still required to pay a good part of the publishing cost himself.

In introducing a recent (and handsomely selling) French edition of *The Theory of the Leisure Class*, Raymond Aron argues that Veblen was better in his social than in his economic perception. With this I agree. The basic idea of *The Theory of Business Enterprise* is a plausible one — I can still remember my excitement when I first read the book in the thirties while a student at Berkeley, where the Veblen influence was strong. There is a conflict between the ordered rationality of the machine process as developed by engineers and technicians and the moneymaking context in which it operates. The moneymakers, through competition and interfirm aggression, and the resolution of the latter by consolidation and monopoly, sabotage the rich possibilities inherent in the machine process. But — though some will still object — the idea has been a blind alley. Organization and management are greater tasks than Veblen implies; so is the problem of accommodating production to social need. And so is that of motivation and incentive. All of this has become evident in the socialist economies, where far more difficulties have been encountered in translating the rationality of the machine process into effective economic performance than Veblen would have supposed. In the thirties, after Veblen's death, the political movement (perhaps more properly the cult) "technocracy" was founded on these ideas by Howard Scott. For a while it flourished. Had the technocrats been given a chance, they would have faced the same problems of management, organization and incentives as have the socialist states. Though much read in the first half of the twentieth century, *The Theory of Business Enterprise,* unlike *The Theory of the Leisure Class,* has not similarly survived.

XIII

Veblen's writing continued, and so, in 1906, did his academic peregrinations. His classes were small, his reputable academic colleagues adverse and his married life perilous — he was increasingly disinclined to resist the aggressions of admiring women. But in a minor way he was famous and thus a possible academic adornment. Harvard, urged by Frank W. Taussig, who had a recurring instinct for dissent, considered inviting him to join its Department of Economics but soon had second thoughts. David Starr Jordan, then creating a new university south of San Francisco, was not so cautious. He invited Veblen to Leland Stanford as an associate professor. Veblen survived there for three years. But his domestic arrangements — sometimes Ellen, sometimes others — were now, for the times, a scandal. Once he responded wearily to a complaint with a query: "What is one to do if the woman moves in on you?" Jordan concluded that there were adornments that Stanford could not afford. Veblen was invited to move on. By the students, at least, he was not greatly missed. Though dozens were attracted to his classes by his reputation, only a handful — once only three — ever survived to the end of the term.

After he left Stanford, another established scholar with an instinct for the dissenter came to his rescue. H. J. Davenport, then one of the major figures in the American economic pantheon, took him to the University of Missouri. There he encountered some of the students on whom he had the most lasting effect. One, Isador Lubin, was later to be a close aide of Franklin D. Roosevelt and a protector of Veblen in the latter's many moments of need. Veblen divorced Ellen and in 1914 married Anne Fessenden Bradley, a gentle, admiring woman who did not long survive. In 1918, she suffered severe mental illness, and in 1920 she died. From Missouri Veblen went to Washington during World War I as one of the less likely participants in the wartime administration. From Washington he went on to New York to experiment with life as an editor and then to teach at the New School for Social Research. His writings continued; as were the early ones, they are sardonic, laconic and filled with brilliant insights.[25] As with *The Theory of Business Enterprise,* many develop points of which there is a hint or more in *The Leisure Class.* The men of established reputation continued to be appalled. Reviewing *The Higher Learning in America* in the *New York Times Review of Books* in 1919, one Brander Matthews said of Veblen, "His vocabulary is limited and he indulges in a fatiguing repetition of a dozen or a score of adjectives. His grammar is woefully defective . . ."[26] The book is, in fact, one of Veblen's most effective tracts. Other reviewers were wiser. Gradually, step by step, it came to be realized that Veblen was a genius — the most penetrating, original and uninhibited source of social thought in his time.

This did not mean that he was much honored or rewarded. Veblen's students and disciples frequently had to come to his support. Employment became harder to find than ever. In the midtwenties, aging, silent, impecunious and tired, he returned reluctantly to California, and there, in 1929, he died.

The Nation, following his death, spoke of Veblen's "mordant wit, his extraordinary gift of . . . discovering wholly new meanings in old facts,"[27] saying in one sentence what I have said in many. Wesley C. Mitchell wrote an obituary note for *The Economic Journal,* the journal of The Royal Economic Society, then the most prestigious economic publication in the world. Saying sadly that "we shall have no more of these investigations, with their curious erudition, their irony, their dazzling phrases, their bewildering reversals of problems and values,"[28] he also observed that *The Economic Journal* had reviewed but one of Veblen's books. In 1925, it had taken notice of the ninth reprinting of *The Theory of the Leisure Class*. This was twenty-six years after its original publication.

NOTES

1. Over the years it had fallen on difficult times. Partly as the result of a television program based on this essay, and my plea to then Governor Wendell Anderson — "only Scandinavians are so negligent of their heroes" — it was acquired as a national historic site, and rehabilitation is in prospect.
2. The letters are in the archives of the Minnesota Historical Society in St. Paul, to which I am grateful.
3. These two letters were written in 1926 to Joseph Dorfman, Veblen's distinguished biographer. Dorfman, alas, did something to perpetuate the legend of deprivation.
4. From Florence Veblen, 1926. In an earlier account of the Veblen family (Orson Veblen, "Thorstein Veblen: Reminiscences of His Brother Orson," *Social Forces*, vol. X, no. 2 [December 1931], pp. 187–195), Florence Veblen also dealt harshly with Ellen. However, an unpublished comment (again in the St. Paul archives) by Andrew Veblen dissents at least in part, noting also that the two women had never met.
5. Letter in the St. Paul archives.
6. Although members of the family have disputed Dorfman on numerous details. In the library of the Minnesota Historical Society there is a heavily annotated copy of Dorfman's book giving Emily Veblen's corrections and dissents. Numerous minor points of family history are challenged; like other members of the family, she protested all suggestions that the family was poor or that it was alienated from the rest of the community. And she thought that Dorfman's picture of Thorstein as a lonely, shabby, excessively introverted boy and student was much overdrawn.
7. Joseph Dorfman, *Thorstein Veblen and His America* (New York: Viking, 1934).
8. Dorfman, pp. 79–80.
9. Wesley C. Mitchell, *What Veblen Taught* (New York: Viking, 1936), p. xx.
10. Mitchell, p. xviii.
11. Thorstein Veblen, *The Theory of the Leisure Class* (Boston: Houghton Mifflin, 1973), p. 77.
12. Thorstein Veblen, p. 78.
13. Thorstein Veblen, p. 44.
14. Thorstein Veblen, p. 89.

15. Thorstein Veblen, p. 65.
16. Chauncey Depew, quoted in Dorfman, p. 122.
17. *The Chicago Journal,* quoted in Dorfman, p. 123.
18. The history of Bemis's discharge is the subject of a study by Harold E. Bergquist, Jr., "The Edward W. Bemis Controversy at the University of Chicago," *AAUP Bulletin,* vol. 58, no. 4 (December 1972), pp. 384–393, which appeared after this article originally went to press. While suggesting more complex circumstances than here implied and also a less than innocent role for J. Laurence Laughlin, Mr. Bergquist's conclusions as to the dismissal of Bemis are much as above.
19. Thorstein Veblen, pp. 245–246.
20. Thorstein Veblen, p. 242.
21. *The Scotch* (Boston: Houghton Mifflin, 1964).
22. Lester F. Ward, quoted in Dorfman, p. 194.
23. William Dean Howells, quoted in Dorfman, p. 196.
24. Thorstein Veblen, p. 29.
25. *The Instinct of Workmanship and the State of the Industrial Arts* (1914); *Imperial Germany and the Industrial Revolution* (1915); *An Inquiry into the Nature of Peace and the Terms of Its Perpetuation* (1917); *The Higher Learning in America; A Memorandum on the Conduct of Universities by Business Men* (1918); *The Vested Interests and the Common Man* (1919); *The Place of Science in Modern Civilisation and Other Essays* (1919); *The Engineers and the Price System* (1921); *Absentee Ownership and Business Enterprise in Recent Times; The Case of America* (1923). At the end of his life Veblen resumed an early interest in his Norseland origins and studied the Icelandic sagas. His last publication was *The Laxdaela Saga* (1925).
26. Brander Matthews, *New York Times Review of Books,* March 16, 1919, p. 125.
27. *The Nation,* vol. 129, no. 3345, p. 157.
28. Wesley C. Mitchell, "Thorstein Veblen: 1857–1929," *The Economic Journal,* vol. 39 (1929), p. 649.

The Mandarin Revolution

[*from* The Age of Uncertainty]

The ideas that made the revolutions of the nineteenth century did not originate with the masses, with the people who, by any reasonable calculation, had the most reason for revolt; they came from intellectuals. In similar fashion, the ideas that saved the reputation of capitalism in the years before and after World War II came not from businessmen, bankers or owners of shares but again from intellectuals, and principally from the British economist John Maynard Keynes. It was to be his fate to be regarded as peculiarly dangerous by the class he rescued.

*   *   *   *

JOHN MAYNARD KEYNES was born in 1883, the year that Karl Marx died. His mother, Florence Ada Keynes, a woman of high intelligence, was diligent in good works, a respected community leader and, in late life, the mayor of Cambridge, England. His father, John Neville Keynes, was an economist, logician and for some fifteen years the Registrary, which is to say the chief administrative officer of the University of Cambridge. Maynard, as he was always known to friends, went to Eton, where his first interest was in mathematics. Then he went to King's College, after Trinity the most prestigious of the Cambridge colleges and the one noted especially for its economists. Keynes was to add both to its prestige in economics and, as its bursar, to its wealth.

Winston Churchill held — where I confess escapes me — that great men usually have had unhappy childhoods. At both Eton and Cambridge, Keynes, by his own account and that of his contemporaries, was exceedingly happy. The point could be important. Keynes never sought to change the world out of any sense of personal dissatisfaction or discontent. Marx swore that the bourgeoisie would suffer for his poverty and his carbuncles. Keynes experienced neither deprivation nor boils; for him the world was excellent.

At King's, Keynes was one of a group of ardent young intellectuals which included Lytton Strachey, Leonard Woolf and Clive Bell. All, with wives — Virginia Woolf, Vanessa Bell — and lovers, would assemble later in London as the Bloomsbury Group. All were much under the influence of the philosopher, G. E. Moore. In later years Keynes told of what he had from Moore. It was the belief that: "The appropriate subjects of passionate contemplation and communion were a beloved person, beauty and truth, and one's prime objects in life were love, the creation and enjoyment of aesthetic experience and the pursuit of knowledge. Of these, love came a long way first."[1] With these thoughts, inevitably, Keynes found his interest shifting from mathematics to economics.

The more important instrument of the change was Alfred Marshall, who was not at King's but along the river in the equally beautiful precincts of St. John's, known as John's. Marshall, who combined the reputation of a prophet with the aura of a saint, presided over the world of Anglo-American economics in nearly undisputed eminence for forty years — from 1885 until his death in 1924. When I was first introduced to economics at Berkeley in 1931, it was Marshall's *Principles* students were required to read. It was a majestic book. It was also superb for discouraging second-rate scholars from any further pursuit of the subject.

When he finished with Cambridge in 1905, Keynes sat for the Civil Service examinations and did badly in economics. His explanation was characteristic: "The examiners presumably knew less than I did."[2] But this deficiency was not fatal, and he went to the India Office. Here he relieved his boredom by working on two books — a technical treatise on the theory of probability and his later book on Indian currency. Neither much changed the world or economic thought; soon he returned to Cambridge on a fellowship provided personally by Alfred Marshall. It was to be the economics of Alfred Marshall — the notion, in particular, of a benign tendency to an equilibrium where all willing workers were employed — that Keynes would do most to make obsolete.

II

When the Great War came, Keynes was not attracted to the trenches. He went to the Treasury, where his job was to take British earnings from trade, proceeds from loans floated in the United States and returns from securities conscripted and sold abroad and make them cover essential overseas war purchases. And he helped the French and the Russians do the same. No magic was involved, as many have since suggested. Economic skill does not extend to getting very much for nothing. But an adept and resourceful mind was useful, and this Keynes had. In the course of time Keynes received a notice to report for military service. He sent it back. When the war was over, he was a natural choice for the British delegation to the Peace Conference. In the later official view, this was an appalling mistake.

The mood in Paris in the early months of 1919 was vengeful, myopic, indifferent to economic realities, and it horrified Keynes. So did his fellow civil servants. So did the politicians. In June he resigned and came home, and, in the next two months, he composed the greatest polemical document of modern times. It argued against the reparations clauses of the Treaty and, as he saw it, the Carthaginian peace.

Europe would only punish itself by exacting, or seeking to exact, more from the Germans than they had the practical capacity to pay. Restraint by the victors was not a matter of compassion but of elementary self-interest. The case was documented with figures and written with passion. In memorable passages Keynes gave his impressions of the men who were writing the peace. Woodrow Wilson he called "this blind and deaf Don Quixote."[3] Of Clemenceau he said: "He had one illusion — France; and one disillusion, mankind . . ."[4] On Lloyd George he was rather severe:

> How can I convey to the reader, who does not know him, any just impression of this extraordinary figure of our time, this syren, this goat-footed bard, this half-human visitor to our age from the hag-ridden magic and enchanted woods of Celtic antiquity.[5]

Alas, no writer is of perfect courage. Keynes deleted this passage on Lloyd George at the last moment.

The Economic Consequences of the Peace was published before the end of 1919. The judgment of the British Establishment was rendered by *The Times:* "Mr. Keynes may be a 'clever' economist. He may have been a useful Treasury official. But in writing this book, he has rendered the Allies a disservice for which their enemies will, doubtless, be grateful."[6] In time there would be a responsible view that Keynes went too far — that in calculating the limits on Germany's ability to pay, he was excessively orthodox. Perhaps he did contribute to the Germans' sense of persecution and injustice that Hitler then so effectively exploited. But the technique of *The Times* attack should also be noticed. It was not that the great men of the Treaty and the Establishment were suffering under the onslaught, although that, of course, was the real point. Rather, the criticism was causing rejoicing to the nation's enemies. It's a device to which highly respectable men regularly resort. "Even if you are right, it is only the Communists who will be pleased."

And it is when they are wrong that great men most resent the breaking of ranks. So they greatly resented Keynes. For the next twenty years he headed an insurance company and speculated in shares, commodities and foreign exchange, sometimes losing, more often winning. He also taught economics, wrote extensively and applied himself to the arts, old books and his Bloomsbury friends. But on public matters he was kept outside: he had broken the rules. As we often see, the intelligent man is not sought out. Rather, he is excluded as a threat.

Keynes's exclusion proved to be his good fortune. The curse of the public man is that he first accommodates his tongue and eventually his thoughts to his public position. Presently saying nothing but saying it nicely becomes a habit. On the outside one can at least have the pleasure of inflicting the truth. Also, as a freelance intellectual, Keynes could marry Lydia Lopokova, who had just enchanted London as the star of Diaghilev's ballet. My memory retains a couplet from somewhere:

> Was there ever such a union of beauty and brains
> As when the lovely Lopokova married John Maynard Keynes?

For a civil servant, even for a Cambridge professor, Lopokova would then have been a bit brave. As it was (according to legend), old family friends in Cambridge asked: Has Maynard married a chorus girl?

Mostly in those years Keynes wrote. Good writing in economics is suspect — and with justification. It can persuade people. It also requires clear thought. No one can express well what he does not understand. So clear writing is perceived as a threat, something deeply damaging to the numerous scholars who shelter mediocrity of mind behind obscurity of prose. Keynes was a superb writer when he chose to try. This added appreciably to the suspicion with which he was regarded.

But while Keynes was kept outside, he could not, as would a Marxist, be ignored. He was a Fellow of King's. He was the Chairman of the National Mutual Insurance Company. He was the director of other companies. So he was heard. It might have been better strategy to have kept him inside and under control.

III

The man who suffered most from Keynes's freedom from constraint was Winston Churchill. In 1925, Churchill presided over one of the most dramatically disastrous errors by a government in modern economic history, and it was Keynes who made it famous.

The mistake was the attempted return to the gold standard at the prewar gold and dollar value of the pound — 123.27 fine grains of gold and 4.86 dollars to the pound. Churchill was Chancellor of the Exchequer.

In retrospect, the error was not an especially subtle one. British prices and wages had risen during the war as they had in other countries. But in the United States they had risen less and had fallen more in the postwar slump. And in France, as elsewhere in Europe, though prices had risen more than in Britain, the exchange value of the local currencies had fallen even more than prices had gone up. When you bought the cheap foreign currencies and then the goods, they were, in comparison with those of Britain, a bargain.

Had Britain gone back to the pound at, say, 4.40 dollars, all might have been well. With sterling bought at that rate, the cost of British commodities, manufactures or services — coal, textiles, machinery, ships, shipping — would have been pretty much in line with those of other countries, given their prices and the cost of their currencies. With pounds bought at 4.86 dollars, British prices were about 10 percent higher than those of her competitors. Ten percent is 10 percent. It was enough to send buyers to France, Germany, the Low Countries, the United States.

Why the mistake? To go back to the old rate of exchange of pounds for gold and dollars was to show that British financial management was again as solid, as reliable, as in the nineteenth century. It proved that the war had changed nothing. It was a thought to which Winston Churchill, eager historian and professional custodian of the British past, was highly susceptible. Also, only a few people participate in such decisions, and the instinct is strongly conformist. The man of greatest public prestige states his position at a meeting; the others hasten to praise his wisdom. Those who have a reputation for dissent, like Keynes, are not invited to take part in the discussion. They are not responsible, serious, effective. It follows that financial decisions, as often those on foreign policy, are carefully orchestrated to protect error.

The country responded well to Churchill's House of Commons announcement of the return to gold. The *New York Times* reported in its headline that he had carried "PARLIAMENT AND NATION TO

HEIGHT OF ENTHUSIASM." Keynes wrote instead to ask why Churchill did "such a silly thing." It was because he had "no instinctive judgment to prevent him from making mistakes."[7] And "lacking this instinctive judgment, he was deafened by the clamorous voices of conventional finance."[8] Also, he was misled by his experts. One cannot believe that Churchill read this exculpation with any pleasure.

If British exports were to continue, British prices had to come down. Prices could come down only if wages came down. And wages could come down in only one of two ways. There could be a horizontal slash, whatever the unions might say. Or there could be unemployment, enough unemployment to weaken union demands, threaten employed workers with idleness and thus bring down wages. This Keynes foresaw.

There was, in the end, both unemployment and a horizontal wage cut. As the mines of the Ruhr came back into production after 1924, world prices of coal fell. To meet this competition with the more expensive pound, the British coal-owners proposed a three-point program: longer hours in the pits, abolition of the minimum wage, lower wages for all. A Royal Commission agreed that the lower wage was necessary. The miners refused; the owners then locked them out. On the fourth of May, 1926, the transport, printing, iron and steel, electricity and gas and most of the building-trades unions came out in support of the miners. This, with some slight exaggeration, was called the General Strike. For quite a few workers it didn't make too much difference; they were already on the dole, for unemployment, the other remedy, was by then well advanced. In these years unemployment ranged between 10 and 12 percent of the British labor force.

The General Strike lasted only nine days. Those who had most ardently applauded the return to gold were the first to see the strike as a threat to constitutional government, a manifestation of anarchy. Churchill took an especially principled stand. The miners remained on strike through most of 1926 but were eventually defeated. Keynes's judgment was redeemed, but he was not forgiven. It had happened again: when the men of great reputation are wrong, it is the worst of personal tactics to be right.

IV

In Europe it was World War I that shook the old certainties. The trenches would linger in social memory as the ultimate horror. In the United States it was the Great Depression of the nineteen-thirties, and its effects spread around the world. The richer the country, the more advanced its industry, the worse, in general, the slump.

Many economists — Lionel Robbins in England, Joseph Schumpeter in the United States — held that depression had a necessary, therapeutic function; the metaphor was that it extruded poisons that had been accumulating in the economic system. Others joined in urging patience, a course of action that is easier when supported by a regular income. And many warned that affirmative measures by government would cause inflation. The practical effect in all cases was to come out for inaction. It was not a good time for economists. Britain did abandon the gold standard and free trade. Otherwise Westminster and Whitehall reacted to the Depression by ignoring the steady flow of advice it was receiving from John Maynard Keynes.

Keynes was wholly clear as to the proper action. He wanted borrowing by the government and the expenditure of the resulting funds; this borrowing would ensure the increase in the money supply — in bank deposits. What was spent would be spent by the government and would then be respent by workers and others receiving the money. The government spending and the further spending by the recipients ensured that there would be no offsetting drop in velocity. You not only created money but enforced its use.

Keynes in these years did have one notable friend. It was the "goat-footed bard," David Lloyd George. Keynes explained helpfully that he supported Lloyd George when he was right and opposed him when he was wrong. But Lloyd George was by now in the political wilderness with the other winners and losers from World War I. Gradually for Keynes there was compensation. He became a prophet with honor except in his own country. The most successful application of his policies was, in fact, where he was all but unknown.

v

The Nazis were not given to books. Their economic reaction was to circumstance, and this served them better than the sound economists served Britain and the United States. From 1933 on, Hitler borrowed money and spent — and he did it liberally as Keynes would have advised. It seemed the obvious thing to do, given the unemployment. At first, the spending was mostly for civilian works — railroads, canals, public buildings, the *Autobahnen.* Exchange control then kept frightened Germans from sending their money abroad and those with rising incomes from spending too much of it on imports.

The results were all a Keynesian could have wished. By late 1935, unemployment was at an end in Germany. By 1936, high income was pulling up prices or making it possible to raise them. Likewise wages were beginning to rise. So a ceiling was put over both prices and wages, and this too worked. Germany, by the late thirties, had full employment at stable prices. It was, in the industrial world, an absolutely unique achievement.

The German example was instructive but not persuasive. British and American conservatives looked at the Nazi financial heresies — the borrowing and spending — and uniformly predicted a breakdown. Only Schacht, the German banker, they said, was keeping things patched together. (They did not know that Schacht, so far as he was aware of what was happening, was opposed.) And American liberals and British socialists looked at the repression, the destruction of the unions, the Brown Shirts, the Black Shirts, the concentration camps, the screaming oratory, and ignored the economics. Nothing good, not even full employment, could come from Hitler. It was the American case that was influential.

At the close of 1933, Keynes addressed a letter to Franklin D. Roosevelt, which, not seeking reticence, he published in the *New York Times.* A single sentence summarized his case: "I lay overwhelming emphasis on the increase of national purchasing power resulting from governmental expenditure which is financed by loans. . . ."[9] The following year he visited FDR, but the letter had been a better means of communication. Each man was puzzled by the face-to-face encounter. The President thought Keynes some kind of "a mathematician rather than a political economist."[10] Keynes was depressed; he had "supposed the President was more literate, economically speaking."[11]

If corporations are large and strong, as they already were in the thirties, they can reduce their prices. And if unions are nonexistent or weak, as they were at the time in the United States, labor can then be forced to accept wage reductions. Action by one company will force action by another. The modern inflationary spiral will work in reverse; the reduced purchasing power of workers will add to its force. Through the National Recovery Administration, Washington was trying to arrest this process — a reasonable and even wise effort, given the circumstances. This Keynes and most economists did not see; he and they believed the NRA wrong, and ever since it has had a poor press. One of FDR's foolish mistakes. Keynes wanted much more vigorous borrowing and spending; he thought the Administration far too cautious. And Washington was, indeed, reluctant.

In the early thirties the Mayor of New York was James J. Walker. Defending a casual attitude toward dirty literature, as it was then called, he said he had never heard of a girl being seduced by a book. Keynes was now, after a fashion, to prove Walker wrong. Having failed by direct, practical persuasion, he proceeded to seduce Washington and the world by way of a book. Further to prove the point against Walker, it was a nearly unreadable one.

V I

The book was *The General Theory of Employment Interest and Money.* (For some reason Keynes omitted the commas.) He at least was not in doubt about its influence.

The General Theory was published long before it was finished. Like the Bible and *Das Kapital,* it is deeply ambiguous, and, as in the case of the Bible and Marx, the ambiguity helped greatly to win converts. I am not reaching for paradox here. When understanding is achieved after much effort, readers hold tenaciously to their belief.

The pain, they wish to think, was worthwhile. And if there are enough contradictions and ambiguities, as there are also in the Bible and Marx, the reader can always find something he wants to believe. This too wins disciples.

Keynes's basic conclusion can, however, be put very directly. Previously it had been held that the economic system, any capitalist system, found its equilibrium at full employment. Left to itself, it was thus that it came to rest. Idle men and idle plant were an aberration, a wholly temporary failing. Keynes showed that the modern economy could as well find its equilibrium with continuing, serious unemployment. Its perfectly normal tendency was to what economists later came to call an underemployment equilibrium.

The ultimate cause of the underemployment equilibrium lay in the effort by individuals and firms to save more from income than it was currently profitable for businessmen to invest. What is saved from income must ultimately be spent or there will be a shortage of purchasing power. Previously for 150 years such a possibility had been excluded in the established economics. The income from producing goods was held always to be sufficient to buy the goods. Savings were always invested. Were there a surplus of savings, interest rates fell, and this ensured their use.

Keynes did not deny that all savings got invested. But he showed that this could be accomplished by a fall in output (and employment) in the economy as a whole. Such a slump reduced earnings, changed business gains into losses, reduced personal incomes, and, while it reduced investment, it reduced savings even more. It was in this way that savings were kept equal to investment. Adjustment, a benign word in economics, could be a chilling thing.

From the foregoing came the remedy. The government should borrow and invest. If it borrowed and invested enough, all savings would be offset by investment at a high, not a low, level of output and employment. *The General Theory* validated the remedy that Keynes had previously urged. It would have been inconvenient if it had come out the other way.

Here is the hard core of the Keynesian Revolution. There was much more, but now, in the next essay, a word on how it spread, came to the United States.

NOTES

1. John Maynard Keynes, "My Early Beliefs," in *Two Memoirs* (London: Rupert Hart-Davis, 1949), p. 83.
2. John Maynard Keynes quoted in R. F. Harrod, *The Life of John Maynard Keynes* (London: Macmillan & Co., 1951), p. 121.
3. John Maynard Keynes, *Essays in Biography* (London: Mercury Books, 1961), p. 20.
4. John Maynard Keynes quoted in Harrod, p. 257.
5. John Maynard Keynes quoted in Harrod, p. 256.
6. Robert Lekachman, *Keynes' General Theory: Reports of Three Decades* (New York: St. Martin's Press, 1964), p. 35.
7. Johh Maynard Keynes, *Essays in Persuasion* (London: Macmillan & Co., 1931), pp. 248–249.
8. John Maynard Keynes quoted in Robert Lekachman, *The Age of Keynes* (New York: Random House, 1966), p. 47.
9. John Maynard Keynes quoted in Harrod, p. 447.
10. Franklin D. Roosevelt quoted in Lekachman, *The Age of Keynes*, p. 123.
11. John Maynard Keynes quoted in Lekachman, *The Age of Keynes*, p. 123.

How Keynes Came to America

[*from* Economics, Peace and Laughter]

The most influential book on economic and social policy in the twentieth century, The General Theory of Employment Interest and Money *by John Maynard Keynes, was published in 1936 in both Britain and the United States. A paperback edition eventually became available in America, and the* New York Times, *discovering to its possible embarrassment that the original edition had not been reviewed, asked me for this comment.*

Quite a few people who took advantage of this bargain were undoubtedly puzzled at the reason for the book's influence; though comfortably aware of their own intelligence, they could not read it. They wondered, accordingly, how it had persuaded so many other people, not all of whom, certainly, were more penetrating or diligent.

*   *   *   *

I believe myself to be writing a book on economic theory which will largely revolutionize — not, I suppose, at once but in the course of the next ten years — the way the world thinks about economic problems.

— Letter from JOHN MAYNARD KEYNES to
GEORGE BERNARD SHAW, New Year's Day, 1935

B Y COMMON, if not yet quite universal, agreement, the Keynesian Revolution was one of the great modern accomplishments in social design. It brought Marxism in the advanced countries to a halt. It led to a level of economic performance that inspired bitter-end conservatives to panegyrics of unexampled banality. Yet those responsible have had no honors and some opprobrium. For a long while, to be known as an active Keynesian was to invite the wrath of those who equate social advance with subversion. Those concerned developed a habit of reticence. As a further consequence, the history of the revolution is, perhaps, the worst-told story of our era.

It is time that we knew better this part of our history and those who made it, and this is a little of the story. Much of it turns on the almost unique unreadability of *The General Theory* and hence the need for people to translate and propagate its ideas to government officials, students and the public at large. As Messiahs go, John Maynard Keynes was deeply dependent on his prophets.

The General Theory appeared in the sixth year of the Great Depression and the fifty-third of Keynes's life. At the time Keynes, like his great contemporary Churchill, was regarded as too candid and inconvenient to be trusted. Public officials are not always admiring of men who say what the right policy should be. Their frequent need, especially in foreign affairs, is for men who will find persuasive reasons for the wrong policy. Keynes had foreseen grave difficulty from the reparations clauses of the Versailles Treaty and had voiced them in *The Economic Consequences of the Peace,* which may well have overstated his case and which certainly was unjust to Woodrow Wilson but which nonetheless provided what proved to be a clearer view of the postwar economic disasters than the men of more stately perception wished anyone to expect.

Later in the twenties, in another book, he was equally untactful toward those who invited massive unemployment in Britain in order to return sterling to the gold standard at its prewar parity with the dollar. The man immediately responsible for this effort, a highly orthodox voice in economic matters at the time, was the then Chancellor of the Exchequer, Winston Churchill, and that book was called *The Economic Consequences of Mr. Churchill.*

From 1920 to 1940, Keynes was sought out by students and intellectuals in Cambridge and London; was well known in London theater and artistic circles; directed an insurance company; made, and on occasion lost, quite a bit of money; and was an influential journalist. But he wasn't really trusted on public questions. The great trade union which identifies trustworthiness with conformity kept him outside. Then came the Depression. There was much unemployment, much suffering. Even respectable men went broke. It was necessary, however unpleasant, to listen to the candid men who had something to say by way of remedy. This listening is the terrible punishment the gods reserve for fair weather statesmen.

It is a measure of how far the Keynesian Revolution has proceeded that the central thesis of *The General Theory* now sounds rather commonplace. Until the book appeared, economists, in the classical (or nonsocialist) tradition, had assumed that the economy, if left to itself, would find its equilibrium at full employment. Increases or decreases in wages and in interest rates would occur as necessary to bring about this agreeable result. If men were unemployed, their wages would fall in relation to prices. With lower wages and wider margins, it would be profitable to employ those from whose toil an adequate return could not previously have been made. It followed that steps to keep wages at artificially high levels, such as might result from (as it was said) the ill-considered efforts by unions, would cause unemployment. Such efforts were, in fact, deemed to be the principal cause of unemployment.

Movements in interest rates played a complementary role by ensuring that all income would ultimately be spent. Thus, were people to decide for some reason to increase their savings, the interest rates on the now-more-abundant supply of loanable funds would fall. This, in turn, would lead to increased investment. The added outlays for investment goods would offset the diminished outlays by the more frugal consumers. In this fashion, changes in consumer spending or in investment decisions were kept from causing any change in total spending that would lead to unemployment.

Keynes argued that neither wage movements nor changes in the rate of interest had, necessarily, any such benign effect. He focused attention on the total of purchasing power in the economy — what freshmen are now taught to call aggregate demand. Wage reductions might not increase employment; in conjunction with other changes, they might merely reduce this aggregate demand. And he held that interest was not the price that was paid to people to save but the price they got for exchanging holdings of cash or its equivalent, their normal preference in assets, for less liquid forms of investment. And it was difficult to reduce interest beyond a certain level. Accordingly, if people sought to save more, this wouldn't necessarily mean lower interest rates and a resulting increase in investment. Instead, the total demand for goods might fall, along with employment and also investment, until savings were brought back into line with investment by the pressure of hardship which had reduced saving in favor of consumption. The economy would find its equilibrium not at full employment but with an unspecified amount of unemployment.

Out of this diagnosis came the remedy. It was to bring aggregate demand back up to the level where all willing workers were employed; and this could be accomplished by supplementing private expenditure with public expenditure. This should be the policy wherever intentions to save exceeded intentions to invest. Since public spending would not perform this offsetting role if there were compensating taxation (which is a form of saving), the public spending should be financed by borrowing — by incurring a deficit. So far as Keynes can be condensed into two paragraphs, this is it. *The General Theory* is more difficult. There are nearly 400 pages, some of them of fascinating obscurity.

Before the publication of *The General Theory*, Keynes had urged his ideas directly on President Roosevelt, most notably in a famous letter to the *New York Times* on December 31, 1933: "I lay overwhelming emphasis on the increase of national purchasing power resulting from government expenditure which is financed by loans." And he visited FDR in the summer of 1934 to press his case, although the session was no great success; each, during the meeting, developed some doubts about the general good sense of the other.

In the meantime, two key Washington officials, Marriner Eccles, the exceptionally able Utah banker, who was to become head of the Federal Reserve Board, and Lauchlin Currie, a recent Harvard instructor who was its assistant director of research and later an economic aide to Roosevelt (and later still a prominent victim of McCarthyite persecution), had on their own account reached conclusions similar to those of Keynes as to the proper course of fiscal policy. When *The General Theory* arrived, they took it as confirmation of the course they had previously been urging. Currie, a brilliant economist and teacher, was also a skilled and influential interpreter of the ideas in the Washington community. Not often have important new ideas on economics entered a government by way of its central bank. Nor should anyone be disturbed. There is not the slightest indication that it will ever happen again.[1]

Paralleling the work of Keynes in the thirties and rivaling it in importance, though not in fame, was that of Simon Kuznets and a group of young economists and statisticians at the University of Pennsylvania, the National Bureau of Economic Research and the United States Department of Commerce. They developed from earlier beginnings the now familiar concepts of National Income and Gross National Product and their components, and made estimates of their amount. Included among the components of National Income and Gross National Product were the saving, investment, aggregate of disposable income and the other magnitudes of which Keynes was talking. As a result, those who were translating Keynes's ideas into action could now know not only what needed to be done but how much. And many who would never have been persuaded by the Keynesian abstractions were compelled to belief by the concrete figures from Kuznets and his inventive colleagues.

However, the trumpet — if the metaphor is permissible for this particular book — that was sounded in Cambridge, England, was heard most clearly in Cambridge, Massachusetts. Harvard was the principal avenue by which Keynes's ideas passed to the United States. Conservatives worry about universities being centers of disquieting innovation. Their worries may be exaggerated but it has occurred.

In the late thirties, Harvard had a large community of young economists, most of them held there by the shortage of jobs that Keynes sought to cure. They had the normal confidence of their years in their ability to remake the world and, unlike less fortunate generations, the opportunity. They also had occupational indication of the need. Massive unemployment persisted year after year. It was degrading to have to continue telling the young that this was merely a temporary departure from the full employment norm and that one need only obtain the needed wage reductions.

Paul Samuelson, who subsequently taught economics to an entire generation and who almost from the outset was the acknowledged leader of the younger Keynesian community, has compared the excitement of the young economists, on the arrival of Keynes's book, to that of Keats on first looking into Chapman's Homer. Some will wonder if economists are capable of such refined emotion, but the effect was certainly great. Here was a remedy for the despair that could be seen just beyond Harvard Yard. It did not overthrow the system but saved it. To the nonrevolutionary, it seemed too good to be true. To the occasional revolutionary, it was. The old economics was still taught by day. But in the evening and almost every evening from 1936 on, almost everyone in the Harvard economic community discussed Keynes.

This might, conceivably, have remained a rather academic discussion. As with the Bible and Marx, obscurity stimulated abstract debate. But in 1938, the practical instincts that economists sometimes suppress with success were catalyzed by the arrival in Cambridge from Minnesota of Alvin H. Hansen. He was then about fifty, an effective teacher and a popular colleague. But, most of all, he was a man for whom economic ideas had no standing apart from their use.

Most economists of established reputation had not taken to Keynes. Faced with the choice between changing one's mind and proving that there is no need to do so, almost everyone gets busy on the proof. So it was then. Hansen had an established reputation, and he did change his mind. Though he had been an effective critic of some central propositions in Keynes's *Treatise on Money*, an immediately preceding work, and was initially rather cool to *The General Theory,* he soon became strongly persuaded of Keynes's importance.

He proceeded to expound the ideas in books, articles and lectures and to apply them to the American scene. He persuaded his students and younger colleagues that they should not only understand the ideas but win understanding in others and then go on to get action. Without ever seeking to do so or being quite aware of the fact, he became the leader of a crusade. In the late thirties Hansen's seminar in Harvard's new Graduate School of Public Administration was regularly visited by the Washington policy-makers. Often the students overflowed into the hall. One felt that it was the most important thing currently happening in the country, and this could have been the case.

The officials took Hansen's ideas, and perhaps even more his sense of conviction, back to Washington. In time there was also a strong migration of his younger colleagues and students to the capital. Among numerous others were Richard Gilbert, later a principal architect of Pakistan's economic development, who was a confidant of Harry Hopkins; Richard Musgrave, later at Princeton and other universities and then once again back at Harvard, who applied Keynes's and Hansen's ideas to the tax system; Alan Sweezy, later of the California Institute of Technology, who went to the Federal Reserve and the WPA; George Jaszi, who went to the Department of Commerce; G. Griffith Johnson, who served at the Treasury, on the National Security Resources Board and in the White House; and Walter Salant, later of the Brookings Institution, who served influentially in several federal agencies. Keynes wrote admiringly of this group of young Washington disciples.

The discussions that had begun in Cambridge continued through the war years in Washington where most of the earlier participants were now serving. One of the leaders, a close friend of Hansen's but not otherwise connected with the Harvard group, was the late Gerhard Colm of the Bureau of the Budget. Colm, a German refugee, had made the transition from a position of influence in Germany to one of major responsibility in the United States government in a matter of some five years. He played a major role in reducing the

Keynesian proposals to workable estimates of costs and quantities. Keynesian policies became central to what was called postwar planning and designs for preventing the re-emergence of massive unemployment.

Meanwhile, others were concerning themselves with a wider audience. Seymour Harris, another of Hansen's colleagues and an early convert to Keynes, became the most prolific exponent of the ideas in the course of becoming one of the most prolific scholars of modern times. He published half a dozen books on Keynes and outlined the ideas in hundreds of letters, speeches, memoranda, Congressional appearances and articles. Professor Samuelson, mentioned above, put the Keynesian ideas into what became the most influential textbook on economics after the great exposition of the classical system by Alfred Marshall. Lloyd Metzler at the University of Chicago applied the Keynesian system to international trade. Lloyd G. Reynolds gathered a talented group of younger economists at Yale and made that university a major center of discussion of the new ideas.

Nor was the Harvard influence confined to the United States. At almost the same time that *The General Theory* arrived in Cambridge, Massachusetts, so did a young Canadian graduate student named Robert Bryce. He was fresh from Cambridge, England, where he had been in Keynes's seminar and had, as a result, a special license to explain what Keynes meant in his more obscure passages. With other Canadian graduate students, Bryce went on to Ottawa and to a succession of senior posts ending as Deputy Minister of Finance. Canada was perhaps the first country to commit itself unequivocally to a Keynesian economic policy.

Meanwhile, with the help of the academic Keynesians, a few businessmen were becoming interested. Two New England industrialists, Henry S. Dennison of the Dennison Manufacturing Company in Framingham, Massachusetts, and Ralph Flanders of the Jones and Lamson Machine Company of Springfield, Vermont (and later United States Senator from Vermont), hired members of the Harvard group to tutor them in the ideas. Before the war they had endorsed them in a book, in which Lincoln Filene of Boston and

Morris E. Leeds of Philadelphia had joined, called *Toward Full Employment*. It was only slightly more readable and even less read than Keynes.[2] In the later war years, the Committee for Economic Development, led in these matters by Flanders and Beardsley Ruml, and again with the help of the academic Keynesians, began evangelizing the business community.

In Washington during the war, the National Planning Association had been a center for academic discussion of the Keynesian ideas. At the end of the war Hans Christian Sonne, an imaginative and liberal New York banker, began underwriting both the NPA and the Keynesian system. With the Committee for Economic Development in which Sonne was also influential, the NPA became another important instrument for explaining the policy to the larger public. (In the autumn of 1949, in an exercise combining imagination with rare diplomacy, Sonne gathered a dozen economists of strongly varying views at Princeton and persuaded them all to sign a specific endorsement of Keynesian fiscal policies. The agreement was later reported to the Congress in well-publicized hearings by Arthur Smithies of Harvard and Simeon Leland of Northwestern University.)

In 1946, ten years after the publication of *The General Theory*, the Employment Act of that year gave the Keynesian system the qualified but still quite explicit support of law. It recognized, as Keynes had urged, that unemployment and insufficient output would respond to positive policies. Not much was said about the specific policies but the responsibility of the federal government to act in some fashion was clearly affirmed. The Council of Economic Advisers became, in turn, a platform for expounding the Keynesian view of the economy, and it was brought promptly into use. Leon Keyserling, as an original member and later chairman, was a tireless exponent of the ideas. And he saw at an early stage the importance of enlarging them to embrace not only the prevention of depression but the maintenance of an adequate rate of economic expansion. Thus in only a decade had the revolution spread.

Those who nurture thoughts of conspiracy and clandestine plots will be saddened to know that this was a revolution without organization. All who participated felt a deep sense of personal responsibility for the ideas; there was a varying but deep urge to persuade. There was a strong feeling in Washington that key economic posts should be held by people who understood the Keynesian system and who would work to establish it. Currie at the White House ran an informal casting office in this regard. But no one ever responded to plans, orders, instructions or any force apart from his own convictions. That perhaps was the most interesting feature of the Keynesian Revolution.

Something more, however, was always suspected. And there was some effort at counterrevolution. Nobody could say that he preferred massive unemployment to Keynes. And even men of conservative mood, when they understood what was involved, opted for the policy — some asking only that it be called by some other name. The Committee for Economic Development, coached by Ruml on semantics, never advocated deficits. Rather, it spoke well of a budget that was balanced only under conditions of high employment. Those who objected to Keynes were also invariably handicapped by the fact that they hadn't (and couldn't) read the book. It was like attacking the original Kama Sutra for pornography without being able to read Sanskrit. Still, where resisting social change is involved, there are men who can surmount any handicap.

Appropriately Harvard, not Washington, was the principal object of attention. In the fifties, a group of graduates of mature years banded together in an organization called the Veritas Foundation and financed a volume called *Keynes at Harvard*. It found that "Harvard was the launching pad for the Keynesian rocket in America." But then it damaged this highly plausible proposition by identifying Keynesianism with socialism, Fabian socialism, Marxism, communism, fascism and also literary incest, meaning that one Keynesian always reviewed the works of another Keynesian.[3] Like so many others in similar situations, the authors sacrificed their chance for credibility by writing not for the public but for those who were paying the bill. The university was comparatively unperturbed, the larger public sadly indifferent. The book continued for a long while to have some circulation on the more thoughtful fringes of the conservative John Birch Society.

As a somewhat less trivial matter, a more influential group of graduates pressed for an investigation of the Department of Economics, employing as their instrument the Visiting Committee that annually reviews the work of the Department on behalf of the Governing Boards. The Keynesian Revolution belongs to our history; so, accordingly, does this investigation.

It was conducted by Clarence Randall, then the unduly articulate head of the Inland Steel Company, with the support of Sinclair Weeks, a leading zipper manufacturer, onetime senator and long a tetrarch of the right wing of the Republican Party in Massachusetts. In due course, the Committee found that Keynes was, indeed, exerting a baneful influence on the Harvard economic mind and that the Department of Economics was unbalanced in his favor. As always, there was the handicap that the investigators, with one or two possible exceptions, had not read *The General Theory* and were thus uncertain as to what they attacked. The Department, including the members most skeptical of Keynes's analysis — no one accepted all of it and some not much — unanimously rejected the Committee's findings. So, as one of his last official acts before becoming High Commissioner to Germany in 1953, did President James Bryant Conant. In consequence of the controversy, there was much bad feeling between the Department and its critics.

In ensuing years there was further discussion of the role of Keynes at Harvard and of related issues. But it became increasingly amicable, for the original investigators had been caught up in one of those fascinating and paradoxical developments with which the history of the Keynesian (and doubtless all other) revolutions is replete. Shortly after the Committee reached its disturbing conclusion, the Eisenhower Administration came to power.

Mr. Randall then became a Presidential assistant and adviser. Mr. Weeks became Secretary of Commerce and almost immediately was preoccupied with the firing of the head of the Bureau of Standards over the question of the efficacy of Glauber's salts as a battery additive. Having staked his public reputation against the nation's scientists and engineers on the issue that a battery could be improved by giving it a laxative (as the late Bernard De Voto put it), Mr. Weeks could hardly be expected to keep open another front against the Harvard economists. But much worse, both he and Mr. Randall were acquiring a heavy contingent liability for the policies of the Eisenhower Administration. And these, it soon developed, had almost as strong a Keynesian coloration as the Department at Harvard.

President Eisenhower's first Chairman of the Council of Economic Advisers was Arthur F. Burns of Columbia University and the National Bureau of Economic Research (and later adviser and Chairman of the Federal Reserve Board under Richard Nixon). Mr. Burns had credentials as a critic of Keynes. A man who always associated respectability with mild obsolescence, his introduction to the 1946 annual report of the National Bureau was called "Economic Research and the Keynesian Thinking of Our Time." He made his own critical interpretation of the Keynesian underemployment equilibrium and concluded, perhaps a trifle heavily, that "the imposing schemes for government action that are being bottomed on Keynes's equilibrium theory must be viewed with skepticism." Alvin Hansen replied rather sharply.

But if Burns regarded Keynes with skepticism, he viewed recessions (including ones for which he might be held responsible) with antipathy. In his 1955 report as Chairman of the Council of Economic Advisers, he said, "Budget policies can help promote the objective of maximum production by wisely allocating resources *first, between private and public uses;* second, among various government programs." (My italics.) Keynes, reading these words carefully — government action to decide as between private and public spending — would have strongly applauded. And, indeed, a spokesman for the National Association of Manufacturers told the Joint Economic Committee that they pointed "directly toward the planned and eventually the socialized economy."

After the departure of Burns, the Eisenhower Administration incurred a deficit of $9.4 billion in the National Income accounts in the course of overcoming the recession of 1958. This was by far the largest deficit ever incurred by an American government in peacetime; it exceeded the total peacetime expenditure by FDR in any year up to 1940. No administration had ever given the economy such a massive dose of Keynesian medicine. With a Republican administration, guided by men like Mr. Randall and Mr. Weeks, following such policies, the academic Keynesians at Harvard and elsewhere were no longer vulnerable. Keynes ceased to be a wholly tactful topic of conversation with such critics.

Presidents Kennedy and Johnson continued what became commonplace policy. Advised by Walter Heller, a remarkably skillful exponent of Keynes's ideas, they added the new device of the deliberate tax reduction to sustain aggregate demand. And they abandoned, at long last, the double talk by which advocates of Keynesian policies combined advocacy of measures to promote full employment and economic growth with promises of a promptly balanced budget. "We have recognized as self-defeating the effort to balance our budget too quickly in an economy operating well below its potential," President Johnson said in his 1965 report.

NOTES

1. Currie failed of promotion at Harvard partly because his ideas, brilliantly anticipating Keynes, were considered to reflect deficient scholarship until Keynes made them respectable. Economics *is* very complicated.
2. I drafted it.
3. The authors also reported encouragingly that "Galbraith is being groomed as the new crown prince of Keynesism [sic]."

The Speculative Episode

[*from* A Short History of Financial Euphoria]

This is a brief glance at the rules governing the events that are chronicled on the pages that follow.

*   *   *   *

> Anyone taken as an individual is tolerably sensible and reasonable — as a member of a crowd, he at once becomes a blockhead.
>
> — FRIEDRICH VON SCHILLER,
> as quoted by BERNARD BARUCH

THAT THE FREE-ENTERPRISE economy is given to recurrent episodes of speculation will be agreed. These — great events and small, involving bank notes, securities, real estate, art and other assets or objects — are, over the years and centuries, part of history. What have not been sufficiently analyzed are the features common to these episodes, the things that signal their certain return and have thus the considerable practical value of aiding understanding and prediction. Regulation and more orthodox economic knowledge are not what protect the individual and the financial institution when euphoria returns, leading on as it does to wonder at the increase in values and wealth, to the rush to participate that drives up prices, and to the eventual crash and its sullen and painful aftermath. There is protection only in a clear perception of the characteristics common to these flights into what must conservatively be described as mass insanity. Only then is the investor warned and saved.

There are, however, few matters on which such a warning is less welcomed. In the short run, it will be said to be an attack, motivated by either deficient understanding or uncontrolled envy, on the wonderful process of enrichment. More durably, it will be thought to demonstrate a lack of faith in the inherent wisdom of the market itself.

The more obvious features of the speculative episode are manifestly clear to anyone open to understanding. Some artifact or some development, seemingly new and desirable — tulips in Holland, gold in Louisiana, real estate in Florida, the superb economic designs of a political leader — captures the financial mind or perhaps, more accurately, what so passes. The price of the object of speculation goes up. Securities, land, objets d'art and other property, when bought today, are worth more tomorrow. This increase and the prospect attract new buyers; the new buyers assure a further increase. Yet more are attracted; yet more buy; the increase continues. The speculation building on itself provides its own momentum.

This process, once it is recognized, is clearly evident, and especially so after the fact. So also, if more subjectively, are the basic attitudes of the participants. These take two forms. There are those who are persuaded that some new price-enhancing circumstance is in control, and they expect the market to stay up and go up, perhaps indefinitely. It is adjusting to a new situation, a new world of greatly, even infinitely increasing returns and resulting values. Then there are those, superficially more astute and generally fewer in number, who perceive or believe themselves to perceive the speculative mood of the moment. They are in to ride the upward wave; their particular genius, they are convinced, will allow them to get out before the speculation runs its course. They will get the maximum reward from the increase as it continues; they will be out before the eventual fall.

For built into this situation is the eventual and inevitable fall. Built in also is the circumstance that it cannot come gently or gradually. When it comes, it bears the grim face of disaster. That is because both of the groups of participants in the speculative situation are programmed for sudden efforts at escape. Something, it matters little what — although it will always be much debated — triggers the ultimate reversal. Those who had been riding the upward wave decide now is the time to get out. Those who thought the increase would be forever find their illusion destroyed abruptly, and they, also, respond to the newly revealed reality by selling or trying to sell. Thus the collapse. And thus the rule, supported by the experience of centuries: the speculative episode always ends not with a whimper but with a bang.

So much, as I've said, is clear. Less understood is the mass psychology of the speculative mood. When it is fully comprehended, it allows those so favored to save themselves from disaster. Given the pressure of this crowd psychology, however, the saved will be the exception to a very broad and binding rule. They will be required to resist two compelling forces: one, the powerful personal interest that develops in the euphoric belief, and the other, the pressure of public and seemingly superior financial opinion that is brought to bear on behalf of such belief. Both stand as proof of Schiller's dictum that the crowd converts the individual from reasonably good sense to the stupidity against which, as he also said, "the very Gods Themselves contend in vain."

Although only a few observers have noted the vested interest in error that accompanies speculative euphoria, it is, nonetheless, an extremely plausible phenomenon. Those involved with the speculation are experiencing an increase in wealth — getting rich or being further enriched. No one wishes to believe that this is fortuitous or undeserved; all wish to think that it is the result of their own superior insight or intuition. The very increase in values thus captures the thoughts and minds of those being rewarded. Speculation buys up, in a very practical way, the intelligence of those involved.

This is particularly true of the first group noted above — those who are convinced that values are going up permanently and indefinitely. But the errors of vanity of those who think they will beat the speculative game are also thus reinforced. As long as they are in, they have a strong pecuniary commitment to belief in the unique personal intelligence that tells them there will be yet more. In the nineteenth century, one of the most astute observers of the euphoric episodes common to those years was Walter Bagehot, financial writer and early editor of *The Economist*. To him we are indebted for the observation that "all people are most credulous when they are most happy."

Strongly reinforcing the vested interest in euphoria is the condemnation that the reputable public and financial opinion directs at those who express doubt or dissent. It is said that they are unable, because of defective imagination or other mental inadequacy, to grasp the new and rewarding circumstances that sustain and secure the increase in values. Or their motivation is deeply suspect. In the winter of 1929, Paul M. Warburg, the most respected banker of his time and one of the founding parents of the Federal Reserve System, spoke critically of the then-current orgy of "unrestrained speculation" and said that if it continued, there would ultimately be a disastrous collapse, and the country would face a serious depression. The reaction to his statement was bitter, even vicious. He was held to be obsolete in his views; he was "sandbagging American prosperity"; quite possibly, he was himself short in the market. There was more than a shadow of anti-Semitism in this response.

Later, in September of that year, Roger Babson, a considerable figure of the time who was diversely interested in statistics, market forecasting, economics, theology and the law of gravity, specifically foresaw a crash and said, "It may be terrific." There would be a 60- to 80-point drop in the Dow, and, in consequence, "Factories will shut down . . . men will be thrown out of work . . . the vicious circle will get in full swing and the result will be a serious business depression."

Babson's forecast caused a sharp break in the market, and the reaction to it was even more furious than that to Warburg's. *Barron's* said he should not be taken seriously by anyone acquainted with the "notorious inaccuracy" of his past statements. The great New York Stock Exchange house of Hornblower and Weeks told its customers, in a remarkably resonant sentence, that "we would not be stampeded into selling stocks because of a gratuitous forecast of a bad break in the market by a well-known statistician." Even Professor Irving Fisher of Yale University, a pioneer in the construction of index numbers and otherwise the most innovative economist of his day, spoke out sharply against Babson. It was a lesson to all to keep quiet and give tacit support to those indulging their euphoric vision.

Without, I hope, risking too grave a charge of self-gratification, I might here cite personal experience. In the late winter of 1955, J. William Fulbright, then the chairman of the Senate Banking and Currency Committee, called hearings to consider a modest speculative buildup in the securities market. Along with Bernard Baruch, the current head of the New York Stock Exchange and other authorities real or alleged, I was invited to testify. I refrained from predicting a crash, contented myself with reminding the committee at some length as to what had happened a quarter of a century earlier, and urged a substantial protective increase in margin requirements — down payments on the purchases of stocks. While I was testifying, the market took a considerable tumble.

The reaction in the next days was severe. The postman each morning staggered in with a load of letters condemning my comments, the most extreme threatening what the CIA was later to call executive action, the mildest saying that prayers were being offered for my richly deserved demise. A few days later I broke my leg in a skiing accident, and newsmen, seeing me in a cast, reported the fact. Letters now came in from speculators saying their prayers had been answered. In a small way I had done something for religion. I posted the most compelling of the communications in a seminar room at Harvard as an instruction to the young. Presently the market recovered, and my mail returned to normal.

On a more immediately relevant occasion, in the autumn of 1986, my attention became focused on the speculative buildup then taking place in the stock market, the casino manifestations in program and index trading and the related enthusiasms emanating from corporate raiding, leveraged buyouts and the mergers-and-acquisitions mania. *The New York Times* asked me to write an article on the subject; I more than willingly complied.

Sadly, when my treatise was completed, it was thought by the *Times* editors to be too alarming. I had made clear that the markets were in one of their classically euphoric moods and said that a crash was inevitable, while thoughtfully avoiding any prediction as to precisely when. In early 1987, *The Atlantic* published with pleasure what the *Times* had declined. (The *Times* later relented and arranged with *The Atlantic* editors for publication of an interview that covered much of the same ground.) However, until the crash of October 19 of that year, the response to the piece was both sparse and unfavorable. "Galbraith doesn't like to see people making money" was one of the more corroding observations. After October 19, however, almost everyone I met told me that he had read and admired the article; on the day of the crash itself, some 40 journalists and television commentators from Tokyo, across the United States and on to Paris and Milan called me for comment. Clearly, given the nature of the euphoric mood and the vested interest therein, the critic must wait until after the crash for any approval, not to say applause.

To summarize: The euphoric episode is protected and sustained by the will of those who are involved, in order to justify the circumstances that are making them rich. And it is equally protected by the will to ignore, exorcise or condemn those who express doubts.

In Goldman, Sachs We Trust

[*from* The Great Crash, 1929]

The most successful book, by publishing standards, that I ever wrote was The Great Crash, 1929. *A history of the 1929 disaster with its later painful repercussions, it first appeared in 1955 and is still in print today; on occasion it sells more copies than all my other books combined. The reason for its durability is simple: a citizen of sense, encountering someone deeply involved with the imaginative technology of recent times and the speculative enthusiasm surrounding it, advises, "You should read Galbraith on 1929."*

The central speculative episode of that earlier age turned on the investment trust, of which a leading sponsor was the reputable firm of Goldman, Sachs. This was their contribution to a by no means rare exercise in financial insanity. Goldman, Sachs has since restored its reputation, but a new set of financial innovations, many of them attached to technology, have taken the place of the investment trust and other ventures of the time.

*   *   *   *

T HE RECONDITE PROBLEMS of Federal Reserve policy were not the only questions that were agitating Wall Street intellectuals in the early months of 1929. There was worry that the country might be running out of common stocks. One reason prices of stocks were so high, it was explained, was that there weren't enough to go around, and, accordingly, they had acquired a "scarcity value." Some issues, it was said, were becoming so desirable that they would soon be taken out of the market and would not reappear at any price.

If, indeed, common stocks were becoming scarce, it was in spite of as extraordinary a response of supply to demand as any in the history of that well-worn relationship. Without doubt, the most striking feature of the financial era which ended in the autumn of 1929 was the desire of people to buy securities and the effect of this on values. But the increase in the number of securities to buy was hardly less striking. And the ingenuity and zeal with which companies were devised in which securities might be sold was as remarkable as anything.

Not all of the increase in the volume of securities in 1928 and 1929 was for the sole purpose of accommodating the speculator. It was a good time to raise money for general corporate purposes. Investors would supply capital with enthusiasm and without tedious questions. (Seaboard Air Line was a speculative favorite of the period in part because many supposed it to be an aviation stock with growth possibilities whereas, in fact, it was a railroad.) In these years of prosperity men with a vision of still greater prosperity stretching on and on and forever naturally saw the importance of being well provided with plant and working capital. This was no time to be niggardly.

Also, it was an age of consolidation, and each new merger required, inevitably, some new capital and a new issue of securities to pay for it. A word must be said about the merger movement of the nineteen-twenties.

It was not the first such movement but, in many respects, it was the first of its kind. Just before and just after the turn of the century, in industry after industry, small companies were combined into large ones. The United States Steel Corporation, International Harvester, International Nickel, American Tobacco and numerous other of the great corporations trace to this period. In these cases the firms which were combined produced the same or related products for the same national market. The primary motivation in all but the rarest cases was to reduce, eliminate or regularize competition. Each of the new giants dominated an industry and henceforth exercised measurable control over prices and production, and perhaps also over investment and the rate of technological innovation.

A few such mergers occurred in the twenties. Mostly, however, the mergers of this period brought together not firms in competition with each other but firms doing the same thing in different communities. Local electric, gas, water, bus and milk companies were united in great regional or national systems. The purpose was to eliminate not competition but rather the incompetence, somnambulance, naïveté or even the unwarranted integrity of local managements. In the twenties, a man in Wall Street or Chicago could take unabashed pride in the fact that he was a financial genius. The local owners and managers were not. There was no false modesty when it came to citing the advantages of displacing yokels with a central management of decent sophistication.

In the case of utilities the instrument for accomplishing this centralization of management and control was the holding company. It bought control of the operating companies. On occasion they bought control of other holding companies, which controlled yet other holding companies, which in turn, directly or indirectly through yet other holding companies, controlled the operating companies. Everywhere local power, gas and water companies passed into the possession of a holding-company system.

Food retailing, variety stores, department stores and motion picture theatres showed a similar, although not precisely identical, development. Here, too, local ownership gave way to central direction and control. The instrument of this centralization, however, was not the holding company but the corporate chain. These chains, more often than not, established new outlets instead of taking over existing businesses.

The holding companies issued securities in order to buy operating properties, and the chains issued securities in order to build new stores and theatres. While in the years before 1929 the burgeoning utility systems — Associated Gas and Electric, Commonwealth and Southern and the Insull companies — attracted great attention, the chains were at least as symbolic of the era. Montgomery Ward was

one of the prime speculative favorites of the period; it owed its eminence to the fact that it was a chain and thus had a particularly
bright future. The same was true of Woolworth, American Stores
and others. Interest in branch and chain banking was also strong,
and it was widely felt that state and federal laws were an archaic barrier to a consolidation which would knit the small-town and small-
city banks into a few regional and national systems. Various arrangements for defeating the intent of the law, most notably bank
holding companies, were highly regarded.

Inevitably promoters organized some new companies merely to
capitalize on the public interest in industries with a new and wide
horizon and to provide securities to sell. Radio and aviation stocks
were believed to have a particularly satisfactory prospect, and companies were formed which never had more than a prospect. In
September 1929, an advertisement in *The New York Times* called attention to the impending arrival of television and said with considerable prescience that the "commercial possibilities of this new art
defy imagination." The ad opined, somewhat less presciently, that
sets would be in use in homes that fall. However, in the main, the
market boom of 1929 was rooted directly or indirectly in existing industries and enterprises. New and fanciful issues for new and fanciful purposes, ordinarily so important in times of speculation,
played a relatively small part. No significant amount of stock was
sold in companies "To make Salt Water Fresh — For building of
Hospitals for Bastard Children — For building of Ships against Pi-
rates — For importing a Number of large Jack Asses from Spain," or
even "For a Wheel of Perpetual Motion," to cite a representative list
of promotions at the time of the South Sea Bubble.[1]

II

The most notable piece of speculative architecture of the late twenties, and the one by which, more than any other device, the public
demand for common stocks was satisfied, was the investment trust
or company. The investment trust did not promote new enterprises
or enlarge old ones. It merely arranged that people could own stock

in old companies through the medium of new ones. Even in the United States, in the twenties, there were limits to the amount of real capital which existing enterprises could use or new ones could be created to employ. The virtue of the investment trust was that it brought about an almost complete divorce of the volume of corporate securities outstanding from the volume of corporate assets in existence. The former could be twice, thrice or any multiple of the latter. The volume of underwriting business and of securities available for trading on the exchanges all expanded accordingly. So did the securities to own, for the investment trusts sold more securities than they bought. The difference went into the call market, real estate or the pockets of the promoters. It is hard to imagine an invention better suited to the time or one better designed to eliminate the anxiety about the possible shortage of common stocks.

The idea of the investment trust is an old one, although, oddly enough, it came late to the United States. Since the eighteen-eighties in England and Scotland, investors, mostly smaller ones, had pooled their resources by buying stock in an investment company. The latter, in turn, invested the funds so secured. A typical trust held securities in from five hundred to a thousand operating companies. As a result, the man with a few pounds, or even a few hundred, was able to spread his risk far more widely than were he himself to invest. And the management of the trusts could be expected to have a far better knowledge of companies and prospects in Singapore, Madras, Capetown and the Argentine, places to which British funds regularly found their way, than could the widow in Bristol or the doctor in Glasgow. The smaller risk and better information well justified the modest compensation of those who managed the enterprise. Despite some early misadventures, the investment trusts soon became an established part of the British scene.

Before 1921 in the United States only a few small companies existed for the primary purpose of investing in the securities of other companies.[2] In that year, interest in investment trusts began to develop, partly as the result of a number of newspaper and magazine articles describing the English and Scottish trusts. The United States, it was pointed out, had not been keeping abreast of the times;

other countries were excelling in fiduciary innovation. Soon, however, we began to catch up. More trusts were organized, and by the beginning of 1927 an estimated 160 were in existence. Another 140 were formed during that year.[3]

The managers of the British trusts normally enjoyed the greatest of discretion in investing the funds placed at their disposal. At first the American promoters were wary of asking for such a vote of confidence. Many of the early trusts were trusts — the investor bought an interest in a specified assortment of securities which were then deposited with a trust company. At the least the promoters committed themselves to a rigorous set of rules on the kinds of securities to be purchased and the way they were to be held and managed. But as the twenties wore along, such niceties disappeared. The investment trust became, in fact, an investment corporation.[4] It sold its securities to the public — sometimes just common stock, more often common and preferred stock, debenture and mortgage bonds — and the proceeds were then invested as the management saw fit. Any possible tendency of the common stockholder to interfere with the management was prevented by selling him non-voting stock or having him assign his voting rights to a management-controlled voting trust.

For a long time the New York Stock Exchange looked with suspicion on the investment trusts; only in 1929 was listing permitted. Even then the Committee on the Stock List required an investment trust to post with the Exchange the book and market value of the securities held at the time of listing and once a year thereafter to provide an inventory of its holdings. This provision confined the listing of most of the investment trusts to the New York Curb Exchange and to the Boston, Chicago or other road company exchanges. Apart from its convenience, this refusal to disclose holdings was thought to be a sensible precaution. Confidence in the investment judgment of the managers of the trusts was very high. To reveal the stocks they were selecting might, it was said, set off a dangerous boom in the securities they favored. Historians have told with wonder of one of the promotions at the time of the South Sea Bubble. It was "for an Undertaking which shall in due time be revealed." The stock is said to have sold exceedingly well. As promotions, the investment trusts were, on the record, more wonderful. They were undertakings the nature of which was never to be revealed, and their stock also sold exceedingly well.

III

During 1928 an estimated 186 investment trusts were organized; by the early months of 1929 they were being promoted at the rate of approximately one each business day, and a total of 265 made their appearance during the course of the year. In 1927 the trusts sold to the public about $400,000,000 worth of securities; in 1929 they marketed an estimated three billions worth. This was at least a third of all the new capital issues in that year; by the autumn of 1929 the total assets of the investment trusts were estimated to exceed eight billions of dollars. They had increased approximately elevenfold since the beginning of 1927.[5]

The parthenogenesis of an investment trust differed from that of an ordinary corporation. In nearly all cases it was sponsored by another company, and by 1929 a surprising number of different kinds of concerns were bringing the trusts into being. Investment banking houses, commercial banks, brokerage firms, securities dealers and, most important, other investment trusts were busy giving birth to new trusts. The sponsors ranged in dignity from the House of Morgan, sponsor of the United and Alleghany Corporations, down to one Chauncey D. Parker, the head of a fiscally perilous investment banking firm in Boston, who organized three investment trusts in 1929 and sold $25,000,000 worth of securities to an eager public. Chauncey then lost most of the proceeds and lapsed into bankruptcy.[6]

Sponsorship of a trust was not without its rewards. The sponsoring firm normally executed a management contract with its offspring. Under the usual terms, the sponsor ran the investment trust, invested its funds and received a fee based on a percentage of capital or earnings. Were the sponsor a stock exchange firm, it also received commissions on the purchase and sale of securities for its trust.

Many of the sponsors were investment banking firms, which meant, in effect, that the firm was manufacturing securities it could then bring to market. This was an excellent way of insuring an adequate supply of business.

The enthusiasm with which the public sought to buy investment trust securities brought the greatest rewards of all. Almost invariably people were willing to pay a sizable premium over the offering price. The sponsoring firm (or *its* promoters) received allotments of stock or warrants which entitled them to stock at the offering price. These they were then able to sell at once at a profit. Thus one of the enterprises of the Mr. Chauncey D. Parker just mentioned — a company with the resounding name of Seaboard Utilities Shares Corporation — issued 1,600,000 shares of common stock on which the company netted $10.32 a share. That, however, was not the price paid by the public. It was the price at which the stock was issued to Parker and his colleagues. They in turn sold their shares to the public at from $11 to $18.25 and split the profit with the dealers who marketed the securities.[7]

Operations of this sort were not confined to the lowly or the vaguely disreputable. J. P. Morgan and Company, which (with Bonbright and Company) sponsored United Corporation in January 1929, offered a package of one share of common stock and one of preferred to a list of friends, Morgan partners included, at $75. This was a bargain. When trading in United Corporation began a week later, the price was 92 bid, 94 asked on the over-the-counter market, and after four days the stock reached 99. Stock that had been taken up at 75 could be and was promptly resold at these prices.[8] That such agreeable incentives greatly stimulated the organization of new investment trusts is hardly surprising.

IV

There were some, indeed, who only regretted that everyone could not participate in the gains from these new engines of financial progress. One of those who had benefited from the United Corporation promotion just mentioned was John J. Raskob. As Chairman of the Democratic National Committee, he was also politically committed to a firm friendship for the people. He believed that everyone should be in on the kind of opportunities he himself enjoyed.

One of the fruits of this generous impulse during the year was an article in the *Ladies' Home Journal* with the attractive title, "Everybody Ought to Be Rich." In it Mr. Raskob pointed out that anyone who saved fifteen dollars a month, invested it in sound common stocks, and spent no dividends would be worth — as it then appeared — some eighty thousand dollars after twenty years. Obviously, at this rate, a great many people could be rich.

But there was the twenty-year delay. Twenty years seemed a long time to get rich, especially in 1929, and for a Democrat and friend of the people to commit himself to such gradualism was to risk being thought a reactionary. Mr. Raskob, therefore, had a further suggestion. He proposed an investment trust which would be specifically designed to allow the poor man to increase his capital just as the rich man was doing.

The plan, which Mr. Raskob released to the public in the early summer of 1929, was worked out in some detail. (The author stated that he had discussed it with "financiers, economists, theorists, professors, bankers, labor leaders, industrial leaders, and many men of no prominence who have ideas.") A company would be organized to buy stocks. The proletarian with, say, $200 would turn over his pittance to the company which would then buy stocks in the rather less meager amount of $500. The additional $300 the company would get from a financial subsidiary organized for the purpose, and with which it would post all of the stock as collateral. The incipient capitalist would pay off his debt at the rate of perhaps $25 a month. He would, of course, get the full benefit of the increase in the value of the stock, and this was something that Mr. Raskob regarded as inevitable. Hammering home the inadequacy of existing arrangements, Mr. Raskob said: "Now all the man with $200 to $500 to invest can do today is to buy Liberty bonds . . ."[9]

The reaction to the Raskob plan was comparable to the response to a new and daring formulation of the relation of mass to energy. "A practical Utopia," one paper called it. Another described it as "the greatest vision of Wall Street's greatest mind." A tired and cynical commentator was moved to say that it looks "more like financial statesmanship than anything that has come out of Wall Street in many a weary moon."[10]

Had there been a little more time, it seems certain that something would have been made of Mr. Raskob's plan. People were full of enthusiasm for the wisdom and perspicacity of such men. This was admirably indicated by the willingness of people to pay for the genius of the professional financier.

v

The measure of this respect for financial genius was the relation of the market value of the outstanding securities of the investment trusts to the value of the securities it owned. Normally the securities of the trust were worth considerably more than the property in its possession. Sometimes they were worth twice as much. There should be no ambiguity on this point. The only property of the investment trust was the common and preferred stocks and debentures, mortgages, bonds and cash that it owned. (Often it had neither office nor office furniture; the sponsoring firm ran the investment trust out of its own quarters.) Yet, had these securities all been sold on the market, the proceeds would invariably have been less, and often much less, than the current value of the outstanding securities of the investment company. The latter, obviously, had some claim to value which went well beyond the assets behind them.

That premium was, in effect, the value an admiring community placed on professional financial knowledge, skill and manipulative ability. To value a portfolio of stocks "at the market" was to regard it only as inert property. But as the property of an investment trust it was much more, for the portfolio was then combined with the precious ingredient of financial genius. Such special ability could invoke a whole strategy for increasing the value of securities. It could join in pools and syndicates to put up values. It knew when others were doing likewise and could go along. Above all, the financial genius was in on things. It had access to what Mr. Lawrence, a Princeton University economist, described as "the stage whereon is focused the world's most intelligent and best informed judgment of the values of the enterprises which serve men's needs."[11] One might make money investing directly in Radio, J. I. Case or Montgomery Ward, but how much safer and wiser to let it be accomplished by the men of peculiar knowledge and wisdom.

By 1929 the investment trusts were aware of their reputation for omniscience, as well as its importance, and they lost no opportunity to enlarge it. To have a private economist was one possibility, and, as the months passed, a considerable competition developed for those men of adequate reputation and susceptibility. It was a golden age for professors. The American Founders Group, an awe-inspiring family of investment trusts, had as a director Professor Edwin W. Kemmerer, the famous Princeton money expert. The staff economist was Dr. Rufus Tucker, also a well-known figure. (That economists were not yet functioning with perfect foresight is perhaps suggested by the subsequent history of the enterprise. United Founders, the largest company in the group, suffered a net contraction in its assets of $301,385,504 by the end of 1935, and its stock dropped from a high of over $75 a share in 1929 to a little under 75 cents.)[12]

Still another great combine was advised by Dr. David Friday, who had come to Wall Street from the University of Michigan. Friday's reputation for both insight and foresight was breathtaking.

A Michigan trust had three college professors — Irving Fisher of Yale, Joseph S. Davis of Stanford and Edmund E. Day then of Michigan — to advise on its policies.[13] The company stressed not only the diversity of its portfolio but also of its counsel. It was fully protected from any parochial Yale, Stanford or Michigan view of the market.

Other trusts urged the excellence of their genius in other terms. Thus one observed that, since it owned stocks in 120 corporations, it benefited from the "combined efficiency of their presidents, officers and the boards of directors." It noted further that "closely allied to these corporations are the great banking institutions." Then, in something of a logical broad jump, it concluded, "The trust, therefore, mobilizes to a large extent the successful business intellect of the country." Another concern, less skilled in logical method, contented itself with pointing out that "investing is a science instead of a 'one-man job.'"[14]

As 1929 wore along, it was plain that more and more of the new investors in the market were relying on the intellect and the science of the trusts. This meant, of course, that they still had the formidable problem of deciding between the good and the bad trusts. That there were some bad ones was (though barely) recognized. Writing in the March 1929 issue of *The Atlantic Monthly,* Paul C. Cabot stated that dishonesty, inattention, inability and greed were among the common shortcomings of the new industry. These were impressive disadvantages, and as an organizer and officer of a promising investment trust, the State Street Investment Corporation, Mr. Cabot presumably spoke with some authority.[15] However, audience response to such warnings in 1929 was very poor. And the warnings were very infrequent.

V I

Knowledge, manipulative skill or financial genius were not the only magic of the investment trust. There was also leverage. By the summer of 1929, one no longer spoke of investment trusts as such. One referred to high-leverage trusts, low-leverage trusts or trusts without any leverage at all.

The principle of leverage is the same for an investment trust as in the game of crack-the-whip. By the application of well-known physical laws, a modest movement near the point of origin is translated into a major jolt on the extreme periphery. In an investment trust leverage was achieved by issuing bonds, preferred stock as well as common stock to purchase, more or less exclusively, a portfolio of common stocks. When the common stock so purchased rose in value, a tendency which was always assumed, the value of the bonds and preferred stock of the trust was largely unaffected.[16] These securities had a fixed value derived from a specified return. Most or all of the gain from rising portfolio values was concentrated on the common stock of the investment trust, which, as a result, rose marvelously.

Consider, by way of illustration, the case of an investment trust organized in early 1929 with a capital of $150 million — a plausible size by then. Let it be assumed, further, that a third of the capital was realized from the sale of bonds, a third from preferred stock, and the rest from the sale of common stock. If this $150 million were invested, and if the securities so purchased showed a normal appreciation, the portfolio value would have increased by midsummer by about 50 percent. The assets would be worth $225 million. The bonds and preferred stock would still be worth only $100 million; their earnings would not have increased, and they could claim no greater share of the assets in the hypothetical event of a liquidation of the company. The remaining $125 million, therefore, would underlie the value of the common stock of the trust. The latter, in other words, would have increased in asset value from $50 million to $125 million, or by 150 percent, and as the result of an increase of only 50 percent in the value of the assets of the trust as a whole.

This was the magic of leverage, but this was not all of it. Were the common stock of the trust, which had so miraculously increased in value, held by still another trust with similar leverage, the common stock of *that* trust would get an increase of between 700 and 800 percent from the original 50 percent advance. And so forth. In 1929 the discovery of the wonders of the geometric series struck Wall Street with a force comparable to the invention of the wheel. There was a rush to sponsor investment trusts which would sponsor investment trusts, which would, in turn, sponsor investment trusts. The miracle of leverage, moreover, made this a relatively costless operation to the man ultimately behind all of the trusts. One trust having been launched and a share of the common stock having been retained, the capital gains from leverage made it relatively easy to swing a second and larger one which enhanced the gains and made possible a third and still bigger trust.

Thus, Harrison Williams, one of the more ardent exponents of leverage, was thought by the Securities and Exchange Commission to have substantial influence over a combined investment trust and holding company system with a market value in 1929 at close to a billion dollars.[17] This had been built on his original control of a smallish concern — the Central States Electric Corporation — which was worth only some six million dollars in 1921.[18] Leverage was also a prime factor in the remarkable growth of the American Founders Group. The original member of this notable family of investment trusts was launched in 1921. The original promoter was, unhappily, unable to get the enterprise off the ground because he was in bankruptcy. However, the following year a friend contributed $500, with which modest capital a second trust was launched, and the two companies began business. The public reception was highly favorable, and by 1927 the two original companies and a third which had subsequently been added had sold between seventy and eighty million dollars worth of securities to the public.[19] But this was only the beginning; in 1928 and 1929 an explosion of activity struck the Founders Group. Stock was sold to the public at a furious rate. New firms with new names were organized to sell still more stock until, by the end of 1929, there were thirteen companies in the group.

At that time the largest company, the United Founders Corporation, had total resources of $686,165,000. The group as a whole had resources with a market value of more than a billion dollars, which may well have been the largest volume of assets ever controlled by an original outlay of $500. Of the billion dollars, some $320,000,000 was represented by inter-company holdings — the investment of one or another company of the group in the securities of yet others. This fiscal incest was the instrument through which control was maintained and leverage enjoyed. Thanks to this long chain of holdings by one company in another, the increases in values in 1928 and 1929 were effectively concentrated in the value of the common stock of the original companies.

Leverage, it was later to develop, works both ways. Not all of the securities held by the Founders were of a kind calculated to rise indefinitely, much less to resist depression. Some years later the portfolio was found to have contained 5000 shares of Kreuger and Toll, 20,000 shares of Kolo Products Corporation, an adventuresome new company which was to make soap out of banana oil, and $295,000 in the bonds of the Kingdom of Yugoslavia.[20] As Kreuger and Toll moved down to its ultimate value of nothing, leverage was also at work — geometric series are equally dramatic in reverse. But this aspect of the mathematics of leverage was still unrevealed in early 1929, and notice must first be taken of the most dramatic of all the investment company promotions of that remarkable year, those of Goldman, Sachs.

VII

Goldman, Sachs and Company, an investment banking and brokerage partnership, came rather late to the investment trust business. Not until December 4, 1928, less than a year before the stock market crash, did it sponsor the Goldman Sachs Trading Corporation, its initial venture in the field. However, rarely, if ever, in history has an enterprise grown as the Goldman Sachs Trading Corporation and its offspring grew in the months ahead.

The initial issue of stock in the Trading Corporation was a million shares, all of which was bought by Goldman, Sachs and Company at $100 a share for a total of $100,000,000. Ninety percent was then sold to the public at $104. There were no bonds and no preferred stocks; leverage had not yet been discovered by Goldman, Sachs and Company. Control of the Goldman Sachs Trading Corporation remained with Goldman, Sachs and Company by virtue of a management contract and the presence of the partners of the company on the board of the Trading Corporation.[21]

In the two months after its formation, the new company sold some more stock to the public, and on February 21 it merged with another investment trust, the Financial and Industrial Securities Corporation. The assets of the resulting company were valued at $235 million, reflecting a gain of well over 100 percent in under three months. By February 2, roughly three weeks before the merger, the stock for which the original investors had paid $104 was selling for $136.50. Five days later, on February 7, it reached $222.50. At this latter figure it had a value approximately twice that of the current total worth of the securities, cash and other assets owned by the Trading Corporation.

This remarkable premium was not the undiluted result of public enthusiasm for the financial genius of Goldman, Sachs. Goldman, Sachs had considerable enthusiasm for itself, and the Trading Corporation was buying heavily its own securities. By March 14 it had bought 560,724 shares of its own stock for a total outlay of $57,021,936.[22] This, in turn, had boomed their value. However, perhaps foreseeing the exiguous character of an investment company which had its investments all in its own common stock, the Trading Corporation stopped buying itself in March. Then it resold part of the stock to the noted speculator William Crapo Durant, who re-resold it to the public as opportunity allowed.

The spring and early summer were relatively quiet for Goldman, Sachs, but it was a period of preparation. By July 26 the company was ready. On that date the Trading Corporation, jointly with Harrison Williams, launched the Shenandoah Corporation, the first of two remarkable trusts. The initial securities issue by Shenandoah was $102,500,000 (there was an additional issue a couple of months later) and it was reported to have been oversubscribed some sevenfold. There were both preferred and common stock, for by now Goldman, Sachs knew the advantages of leverage. Of the five million shares of common stock in the initial offering, two million were taken by the Trading Corporation, and two million by Central States Electric Corporation on behalf of the co-sponsor, Harrison Williams. Williams was a member of the small board along with partners in Goldman, Sachs. Another board member was a prominent New York attorney whose lack of discrimination in this instance may perhaps be attributed to youthful optimism. It was Mr. John Foster Dulles. The stock of Shenandoah was issued at $17.50. There was brisk trading on a "when issued" basis. It opened at 30, reached a high of 36, and closed at 36, or 18.5 above the issue price. (By the end of the year the price was 8 and a fraction. It later touched fifty cents.)

Meanwhile Goldman, Sachs was already preparing its second tribute to the countryside of Thomas Jefferson, the exponent of small and simple enterprises. This was the even mightier Blue Ridge Corporation, which made its appearance on August 20. Blue Ridge had a capital of $142,000,000, and nothing about it was more remarkable than the fact that it was sponsored by Shenandoah, its precursor by precisely twenty-five days. Blue Ridge had the same board of directors as Shenandoah, including the still optimistic Mr. Dulles, and of its 7,250,000 shares of common stock (there was also a substantial issue of preferred) Shenandoah subscribed a total of 6,250,000. Goldman, Sachs by now was applying leverage with a vengeance.

An interesting feature of Blue Ridge was the opportunity it offered the investor to divest himself of routine securities in direct exchange for the preferred and common stock of the new corporation. A holder of American Telephone and Telegraph Company could receive $4^{70}\!/_{715}$ shares each of Blue Ridge Preference and Common for each share of Telephone stock turned in. The same privilege was extended to holders of Allied Chemical and Dye, Santa Fe, Eastman Kodak, General Electric, Standard Oil of New Jersey and some fifteen other stocks. There was much interest in this offer.

August 20, the birthday of Blue Ridge, was a Tuesday, but there was more work to be done by Goldman, Sachs that week. On Thursday, the Goldman Sachs Trading Corporation announced the acquisition of the Pacific American Associates, a West Coast investment trust which, in turn, had recently bought a number of smaller investment trusts and which owned the American Trust Company, a large commercial bank with numerous branches throughout California. Pacific American had a capital of around a hundred million. In preparation for the merger, the Trading Corporation had issued another $71,400,000 in stock which it had exchanged for capital stock of the American Company, the holding company which owned over 99 percent of the common stock of the American Trust Company.[23]

Having issued more than a quarter of a billion dollars worth of securities in less than a month — an operation that would not then have been unimpressive for the United States Treasury — activity at Goldman, Sachs subsided somewhat. Its members had not been the only busy people during this time. It was a poor day in August and September of that year when no new trust was announced or no large new issue of securities was offered by an old one. Thus, on

August 1, the papers announced the formation of Anglo-American Shares, Inc., a company which, with a touch not often seen in a Delaware corporation, had among its directors the Marquess of Carisbrooke, GCB, GCVO, and Colonel, the Master of Sempill, AFC, otherwise identified as the President of the Royal Aeronautical Society, London. American Insuranstocks Corporation was launched the same day, though boasting no more glamorous a director than William Gibbs McAdoo. On succeeding days came Gude Winmill Trading Corporation, National Republic Investment Trust, Insull Utility Investments, Inc., International Carriers, Ltd., Tri-Continental Allied Corporation and Solvay American Investment Corporation. On August 13 the papers also announced that an Assistant U.S. Attorney had visited the offices of the Cosmopolitan Fiscal Corporation and also an investment service called the Financial Counselor. The law, no less. In both cases the principals were absent. The offices of the Financial Counselor were equipped with a peephole like a speakeasy.

Even more investment trust securities were offered in September of 1929 than in August — the total was above $600 million.[24] However, the nearly simultaneous promotion of Shenandoah and Blue Ridge was to stand as the pinnacle of new era finance. It is difficult not to marvel at the imagination which was implicit in this gargantuan insanity. If there must be madness, something may be said for having it on a heroic scale.

Some years later, on a gray dawn in Washington, the following colloquy occurred before a committee of the United States Senate:[25]

> *Senator Couzens.* Did Goldman, Sachs and Company organize the Goldman Sachs Trading Corporation?
> *Mr. Sachs.* Yes, sir.
> *Senator Couzens.* And it sold its stock to the public?
> *Mr. Sachs.* A portion of it. The firm invested originally in 10 percent of the entire issue for the sum of $10,000,000.
> *Senator Couzens.* And the other 90 percent was sold to the public?
> *Mr. Sachs.* Yes, sir.
> *Senator Couzens.* At what price?

Mr. Sachs. At 104. That is the old stock . . . the stock was split two
for one.
Senator Couzens. And what is the price of the stock now?
Mr. Sachs. Approximately 1¾.

NOTES

1. Walter Bagehot, *Lombard Street,* 1922 ed. (London: John Murray, 1922),
   pp. 130, 131.
2. One estimate puts the number at about forty. Cf. *Investment Trusts and
   Investment Companies,* Pt. I, Report of the Securities and Exchange
   Commission (Washington, 1939), p. 36.
3. Ibid.
4. And would be more accurately described as an investment company or
   investment corporation. However, I have kept here to the less precise
   but more customary usage.
5. The estimates in this paragraph are all from *Investment Trusts and Investment Companies,* Pt. III, Ch. 1, pp. 3, 4.
6. *Investment Trusts and Investment Companies,* Pt. III, Ch. 2, pp. 37 ff.
7. *Investment Trusts and Investment Companies,* Pt. III, Ch. 2, p. 39.
8. *Stock Exchange Practices,* Report (Washington, 1934), pp. 103–104.
9. *The Literary Digest,* June 1, 1929.
10. Ibid.
11. Joseph Stagg Lawrence, *Wall Street and Washington* (Princeton, N.J.:
    Princeton University Press, 1929), p. 163.
12. Bernard J. Reis, *False Security* (New York: Equinox, 1937), pp. 117 ff. and
    296.
13. *Investment Trusts and Investment Companies,* Pt. I, p. 111.
14. *Investment Trusts and Investment Companies,* Pt. I, pp. 61, 62.
15. *Investment Trusts and Investment Companies,* Pt. III, Ch. 1, p. 53.
16. Assuming they were reasonably orthodox. Bonds and preferred stock,
    in these days, were issues with an almost infinite variety of conversion
    and participation rights.
17. Part of it shared with Goldman, Sachs, as will be noted presently. The
    line between a holding company, which has investment in and control
    of an operating company (or another holding company), and an in-
    vestment trust or company, which has investment but which is pre-
    sumed not to have control, is often a shadowy one. The pyramiding of
    holding companies and concomitant leverage effects was also a striking
    feature of the period.
18. *Investment Trusts and Investment Companies,* Pt. III, Ch. 1, pp. 5, 6.

19. *Investment Trusts and Investment Companies,* Pt. I, pp. 98–100.
20. Reis, p. 124.
21. *Stock Exchange Practices,* Hearings, April–June 1932, Pt. 2, pp. 566, 567.
22. Details here are from *Investment Trusts and Investment Companies,* Pt. III, Ch. 1, pp. 6 ff. and 17 ff.
23. Details on Shenandoah, Blue Ridge and the Pacific American merger which are not from the *New York Times* of the period are from *Investment Trusts and Investment Companies,* Pt. III, Ch. 1, pp. 5–7.
24. E. H. H. Simmons, *The Principal Causes of the Stock Market Crisis of Nineteen Twenty-Nine* (address issued in pamphlet form by the New York Stock Exchange, January 1930), p. 16.
25. *Stock Exchange Practices,* Hearings, April–June 1932, Pt. 2, pp. 566–567.

The Crash

[*from* The Great Crash, 1929]

No author can be fully trusted when describing the quality of his own work; I verge on dangerous ground when writing about this piece. It, like the preceding chapter, which was also from The Great Crash, 1929, *has been wonderfully received over the almost fifty years since its publication and in some measure is recognized as* the *history of the great days of that event.*

*   *   *   *

Accorecording to the accepted view of events, by the autumn of 1929 the economy was well into a depression. In June the indexes of industrial and of factory production both reached a peak and turned down. By October, the Federal Reserve index of industrial production stood at 117 as compared with 126 four months earlier. Steel production declined from June on; in October freight-car loadings fell. Home-building, a most mercurial industry, had been falling for several years, and it slumped still farther in 1929. Finally, down came the stock market. A penetrating student of the economic behavior of this period has said that the market slump "reflected, in the main, the change which was already apparent in the industrial situation."[1]

Thus viewed, the stock market is but a mirror which, perhaps as in this instance somewhat belatedly, provides an image of the underlying or *fundamental* economic situation. Cause and effect run from the economy to the stock market, never the reverse. In 1929 the economy was headed for trouble. Eventually that trouble was violently reflected in Wall Street.

In 1929 there were good, or at least strategic, reasons for this view, and it is easy to understand why it became high doctrine. In Wall Street, as elsewhere in 1929, few people wanted a bad depression. In Wall Street, as elsewhere, there is deep faith in the power of incantation. When the market fell, many Wall Street citizens immediately sensed the real danger, which was that income and employment — prosperity in general — would be adversely affected. This had to be prevented. Preventive incantation required that as many important people as possible repeat as firmly as they could that it wouldn't happen. This they did. They explained how the stock market was merely the froth and that the real substance of economic life rested in production, employment and spending, all of which would remain unaffected. No one knew for sure that this was so. As an instrument of economic policy, incantation does not permit of minor doubts or scruples.

In the later years of depression it was important to continue emphasizing the unimportance of the stock market. The depression was an exceptionally disagreeable experience. Wall Street has not always been a cherished symbol in our national life. In some of the devout regions of the nation, those who speculate in stocks — the even more opprobrious term *gamblers* is used — are not counted the greatest moral adornments of our society. Any explanation of the depression that attributed importance to the market collapse would, accordingly, have been taken very seriously, and it would have meant serious trouble for Wall Street. Wall Street, no doubt, would have survived, but there would have been scars. We should be clear that no deliberate conspiracy existed to minimize the consequences of the Wall Street crash for the economy. Rather, it merely appeared to everyone with an instinct for conservative survival that Wall Street had better be kept out of it. It was vulnerable.

In fact, any satisfactory explanation of the events of the autumn of 1929 and thereafter must accord a solid role to the speculative boom and ensuing collapse. Until September or October of 1929, the decline in economic activity was very modest. As I shall argue later, until after the market crash one could reasonably assume that this downward movement might soon reverse itself, as a similar movement had reversed itself in 1927. There were no reasons for expecting disaster. No one could foresee that production, prices, incomes and all other indicators would continue to shrink through three long and dismal years. Only after the market crash were there plausible grounds to suppose that things might now for a long while get a lot worse.

From the foregoing it follows that the crash did not come — as some have suggested — because the market suddenly became aware that a serious depression was in the offing. A depression, serious or otherwise, could not be foreseen when the market fell. There is still the possibility that the downturn in the indexes frightened the speculators, led them to unload their stocks and so punctured a bubble that had, in any case, to be punctured one day. This is more plausible. Some people who were watching the indexes may have been persuaded by this intelligence to sell, and others may then have been encouraged to follow. This is not very important, for it is in the nature of a speculative boom that almost anything can collapse it. Any serious shock to confidence can cause sales by those speculators who have always hoped to get out before the final collapse but after all possible gains from rising prices have been reaped. Their pessimism will infect those simpler souls who had thought the market might go up forever but who now will change their minds and sell. Soon there will be margin calls, and still others will be forced to sell. So the bubble breaks.

Along with the downturn of the indexes, Wall Street has always attributed importance to two other events in the pricking of the bubble. In England on September 20, 1929, the enterprises of Clarence Hatry suddenly collapsed. Hatry was one of those curiously un-English figures with whom the English periodically find themselves unable to cope. Although his earlier financial history had been anything but reassuring, Hatry had built up an industrial and financial empire in the nineteen-twenties of truly impressive proportions. The nucleus, all the more remarkably, was a line of coin-in-the-slot vending and automatic photograph machines. From these unprepossessing enterprises he had marched on into investment trusts and high finance. His expansion owed much to the issuance of unauthorized stock, the increase of assets by the forging of stock certificates and other equally informal financing. In the lore of 1929, the unmasking of Hatry in London is supposed to have struck a sharp blow to confidence in New York.[2]

Ranking with Hatry in this lore was the refusal on October 11 of the Massachusetts Department of Public Utilities to allow Boston Edison to split its stock four to one. As the company argued, such split-ups were much in fashion. To avoid going along was to risk being considered back in the corporate gaslight era. The refusal was unprecedented. Moreover, the Department added insult to injury by announcing an investigation of the company's rates and by suggesting that the present value of the stock, "due to the action of speculators," had reached a level where "no one, in our judgment . . . on the basis of its earnings, would find it to his advantage to buy it."

These were uncouth words. They could have been as important as, conceivably, the exposure of Clarence Hatry. But it could also be that the inherently unstable equilibrium was shattered simply by a spontaneous decision to get out. On September 22, the financial pages of the New York papers carried an advertisement of an investment service with the arresting headline, OVERSTAYING A BULL MARKET. Its message read as follows: "Most investors make money in a bull market, only to lose all profits made — and sometimes more — in the readjustment that inevitably follows." Instead of the downturn in the Federal Reserve industrial index, the exposure of Hatry or the unnatural obstinacy of the Massachusetts Department of Public Utilities, it could have been such thoughts stirring first in dozens and then in hundreds and finally in thousands of breasts which finally brought an end to the boom. What first stirred these doubts we do not know, but neither is it very important that we know.

I I

Confidence did not disintegrate at once. As noted, through September and into October, although the trend of the market was generally down, good days came with the bad. Volume was high. On the New York Stock Exchange sales were nearly always above four million, and frequently above five. In September new issues appeared in even greater volume than in August, and they regularly commanded a premium over the offering price. On September 20 the *Times* noted that the stock of the recently launched Lehman Corporation which had been offered at $104 had sold the day before at $136. (In the case of this well-managed investment trust the public enthusiasm was not entirely misguided.) During September brokers' loans increased by nearly $670 million, by far the largest increase of any month to date. This showed that speculative zeal had not diminished.

Other signs indicated that the gods of the New Era were still in their temples. In its October 12 issue, the *Saturday Evening Post* had a lead story by Isaac F. Marcosson on the notorious Ivar Kreuger. This was a scoop, for Kreuger had previously been inaccessible to journalists. "Kreuger," Marcosson observed, "like Hoover, is an engineer. He has consistently applied engineer precision to the welding of his far-flung industry." And this was not the only resemblance. "Like Hoover," the author added, "Kreuger rules through pure reason."

In the interview Kreuger was remarkably candid on one point. He told Mr. Marcosson: "Whatever success I have had may perhaps be attributable to three things: One is silence, the second is more silence, while the third is still more silence." This was so. Two and a half years later Kreuger committed suicide in his Paris apartment, and shortly thereafter it was discovered that his aversion to divulging information, especially if accurate, had kept even his most intimate acquaintances in ignorance of the greatest fraud in history. His American underwriters, the eminently respectable firm of Lee, Higginson and Company of Boston, had heard nothing and knew nothing. One of the members of the firm, Donald Durant, was a member of the board of directors of the Kreuger enterprises. He had never attended a directors' meeting, and it is certain that he would have been no wiser had he done so.

During the last weeks of October, *Time* magazine, young and not yet omniscient, also featured Kreuger on its cover — "a great admirer of Cecil Rhodes." Then a week later, as though to emphasize its faith in the New Era, it went on to the equally notorious Samuel Insull. (A fortnight after that, its youthful illusions shattered, the weekly newsmagazine gave the place of historic honor to Warden Lawes of Sing Sing.) In these same Indian summer days, *The Wall Street Journal* took notice of the official announcement that Andrew Mellon would remain in the cabinet at least until 1933 (there had been rumors that he might resign) and observed: "Optimism again prevails . . . the announcement . . . did more to restore confidence than anything else." In Germany Charles E. Mitchell, the famous banker, announced that the "industrial condition of the United States is absolutely sound," that too much attention was being paid to brokers' loans, and that "nothing can arrest the upward movement." On October 15, as he sailed for home, he enlarged on the point: "The markets generally are now in a healthy condition . . . values have a sound basis in the general prosperity of our country." That same evening Professor Irving Fisher made his historic announcement that "stock prices have reached what looks like a permanently high plateau" and added, "I expect to see the stock market a good deal higher than it is today within a few months." Indeed, the only disturbing thing, in these October days, was the fairly steady downward drift in the market.

III

On Saturday, October 19, Washington dispatches reported that Secretary of Commerce Lamont was having trouble finding the $100,000 in public funds that would be required to pay the upkeep of the yacht *Corsair* which J. P. Morgan had just given the government. (Morgan's deprivation was not extreme: a new $3,000,000

Corsair was being readied at Bath, Maine.) There were other and more compelling indications of an unaccustomed stringency. The papers told of a very weak market the day before — there were heavy declines on late trading, and the *Times* industrial average had dropped about 7 points. Steel had lost 7 points; General Electric, Westinghouse and Montgomery Ward all lost 6. Meanwhile, that day's market was behaving very badly. In the second heaviest Saturday trading in history, 3,488,100 shares changed hands. At the close the *Times* industrials were down 12 points. The blue chips were seriously off, and speculative favorites had gone into a nosedive. J. I. Case, for example, had fallen a full 40 points.

On Sunday the market was front-page news — the *Times* headline read, "Stocks driven down as wave of selling engulfs the market," and the financial editor the next day reported for perhaps the tenth time that the end had come. (He had learned, however, to hedge. "For the time at any rate," he said, "Wall Street seemed to see the reality of things.") No immediate explanation of the break was forthcoming. The Federal Reserve had long been quiet. Babson had said nothing new. Hatry and the Massachusetts Department of Public Utilities were from a week to a month in the past. They became explanations only later.

The papers that Sunday carried three comments which were to become familiar in the days that followed. After Saturday's trading, it was noted, quite a few margin calls went out. This meant that the value of stock which the recipients held on margin had declined to the point where it was no longer sufficient collateral for the loan that had paid for it. The speculator was being asked for more cash.

The other two observations were more reassuring. The papers agreed, and this was also the informed view on Wall Street, that the worst was over. And it was predicted that on the following day the market would begin to receive organized support. Weakness, should it appear, would be tolerated no longer.

Never was there a phrase with more magic than "organized support." Almost immediately it was on every tongue and in every news story about the market. Organized support meant that powerful people would organize to keep prices of stocks at a reasonable level.

Opinions differed as to who would organize this support. Some had in mind the big operators like Cutten, Durant and Raskob. They, of all people, couldn't afford a collapse. Some thought of the bankers — Charles Mitchell had acted once before, and certainly if things got bad, he would act again. Some had in mind the investment trusts. They held huge portfolios of common stocks, and obviously they could not afford to have them become cheap. Also, they had cash. So if stocks did become cheap, the investment trusts would be in the market picking up bargains. This would mean that the bargains wouldn't last. With so many people wanting to avoid a further fall, a further fall would clearly be avoided.

In the ensuing weeks the Sabbath pause had a marked tendency to breed uneasiness, doubts, pessimism and a decision to get out on Monday. This, it seems certain, was what happened on Sunday, October 20.

IV

Monday, October 21, was a very poor day. Sales totaled 6,091,870, the third greatest volume in history, and some tens of thousands who were watching the market throughout the country made a disturbing discovery. There was no way of telling what was happening. Previously on big days of the bull market the ticker had often fallen behind, and one didn't discover until well after the market closed how much richer one had become. But the experience with a falling market had been much more limited. Not since March had the ticker fallen seriously behind on declining values. Many now learned for the first time that they could be ruined, totally and forever, and not even know it. And if they were not ruined, there was a strong tendency to imagine it. From the opening on the 21st, the ticker lagged, and by noon it was an hour late. Not until an hour and forty minutes after the close of the market did it record the last transaction. Every ten minutes prices of selected stocks were printed on the bond ticker, but the wide divergence between these and the prices on the tape only added to the uneasiness — and to the growing conviction that it might be best to sell.

Things, though bad, were still not hopeless. Toward the end of Monday's trading the market rallied, and final prices were above the lows for the day. The net losses were considerably less than on Saturday. Tuesday brought a somewhat shaky gain. As so often before, the market seemed to be showing its ability to come back. People got ready to record the experience as merely another setback, of which there had been so many previously.

In doing so, they were helped by the two men who now were recognized as Wall Street's official prophets. On Monday in New York, Professor Irving Fisher said that the decline had represented only a "shaking out of the lunatic fringe." He went on to explain why he felt that the prices of stocks during the boom had not caught up with their real value and would go higher. Among other things, the market had not yet reflected the beneficent effects of prohibition which had made the American worker "more productive and dependable."

On Tuesday, Charles E. Mitchell dropped anchor in New York with the observation that "the decline had gone too far." (Time and sundry congressional and court proceedings were to show that Mr. Mitchell had strong personal reasons for feeling that way.) He added that conditions were "fundamentally sound," said again that too much attention had been paid to the large volume of brokers' loans, and concluded that the situation was one which would correct itself if left alone. However, another jarring suggestion came from Babson. He recommended selling stocks and buying gold.

By Wednesday, October 23, the effect of this cheer was somehow dissipated. Instead of further gains there were heavy losses. The opening was quiet enough, but toward midmorning motor accessory stocks were sold heavily, and volume began to increase throughout the list. The last hour was quite phenomenal — 2,600,000 shares changed hands at rapidly declining prices. The *Times* industrial average for the day dropped from 415 to 384, giving up all of its gains since the end of the previous June. Tel and Tel lost 15 points; General Electric, 20; Westinghouse, 25; and J. I. Case, another 46. Again the ticker was far behind, and to add to the uncertainty an ice storm in the Middle West caused widespread disruption of communications. That afternoon and evening thousands of speculators decided to get out while — as they mistakenly supposed — the getting was good. Other thousands were told they had no choice but to get out unless they posted more collateral, for, as the day's business came to an end, an unprecedented volume of margin calls went out. Speaking in Washington, even Professor Fisher was fractionally less optimistic. He told a meeting of bankers that "security values *in most instances* were not inflated." However, he did not weaken on the unrealized efficiencies of prohibition.

The papers that night went to press with a souvenir of a fast departing era. Formidable advertisements announced subscription rights in a new offering of certificates in Aktiebolaget Kreuger and Toll at $23. There was also one bit of cheer. It was predicted that on the morrow the market would surely begin to receive "organized support."

V

Thursday, October 24, is the first of the days that history — such as it is on the subject — identifies with the panic of 1929. Measured by disorder, fright and confusion, it deserves to be so regarded. That day 12,894,650 shares changed hands, many of them at prices which shattered the dreams and the hopes of those who had owned them. Of all the mysteries of the stock exchange there is none so impenetrable as why there should be a buyer for everyone who seeks to sell. October 24, 1929, showed that what is mysterious is not inevitable. Often there were no buyers, and only after wide vertical declines could anyone be induced to bid.

The panic did not last all day. It was a phenomenon of the morning hours. The market opening itself was unspectacular, and for a while prices were firm. Volume, however, was very large, and soon prices began to sag. Once again the ticker dropped behind. Prices fell farther and faster, and the ticker lagged more and more. By eleven o'clock the market had degenerated into a wild, mad scramble to sell. In the crowded boardrooms across the country the ticker told of a frightful collapse. But the selected quotations coming in over the bond ticker also showed that current values were far below the ancient history of the tape. The uncertainty led more and more people to try to sell. Others, no longer able to respond to margin calls, were sold out. By eleven-thirty the market had surrendered to blind, relentless fear. This, indeed, was panic.

Outside the Exchange in Broad Street a weird roar could be heard. A crowd gathered. Police Commissioner Grover Whalen became aware that something was happening and dispatched a special police detail to Wall Street to insure the peace. More people came and waited, though apparently no one knew for what. A workman appeared atop one of the high buildings to accomplish some repairs, and the multitude assumed he was a would-be suicide and waited impatiently for him to jump. Crowds also formed around the branch offices of brokerage firms throughout the city and, indeed, throughout the country. Word of what was happening, or what was thought to be happening, was passed out by those who were within sight of the board. An observer thought that people's expressions showed "not so much suffering as a sort of horrified incredulity."[3] Rumor after rumor swept Wall Street. Stocks were now selling for nothing. The Chicago and Buffalo Exchanges had closed. A suicide wave was in progress, and eleven well-known speculators had already killed themselves.

At twelve-thirty the officials of the New York Stock Exchange closed the visitors gallery on the wild scenes below. One of the visitors who had just departed was showing his remarkable ability to be on hand for history. He was the former Chancellor of the Exchequer, Mr. Winston Churchill. It was he who in 1925 returned Britain to the gold standard and the overvalued pound. Accordingly, he was responsible for the strain which sent Montagu Norman to plead in New York for easier money, which caused credit to be eased at the fatal time, which, in this academy view, in turn caused the boom. Now Churchill, it could be imagined, was viewing his awful handiwork.

There is no record of anyone's having reproached him. Economics was never his strong point, so (and wisely) it seems most unlikely that he reproached himself.

VI

In New York at least, the panic was over by noon. At noon the organized support appeared.

At twelve o'clock reporters learned that a meeting was convening at 23 Wall Street at the offices of J. P. Morgan and Company. The word quickly passed as to who was there — Charles E. Mitchell, the Chairman of the Board of the National City Bank, Albert H. Wiggin, the Chairman of the Chase National Bank, William C. Potter, the President of the Guaranty Trust Company, Seward Prosser, the Chairman of the Bankers Trust Company, and the host, Thomas W. Lamont, the senior partner of Morgan's. According to legend, during the panic of 1907 the elder Morgan had brought to a halt the discussion of whether to save the tottering Trust Company of America by saying that the place to stop the panic was there. It was stopped. Now, twenty-two years later, that drama was being re-enacted. The elder Morgan was dead. His son was in Europe. But equally determined men were moving in. They were the nation's most powerful financiers. They had not yet been pilloried and maligned by New Dealers. The very news that they would act would release people from the fear to which they had surrendered.

It did. A decision was quickly reached to pool resources to support the market.[4] The meeting broke up, and Thomas Lamont met with reporters. His manner was described as serious, but his words were reassuring. In what Frederick Lewis Allen later called one of the most remarkable understatements of all time,[5] he told the newspapermen, "There has been a little distress selling on the Stock Exchange." He added that this was "due to a technical condition of the market" rather than any fundamental cause, and told the newsmen that things were "susceptible to betterment." The bankers, he let it be known, had decided to better things.

The news had already reached the floor of the Exchange that the bankers were meeting, and the ticker had spread the magic word afield. Prices firmed at once and started to rise. Then at one-thirty Richard Whitney appeared on the floor and went to the post where U.S. Steel was traded. Whitney was perhaps the best-known figure on the floor. He was one of the group of men of good background and appropriate education who, in that time, were expected to manage the affairs of the Exchange. Currently he was vice-president of the Exchange, but in the absence of E. H. H. Simmons in Hawaii he was serving as acting president. What was much more important at the moment, he was known as the floor trader for Morgan's and, indeed, his older brother was a Morgan partner.

As he made his way through the teeming crowd, Whitney appeared debonair and self-confident — some later described his manner as jaunty. (His own firm dealt largely in bonds, so it is improbable that he had been much involved in the turmoil of the morning.) At the Steel post he bid 205 for 10,000 shares. This was the price of the last sale, and the current bids were several points lower. In an operation that was totally devoid of normal commercial reticence, he got 200 shares and then left the rest of the order with the specialist. He continued on his way, placing similar orders for fifteen or twenty other stocks.

This was it. The bankers, obviously, had moved in. The effect was electric. Fear vanished and gave way to concern lest the new advance be missed. Prices boomed upward.

The bankers had, indeed, brought off a notable coup. Prices as they fell that morning kept crossing a large volume of stop-loss orders — orders calling for sales whenever a specified price was reached. Brokers had placed many of these orders for their own protection on the securities of customers who had not responded to calls for additional margin. Each of these stop-loss orders tripped more securities into the market and drove prices down farther. Each spasm of liquidation thus insured that another would follow. It was this literal chain reaction the bankers checked, and they checked it decisively.

In the closing hour, selling orders continuing to come in from across the country turned the market soft once more. Still, in its own way, the recovery on Black Thursday was as remarkable as the selling that made the day so black. The *Times* industrials were off only 12 points, or a little more than a third of the loss of the previous day. Steel, the stock that Whitney had singled out to start the recovery, had opened that morning at 205½, a point or two above the previous close. At the lowest it was down to 193½ for a 12-point loss.[6] Then it recovered to close at 206 for a surprising net gain of 2 points for the day. Montgomery Ward, which had opened at 83 and gone to 50, came back to 74. General Electric was at one point 32 points below its opening price and then came back 25 points. On the Curb, Goldman Sachs Trading Corporation opened at 81, dropped to 65, and then came back to 80. J. I. Case, maintaining a reputation for eccentric behavior that had brought much risk capital into the threshing-machine business, made a new gain of 7 points for the day. Many had good reason to be grateful to the financial leaders of Wall Street.

VII

Not everyone could be grateful, to be sure. Across the country people were only dimly aware of the improvement. By early afternoon, when the market started up, the ticker was hours behind. Although the spot quotations on the bond ticker showed the improvement, the ticker itself continued to grind out the most dismal of news. And the news on the ticker was what counted. To many, many watchers it meant that they had been sold out and that their dream — in fact, their brief reality — of opulence had gone glimmering, together with home, car, furs, jewelry and reputation. That the market, after breaking them, had recovered was the most chilling of comfort.

It was eight and a half minutes past seven that night before the ticker finished recording the day's misfortunes. In the boardrooms speculators who had been sold out since morning sat silently watching the tape. The habit of months or years, however idle it had now become, could not be abandoned at once. Then, as the final trades were registered, the ruined investors, sorrowfully or grimly according to their nature, made their way out into the gathering night.

In Wall Street itself lights blazed from every office as clerks struggled to come abreast of the day's business. Messengers and boardroom boys, caught up in the excitement and untroubled by losses, went skylarking through the streets until the police arrived to quell them. Representatives of thirty-five of the largest wire houses assembled at the offices of Hornblower and Weeks and told the press on departing that the market was "fundamentally sound" and "technically in better condition than it has been in months." It was the unanimous view of those present that the worst had passed. The host firm dispatched a market letter which stated that "commencing with today's trading the market should start laying the foundation for the constructive advance which we believe will characterize 1930." Charles E. Mitchell announced that the trouble was "purely technical" and that "fundamentals remained unimpaired." Senator Carter Glass said the trouble was due largely to Charles E. Mitchell. Senator Wilson of Indiana attributed the crash to Democratic resistance to a higher tariff.

VIII

On Friday and Saturday trading continued heavy — just under six million on Friday and over two million at the short session on Saturday. Prices, on the whole, were steady — the averages were a trifle up on Friday but slid off on Saturday. It was thought that the bankers were able to dispose of most of the securities they had acquired while shoring up the market on Thursday. Not only were things better, but everyone was clear as to who had made them so. The bankers had shown both their courage and their power, and the people applauded warmly and generously. The financial community, the *Times* said, now felt "secure in the knowledge that the most powerful banks in the country stood ready to prevent a recurrence [of panic]." As a result it had "relaxed its anxiety."

Perhaps never before or since have so many people taken the measure of economic prospects and found them so favorable as in the two days following the Thursday disaster. The optimism even included a note of self-congratulation. Colonel Ayres, a notable figure in Cleveland, thought that no other country could have come through such a bad crash so well. Others pointed out that the prospects for business were good and that the stock market debacle would not make them any less favorable. No one knew, but it cannot be stressed too frequently, that for effective incantation knowledge is neither necessary nor assumed.

Eugene M. Stevens, the President of the Continental Illinois Bank, said, "There is nothing in the business situation to justify any nervousness." Walter Teagle said there had been no "fundamental change" in the oil business to justify concern; Charles M. Schwab said that the steel business had been making "fundamental progress" toward stability and added that this "fundamentally sound condition" was responsible for the prosperity of the industry; Samuel Vauclain, Chairman of the Baldwin Locomotive Works, declared that "fundamentals are sound"; President Hoover said that "the fundamental business of the country, that is production and distribution of commodities, is on a sound and prosperous basis." The President was asked to say something more specific about the market — for example, that stocks were now cheap — but he refused.[7]

Many others joined in. Howard C. Hopson, the head of Associated Gas and Electric, omitted the standard reference to fundamentals and thought it was "undoubtedly beneficial to the business interests of the country to have the gambling type of speculator eliminated." (Mr. Hopson, himself a speculator, although more of the sure-thing type, was also eliminated in due course.) A Boston investment trust took space in *The Wall Street Journal* to say, "S-T-E-A-D-Y Everybody! Calm thinking is in order. Heed the words of America's greatest bankers." A single dissonant note, though great in portent, went unnoticed. Speaking in Poughkeepsie, Governor Franklin D. Roosevelt criticized the "fever of speculation."

On Sunday there were sermons suggesting that a certain measure of divine retribution had been visited on the Republic and that it had not been entirely unmerited. People had lost sight of spiritual values in their single-minded pursuit of riches. Now they had had their lesson.

Almost everyone believed that the heavenly knuckle-rapping was over and that speculation could now be resumed in earnest. The papers were full of the prospects for next week's market.

Stocks, it was agreed, were again cheap, and, accordingly, there would be a heavy rush to buy. Numerous stories from the brokerage houses, some of them possibly inspired, told of a fabulous volume of buying orders which was piling up in anticipation of the opening of the market. In a concerted advertising campaign in Monday's papers, stock market firms urged the wisdom of picking up these bargains promptly. "We believe," said one house, "that the investor who purchases securities at this time with the discrimination that is always a condition of prudent investing, may do so with utmost confidence." On Monday the real disaster began.

NOTES

1. Thomas Wilson, *Fluctuations in Income and Employment,* 3rd ed. (New York: Pitman, 1948), p. 143.
2. Hatry pleaded guilty and early in 1930 was given a long jail sentence.
3. Edwin Lefèvre, "The Little Fellow in Wall Street," *The Saturday Evening Post,* January 4, 1930.
4. The amounts to be contributed or otherwise committed were never specified. Frederick Lewis Allen (*Only Yesterday* [New York: Harper, 1931], pp. 329–330) says that each of the institutions, along with George F. Baker, Jr., of the First National, who later joined the pool, put up $40 million. This total — $240 million — seems much too large to be plausible. *The New York Times* subsequently suggested (March 9, 1938) that the total was some $20 to $30 million.
5. Allen, p. 330.
6. Quotations have normally been rounded to the nearest whole number in this history. The Steel quotation on this day seems to call for an exception.
7. This was stated by Garet Garrett in *The Saturday Evening Post* (December 28, 1929) and it is generally confirmed by Mr. Hoover in his memoirs. According to Mr. Garrett the bankers' consortium asked the President for the statement, which suggests that the reassurance, like the support, was tolerably well organized.

Things Become More Serious

[*from* The Great Crash, 1929]

As do all periods of financial exuberance and insanity, the turbulent year of 1929 came to an end. The crash in October was a major episode in American history. Much of what was subsequently written focused on October 24, although a large part of the sorrow, suffering and financial disaster came in the aftermath.

*   *   *   *

IN THE AUTUMN of 1929, the New York Stock Exchange, under roughly its present constitution, was 112 years old. During this lifetime it had seen some difficult days. On September 18, 1873, the firm of Jay Cooke and Company failed, and, as a more or less direct result, so did fifty-seven other Stock Exchange firms in the next few weeks. On October 23, 1907, call money rates reached 125 percent in the panic of that year. On September 16, 1920 — the autumn months are the off season in Wall Street — a bomb exploded in front of Morgan's next door, killing thirty people and injuring a hundred more.

A common feature of all these earlier troubles was that having happened, they were over. The worst was reasonably recognizable as such. The singular feature of the Great Crash of 1929 was that the worst continued to worsen. What looked one day like the end proved on the next day to have been only the beginning. Nothing could have been more ingeniously designed to maximize the suffering, and also to insure that as few as possible escaped the common misfortune. The fortunate speculator who had funds to answer the first margin call presently got another and equally urgent one, and if he met that, there would still be another. In the end, all the money he had was extracted from him and lost. The man with the smart money, who was safely out of the market when the first crash came, naturally went back in to pick up bargains. (Not only were a recorded 12,894,650 shares sold on October 24; precisely the same number were bought.) The bargains then suffered a ruinous fall. Even the man who waited out all of October and all of November, who saw the volume of trading return to normal and saw Wall Street become as placid as a produce market and who then bought common stocks, would see their value drop to a third or a fourth of the purchase price in the next twenty-four months. The Coolidge bull market was a remarkable phenomenon. The ruthlessness of its liquidation was, in its own way, equally remarkable.

II

Monday, October 28, was the first day on which this process of climax and anticlimax *ad infinitum* began to reveal itself. It was another terrible day. Volume was huge, although below the previous Thursday — nine and a quarter million shares as compared with nearly thirteen. But the losses were far more severe. The *Times* industrials were down 49 points for the day. General Electric was off 48; Westinghouse, 34; Tel and Tel, 34. Steel went down 18 points. Indeed, the decline on this one day was greater than that of all the preceding week of panic. Once again a late ticker left everyone in ignorance of what was happening, save that it was bad.

On this day there was no recovery. At one-ten Charles E. Mitchell was observed going into Morgan's, and the news ticker carried the magic word. Steel rallied and went from 194 to 198. But Richard Whitney did not materialize. It seems probable in light of later knowledge that Mitchell was on the way to float a personal loan.

The market weakened again, and in the last hour a phenomenal three million shares — a big day's business before and ever since — changed hands at rapidly falling prices.

At four-thirty in the afternoon the bankers assembled once more at Morgan's, and they remained in session until six-thirty. They were described as taking a philosophical attitude, and they told the press that the situation "retained hopeful features," although these were not specified. But the statement they released after the meeting made clear what had been discussed for the two hours. It was no part of the bankers' purpose, the statement said, to maintain any particular level of prices or to protect anyone's profit. Rather, the aim was to have an orderly market, one in which offers would be met by bids at some price. The bankers were only concerned that "air holes," as Mr. Lamont had dubbed them, did not appear.

Like many lesser men, Mr. Lamont and his colleagues had suddenly found themselves overcommitted to a falling market. The time had come to go short on promises. Support, organized or otherwise, could not contend with the overwhelming, pathological desire to sell. The meeting had considered how to liquidate the commitment to support the market without adding to the public perturbation.

The formula that was found was a chilling one. On Thursday, Whitney had supported prices and protected profits — or stopped losses. This was what people wanted. To the man who held stock on margin, disaster had only one face and that was falling prices. But now prices were to be allowed to fall. The speculator's only comfort, henceforth, was that his ruin would be accomplished in an orderly and becoming manner.

There were no recriminations at the time. Our political life favors the extremes of speech; the man who is gifted in the arts of abuse is bound to be a notable, if not always a great, figure. In business things are different. Here we are surprisingly gentle and forbearing. Even preposterous claims or excuses are normally taken, at least for all public purposes, at their face value. On the evening of the 28th no one any longer could feel "secure in the knowledge that the most powerful banks stood ready to prevent a recurrence" of panic. The market had reasserted itself as an impersonal force beyond the power of any person to control, and, while this is the way markets are supposed to be, it was horrible. But no one assailed the bankers for letting the people down. There was even some talk that on the next day the market might receive organized support.

III

Tuesday, October 29, was the most devastating day in the history of the New York stock market, and perhaps the most devastating day in the history of markets. It combined all of the bad features of all of the bad days before. Volume was immensely greater than on Black Thursday; the drop in prices was almost as great as on Monday. Uncertainty and alarm were as great as on either.

Selling began as soon as the market opened and in huge volume. Great blocks of stock were offered for what they would bring; in the first half hour sales were at a 33,000,000-a-day rate. The air holes, which the bankers were to close, opened wide. Repeatedly and in many issues there was a plethora of selling orders and no buyers at all. The stock of White Sewing Machine Company, which had reached a high of 48 in the months preceding, had closed at 11 the night before. During the day someone — according to Frederick Lewis Allen it was thought to have been a bright messenger boy for the Exchange — had the happy idea of entering a bid for a block of stock at a dollar a share. In the absence of any other bid, he got it.[1] Once again, of course, the ticker lagged — at the close it was two and a half hours behind. By then, 16,410,030 sales had been recorded on the New York Stock Exchange — some certainly went unrecorded — or more than three times the number that was once considered a fabulously big day. The *Times* industrial averages were down 43 points, canceling all of the gains of the twelve wonderful months preceding.

The losses would have been worse had there not been a closing rally. Thus Steel, for which Whitney had bid 205 on Thursday, reached 167 during the course of the day, although it rallied to 174 at the close. American Can opened at 130, dropped to 110, and rose to

120. Westinghouse opened at 131 — on September 3 it had closed at 286 — and dropped to 100. Then it rallied to 126. But the worst thing that happened on this terrible day was to the investment trusts. Not only did they go down, but it became apparent that they could go practically to nothing. Goldman Sachs Trading Corporation had closed at 60 the night before. During the day it dropped to 35 and closed at that level, off by not far short of half. Blue Ridge, its off-spring once removed, on which the magic of leverage was now working in reverse, did much worse. Early in September it had sold at 24. By October 24 it was down to 12, but it resisted rather well the misfortunes of that day and the day following. On the morning of October 29 it opened at 10 and promptly slipped to 3, giving up more than two thirds of its value. It recovered later but other invest-ment trusts did less well; their stock couldn't be sold at all.

The worst day on Wall Street came eventually to an end. Once again the lights blazed all night. Members of the Exchange, their employees and the employees of the Stock Exchange by now were reaching the breaking point from strain and fatigue. In this condi-tion they faced the task of recording and handling the greatest vol-ume of transactions ever. All of this was without the previous cer-tainty that things might get better. They might go on getting worse. In one house an employee fainted from exhaustion, was revived and put back to work again.

IV

In the first week the slaughter had been of the innocents. During this second week there is some evidence that it was the well-to-do and the wealthy who were being subjected to a leveling process comparable in magnitude and suddenness to that presided over a decade before by Lenin. The size of the blocks of stock which were offered suggested that big speculators were selling or being sold. An-other indication came from the boardrooms. A week before, they were crowded, now they were nearly empty. Many of those now in trouble had facilities for suffering in private.

The bankers met twice on the 29th — at noon and again in the evening. There was no suggestion that they were philosophical. This was hardly remarkable because during the day, an appalling rumor had swept the Exchange. It was that the bankers' pool, so far from stabilizing the market, was actually selling stocks! The prestige of the bankers had, in truth, been falling even more rapidly than the market. After the evening session, Mr. Lamont met the press with the disenchanting task of denying that they had been liquidating securities — or participating in a bear raid. After explaining again, somewhat redundantly in view of the day's events, that it was not the purpose of the bankers to maintain a particular level of prices, he concluded: "The group has continued and will continue in a co-operative way to support the market and has not been a seller of stocks." In fact, as later intelligence revealed, Albert H. Wiggin of the Chase was personally short at the time to the tune of some millions. His cooperative support, which if successful would have cost him heavily, must have had an interesting element of ambivalence.

So ended the organized support. The phrase recurred during the next few days, but no one again saw in it any ground for hope. Few men ever lost position so rapidly as did the New York bankers in the five days from October 24 to October 29. The crash on October 24 was the signal for corporations and out-of-town banks, which had been luxuriating in the 10 percent and more rate of interest, to recall their money from Wall Street. Between October 23 and October 30, as values fell and margin accounts were liquidated, the volume of brokers' loans fell by over a billion. But the corporations and the out-of-town banks responded to the horrifying news from New York — although, in fact, their funds were never seriously endangered — by calling home over two billion. The New York banks stepped into the gaping hole that was left by these summer financiers, and during that first week of crisis they increased their loans by about a billion. This was a bold step. Had the New York banks succumbed to the general fright, a money panic would have been added to the other woes. Stocks would have been dumped because their owners could not have borrowed money at any price to carry them. To prevent this was a considerable achievement for which all who owned stocks should have been thankful. But the banks received no credit. People remembered only that they had bravely undertaken to stem the price collapse and had failed.

Despite a flattering supposition to the contrary, people come readily to terms with power. There is little reason to think that the power of the great bankers, while they were assumed to have it, was much resented. But as the ghosts of numerous tyrants will testify, people are very hard on those who, having had power, lose it or are destroyed. Then anger at past arrogance is joined with contempt for present weakness. The victim or his corpse is made to suffer all available indignities.

Such was the fate of the bankers. For the next decade they were fair game for congressional committees, courts, the press and the comedians. The great pretensions and the great failures of these days were a cause. A banker need not be popular; indeed, a good banker in a healthy capitalist society should probably be much disliked. People do not wish to trust their money to a hail-fellow-well-met but to a misanthrope who can say no. However, a banker must not seem futile, ineffective or vaguely foolish. In contrast with the stern power of Morgan in 1907, that was precisely how his successors seemed, or were made to seem, in 1929.

The failure of the bankers did not leave the community entirely without constructive leadership. There was New York Mayor James J. Walker. Appearing before a meeting of motion picture exhibitors on that Tuesday, he appealed to them to "show pictures which will reinstate courage and hope in the hearts of the people."

v

On the Exchange itself, there was a strong feeling that courage and hope might best be restored by just closing up for a while. This feeling had, in fact, been gaining force for several days. Now it derived support from the simple circumstance that everyone was badly in need of sleep. Employees of some Stock Exchange firms had not been home for days. Hotel rooms in downtown New York were at a premium, and restaurants in the financial area had gone on to a fifteen- and twenty-hour day. Nerves were bad, and mistakes were becoming increasingly common. After the close of trading on Tuesday, a broker found a large waste basket of unexecuted orders which he had set aside for early attention and had totally forgotten.[2] One customer, whose margin account was impaired, was sold out twice. A number of firms needed some time to see if they were still solvent. There were, in fact, no important failures by Stock Exchange firms during these days, although one firm had reported itself bankrupt as the result of a clerical error by an employee who was in the last stages of fatigue.[3]

Yet to close the Exchange was a serious matter. It might somehow signify that stocks had lost all their value, with consequences no one could foresee. In any case, securities would immediately become a badly frozen asset. This would be hard on the wholly solvent investors who might still need to realize on them or use them as collateral. And sooner or later a new "gutter" market would develop in which individuals would informally dispose of stocks to those increasingly exceptional individuals who still wanted to buy them.

In 1929 the New York Stock Exchange was, in principle, a sovereignty of its members. Apart from the general statutes relating to the conduct of business and the prevention of fraud, it was subject to no important state or federal regulation. This meant a considerable exercise of self-government. Legislation governing the conduct of trading had to be kept under review and enforced. Stocks had to be approved for listing. The building and other facilities of the Exchange had to be managed. As with the United States Congress, most of this work was done in committees. (These, in turn, were dominated by a somewhat smaller group of members who were expected and accustomed to run things.) A decision to close the Exchange had to be taken by the Governing Committee, a body of about forty members. The mere knowledge that this body was meeting would almost certainly have an unfavorable effect on the market.

Nonetheless, at noon on Tuesday, the 29th, a meeting was held. The members of the committee left the floor in twos and threes and went, not to the regular meeting room, but to the office of the President of the Stock Clearing Corporation directly below the trading floor. Some months later, Acting President Whitney described the session with considerable graphic talent. "The office they met in was never designed for large meetings of this sort, with the result that most of the Governors were compelled to stand, or to sit on tables. As the meeting proceeded, panic was raging overhead on the floor. Every few minutes the latest prices were announced, with quotations moving swiftly and irresistibly downwards. The feeling of those present was revealed by their habit of continually lighting cigarettes, taking a puff or two, putting them out and lighting new ones — a practice which soon made the narrow room blue with smoke and extremely stuffy."

The result of these nervous deliberations was a decision to meet again in the evening. By evening the late rally had occurred, and it was decided to stay open for another day. The next day a further formula was hit upon. The Exchange would stay open. But it would have some special holidays and then go on short hours, and this would be announced just as soon as the market seemed strong enough to stand it.

Many still wanted to close. Whitney said later, although no doubt with some exaggeration, that in the days to come "the authorities of the Exchange led the life of hunted things, until [eventually] the desirability of holding the market open became apparent to all."

VI

The next day those forces were at work which on occasion bring salvation precisely when salvation seems impossible. Stocks rose wonderfully, miraculously, though still on enormous volume. The *Times* industrials were up 31 points for the day, thus recouping a large part of the terrible losses of the day before. Why this recovery occurred no one will ever know. Organized support can have no credit. Organized reassurance has a somewhat better claim. On the evening of the 29th, Dr. Julius Klein, Assistant Secretary of Commerce, friend of President Hoover and the senior apostle of the official economic view, took to the radio to remind the country that President Hoover had said that the "fundamental business of the country" was sound.

He added firmly, "The main point which I want to emphasize is the fundamental soundness of [the] great mass of economic activities." On Wednesday, Waddill Catchings, of Goldman, Sachs, announced on return from a western trip that general business conditions were "unquestionably fundamentally sound." (The same, by then, could not unquestionably be said of all Goldman, Sachs.) Arthur Brisbane told Hearst readers: "To comfort yourself, if you lost, think of the people living near Mount Pelee, ordered [by an earthquake warning] to abandon their homes."

Most important, perhaps, from Pocantico Hills came the first public statement by John D. Rockefeller in several decades. So far as the record shows, it was spontaneous. However, someone in Wall Street — perhaps someone who knew that another appeal to President Hoover to say something specifically encouraging about stocks would be useless — may have realized that a statement from Rockefeller would, if anything, be better. The statement ran: "Believing that fundamental conditions of the country are sound . . . my son and I have for some days been purchasing sound common stocks." The statement was widely applauded, although Eddie Cantor, describing himself as Comedian, Author, Statistician and Victim, said later, "Sure, who else had any money left?"[4]

The accepted Wall Street explanation of Wednesday's miracle was not the reassurance but the dividend news of the day before. This also, without much question, was somewhat organized. U.S. Steel had declared an extra dividend; American Can had not only declared an extra but had increased its regular dividend. These errant sunbeams were deeply welcome in the dark canyons of lower Manhattan.

Just before the Rockefeller statement arrived, things looked good enough on the Exchange so that Richard Whitney felt safe in announcing that the market would not open until noon the following day (Thursday) and that on Friday and Saturday it would stay shut. The announcement was greeted by cheers. Nerves were clearly past the breaking point. On La Salle Street in Chicago a boy exploded a firecracker. Like wildfire the rumor spread that gangsters whose margin accounts had been closed out were shooting up the street.

Several squad cars of police arrived to make them take their losses like honest men. In New York the body of a commission merchant was fished out of the Hudson. The pockets contained $9.40 in change and some margin calls.

VII

At the short session of three hours on Thursday, October 31, well over seven million shares were traded, and the market made another good gain. The *Times* industrials were up 21 points. The weekly return of the Federal Reserve Bank showed a drop in brokers' loans by more than a billion, the largest weekly drop on record. Margin requirements had already been cut to 25 percent; now the Federal Reserve Banks lowered the rediscount rate from 6 to 5 percent. The Reserve Banks also launched vigorous open-market purchases of bonds to ease money rates and liberalize the supply of credit. The boom had collapsed; the restraint that had previously been contemplated could now give way to a policy of active encouragement to the market. On all these happy portents the market closed down for Friday, Saturday and Sunday. They were not days of rest. Brokerage offices were fully staffed, and the Exchange floor was open for completion of trades and also for straightening out innumerable misunderstandings and mistakes. It was noted that on Friday a visitor to the galleries could not have told that the market was suspended.

The weekend brought one piece of bad news. That was the announcement on Saturday of the failure of the $20,000,000 Foshay enterprises of Minneapolis. Foshay owned utilities in some twelve states, Canada, Mexico and Central America, and an assortment of hotels, flour mills, banks, manufacturing and retail establishments wherever he had happened to buy them. The 32-story obelisk, commemorating the enterprise, which still dominates the Minneapolis skyline, had been opened with fitting ceremony by Secretary of War James W. Good, only in August. (Secretary Good had referred to it as the "Washington Monument of the Northwest.")[5] By all but the most technical of considerations, Foshay was bankrupt at that festive time. His survival depended on his ability to continue merchandising stock to the public. The market crash eliminated this source of revenue and made him dependent on the wholly inadequate earnings of his enterprises.

On all other fronts the news was all good. Alfred P. Sloan, Jr., President of the General Motors Corporation, said: "Business is sound." The Ford Motor Company emphasized a similar conviction by announcing a general reduction in its prices: ". . . we feel that such a step is the best contribution that could be made to assure a continuation of good business." The Roadster was cut from $450 to $435; the Phaeton from $460 to $440; the Tudor Sedan from $525 to $500. For the three days that the market was closed the papers carried stories of the accumulation of buying orders, and, in some indefinable way, the stories had a greater ring of conviction than the week before. The market, after all, had closed after an excellent two-day rally. As *Barron's* pointed out, it could now be believed that stocks were selling "ex-hopes and romance." On Monday, the Commercial National Bank and Trust Company took five columns in the *Times* to advertise ". . . our belief and conviction that the general industrial and business condition of the country is fundamentally sound and is essentially unimpaired."

That day the market started on another ghastly slump.

VIII

Over the weekend the financial community had almost certainly been persuaded by its own organized and spontaneous efforts at cheer. The papers described the reaction of professional Wall Street to Monday's market as one of stunned surprise, disbelief and shock. Volume was smaller than the week before but still well above six million. The whole list was weak; individual issues made big losses; the *Times* industrials were down 22 points for the day. Compared with anything but the week before, this was very bad. When measured against the bright hopes for that day, it was most distressing.

Explanations varied. The rumor recurred that the "organized support" was selling stocks, and Mr. Lamont, on meeting the press, added a minor footnote to this now completed story. He said he didn't know — the organized support was really not that well organized. The most plausible explanation is that everyone was feeling cheerful but the public. As before and later, the weekend had been a time of thought, and out of thought had come pessimism and a decision to sell. So, as on other Mondays, no matter how cheerful the superficial portents, the selling orders poured in in volume.

By now it was also evident that the investment trusts, once considered a buttress of the high plateau and a built-in defense against collapse, were really a profound source of weakness. The leverage, of which people only a fortnight before had spoken so knowledgeably and even affectionately, was now fully in reverse. With remarkable celerity it removed all of the value from the common stock of a trust. As before, the case of a typical trust, a small one, is worth contemplating. Let it be supposed that it had securities in the hands of the public which had a market value of $10,000,000 in early October. Of this, half was in common stock, half in bonds and preferred stock. These securities were fully covered by the current market value of the securities owned. In other words, the trust's portfolio contained securities with a market value also of $10,000,000.

A representative portfolio of securities owned by such a trust would, in the early days of November, have declined in value by perhaps half. (Values of many of these securities by later standards would still be handsome; on November 4, the low for Tel and Tel was still 233, for General Electric it was 234 and for Steel 183.) The new portfolio value, $5,000,000, would be only enough to cover the prior claim on assets of the bonds and preferred stock. The common stock would have nothing behind it. Apart from expectations, which were by no means bright, it was now worthless.

This geometrical ruthlessness was not exceptional. On the contrary, it was everywhere at work on the stock of the leverage trusts. By early November, the stock of most of them had become virtually unsalable. To make matters worse, many of them were traded on the Curb or the out-of-town exchanges where buyers were few and the markets thin.

Never was there a time when more people wanted more money more urgently than in those days. The word that a man had "got caught" by the market was the signal for his creditors to descend on him like locusts. Many who were having trouble meeting their margin calls wanted to sell some stocks so they could hold the rest and thus salvage something from their misfortunes. But such people now found that their investment trust securities could not be sold for any appreciable sum and perhaps not at all. They were forced, as a result, to realize on their good securities. Standard stocks like Steel, General Motors, Tel and Tel were thus dumped on the market in abnormal volume, with the effect on prices that had already been fully revealed. The great investment trust boom had ended in a unique manifestation of Gresham's Law in which the bad stocks were driving out the good.

The stabilizing effects of the huge cash resources of the investment trusts had also proved a mirage. In the early autumn the cash and liquid resources of the investment trusts were large. Many trusts had been attracted by the handsome returns in the call market. (The speculative circle had been closed. People who speculated in the stock of investment trusts were, in effect, investing in companies which provided the funds to finance their own speculation.) But now, as reverse leverage did its work, investment trust managements were much more concerned over the collapse in the value of their own stock than in the adverse movements in the stock list as a whole. The investment trusts had invested heavily in each other. As a result, the fall in Blue Ridge hit Shenandoah, and the resulting collapse in Shenandoah was even more horrible for the Goldman Sachs Trading Corporation.

Under these circumstances, many of the trusts used their available cash in a desperate effort to support their own stock. However, there was a vast difference between buying one's stock now when the public wanted to sell and buying during the previous spring — as Goldman Sachs Trading Corporation had done — when the public wanted to buy and the resulting competition had sent prices higher and higher. Now the cash went out and the stock came in, and prices were either not perceptibly affected or not for long. What six months before had been a brilliant financial maneuver was now a form of fiscal self-immolation. In the last analysis, the purchase by a firm of its own stock is the exact opposite of the sale of stocks. It is by the sale of stock that firms ordinarily grow.

However, none of this was immediately apparent. If one has been a financial genius, faith in one's genius does not dissolve at once. To the battered but unbowed genius, support of the stock of one's own company still seemed a bold, imaginative and effective course. Indeed, it seemed the only alternative to slow but certain death. So, to the extent that their cash resources allowed, the managements of the trusts chose faster, though equally certain death. They bought their own worthless stock. Men have been swindled by other men on many occasions. The autumn of 1929 was, perhaps, the first occasion when men succeeded on a large scale in swindling themselves.

NOTES

1. Frederick Lewis Allen, *Only Yesterday* (New York: Harper, 1931), p. 333.
2. Allen, p. 334.
3. *The Work of the Stock Exchange in the Panic of 1929,* an address by Richard Whitney before the Boston Association of Stock Exchange Firms (Boston: June 10, 1930), pp. 16, 17. Whitney's account, on p. 300, of the events of October 29 and thereafter is from the same source.
4. *Caught Short! A Saga of Wailing Wall Street* (New York: Simon and Schuster, 1929 A.C. [After Crash]), p. 31.
5. *Investment News,* October 16, 1929, p. 538.

The Unfinished Business
of the Century

[The London School of Economics, 1999]

This was a lecture given at the London School of Economics (LSE) in June 1999, on the occasion of my receiving an honorary degree. As I said in the preface, it has been the most widely republished discourse I have ever given.

*　　*　　*　　*

SIXTY-TWO YEARS AGO I spent a year in what is known at Harvard as the other Cambridge. It was then in the high pulse of the Keynesian Revolution. Economic discussion was constant, intense, but London also called; once a week I came up to seminars here at the London School of Economics. A major attraction was Friedrich von Hayek, the noted conservative, author of "A Road to Serfdom," his widely read analysis of the disastrous but emerging welfare state. He, however, was only slightly heard. The two hours were given over, all but exclusively, to telling him he was wrong. I found myself in support of this correction; it was education by the rebuke of error. (I trust that will not be the tendency on this pleasant and, for me, nostalgic occasion.) Over the years I've often presented myself to ardent conservatives as a student of von Hayek; it has added in an agreeable way to their normal confusion.

My subject today is "The Unfinished Business of the Century" and, needless to say, "The Millennium." We have had frequent word on the achievements of the past; what we should think about more is the needs of the future. There is a great deal to be said on this; any fears you harbor as to the possible length of this lecture could be well founded.

Much has, indeed, been accomplished in the last century. In what we choose to call the advanced countries there has been an enormous change in the basic activities of life, particularly in the production of food, shelter, clothing, other manufactured artifacts, the provision of health care and the improvement of the means of transportation and communication.

I began my life in economics with the study of agriculture. At that time just under half of all those gainfully employed in the United States were engaged in producing food, tobacco and cotton, as most of the workforce had been for centuries before. Now fewer than five percent are so employed. In this last century men and women have escaped the repetitive and often dismal exertion that keeps people fed and clothed. The amenities of rural life were always greatly praised — it was praise partly designed to conceal the lonely effort involved. I was born and reared on a farm in Canada, and to this day I never awaken in the morning without a sense of satisfaction that I will not have to spend the next hours in that monotonous but richly commended toil. One of the achievements of this century has been the general escape from what Marx, with some slight exaggeration, called the idiocy of rural life.

We have also seen a wonderful lengthening of the years of health and well-being. Being alive and in good health surely enlarges the aggregate of human pleasure. There are other effects. If at the beginning of the century I had been my present age and been asked to speak to you tonight, it would have had to have been from the next world. Some of you would have been there as well. Others, alive and still here, would happily have escaped this lecture.

We have also now the much-celebrated technological supplements to human intelligence, including the computer world. These, in some aspects, are serviceable and good, in others contrived and diversionary. Still, there can be no doubt that greater equality in mental achievement has come from the economic advance of this past century.

More important, there has been a general escape from the worst feature of modern existence — something to which I have already alluded. That is hard, tedious, boring toil. This has not yet been eliminated, but one of the greatest accomplishments of the last hundred years in the favored lands has been the reduction in the proportion of people so engaged.

In this connection we must note that the word *work* is our most misleading social term. It designates the occupation of those who would be very unhappy without it, including many to whom I speak tonight. And it is also the term we use when we speak of arduous, repetitive, even physically painful toil. No word in the English language stretches over such different conditions. There is the further perverse fact that those who most enjoy what is called work are those who are best paid. And they are also allowed the greatest leisure.

The most enduring American social classic of the nineteenth century, coming just at its end, was Thorstein Veblen's *The Theory of the Leisure Class*. It assumed almost without argument that if rich enough, you, and certainly your dependents, did not need to work. There is no question that this book has a continuing effect today. Over the sixty years I have been teaching at Harvard, I have often, while crossing the Yard, been stopped by one of my colleagues with the question, "Aren't you working a bit too hard?" Leisure is thought essential for the affluent and also for those of us for whom work is pleasant, even mentally rewarding. For those who must truly toil, however, leisure is viewed as an escape from social virtue. Nonetheless, here too there has been progress. In the century just passing many have graduated from the miseries to the enjoyments of work. That more can do so is a major hope for the time ahead.

IV

I turn now to urge a more discriminating scrutiny of what is considered the greatest achievement of the twentieth century: economic success and therewith the way we measure it.

Of the economic success, to which I've already adverted, there is no doubt. In the fortunate countries there has been an enormous increase in the production of goods and services, the wherewithal of life. The size of the increase, the annual rise in Gross Domestic Product, has become the prime indicator of human progress. I do not suggest that an increase in GDP and its measurement is unimportant; our debt to my well-loved colleague at Harvard, Simon Kuznets, who first measured Gross National Product (as it once was), is indeed profound. But there are limits.

This summer thousands of visitors will descend on Florence, Italy. In its greatest days it was a city of small, even insignificant income by all modern standards. William Shakespeare lived in a country with a very low Gross Domestic Product. Paris in the years of the Impressionists was appreciably less affluent than it is now. So, also, was the world that gave us Charles Darwin, and no one since has so challenged embodied belief. It is clear that success that is measured by economic output bears no close relationship to human achievement. Today the most ardent artistic effort is devoted not to the arts but to promoting the sale of goods and services. So also much of our scientific effort. Darwin's successors now concentrate heavily on the creation of new products for the market.

V

If the history of the arts and of science gives us pause as to the measurement of present achievement, there are also problems within economies as well. The most serious is the ancient and unsolved problem of instability — the enduring sequence of boom and bust. The history goes back for centuries to the Tulipmania in Holland in 1637 (and perhaps before) and to the early eighteenth-century promise in Paris of gold not yet discovered in Louisiana and to the South Sea Bubble in England. (In later years there was the wonderful prospect for draining the Red Sea to recover the treasure left behind at the crossing of the Israelites.) In the United States in the twentieth century, there was a sequence of boom and bust virtually every thirty years, including the Great Crash of 1929. The speculative crash, now called a correction, has been a basic feature of the system. In the United States we are now having another exercise in speculative optimism following the partial reversal in 1998.

We have far more people selling derivatives, index funds and mutual funds (as we call them) than there is intelligence for the task. I am cautious about prediction; I discovered years ago that my correct predictions are forgotten, the others meticulously remembered. But some things are definite; when you hear it being said that we have entered a new economy of permanent prosperity with prices of financial instruments reflecting that happy fact, you should take cover. This has been the standard justification of speculative excess for several centuries — for a good part of the millennium. My onetime Harvard colleague Joseph Schumpeter thought inevitable and even beneficial what he called "creative destruction" — the cyclical process by which the system eliminates the people and institutions which are mentally too vulnerable for useful economic service. Unfortunately the process has larger and less benign effects, including the possibility of painful recession or depression.

Let us not assume that the age of slump, recession, depression is past. Let us have both the needed warnings against speculative excess and awareness that the ensuing slump can be painful, which will inevitably make necessary specific remedial action by the government. John Maynard Keynes, one regularly reads, is out of fashion; his, indeed, is a cyclical legacy that fades in good times, returns with recession. So others who accept government action as a necessary stabilizing force.

VI

I come to two pieces of the unfinished business of the century and millennium that have high visibility and urgency. The first is the very large number of the very poor even in the richest of countries and notably in the United States. Once the impoverished were scattered over the countryside — especially in our case in the rural South. Now everywhere they are in the great cities, melding in with the larger urban mass. In the fortunate lands poverty, urban poverty, is the most evident and painful of the economic and social legacies from earlier centuries.

The answer or part of the answer is rather clear: everybody should be guaranteed a decent basic income. A rich country such as the United States can well afford to keep all its citizens out of poverty. Some, it will be said, will seize upon the income and not work. So it is now with more limited welfare, as it is called. I've already discussed the issue of leisure and work. Let us accept some resort to leisure by the poor as well as by the rich.

There is more. In the modern economic system, and especially in the United States, we have a bizarre problem in the distribution of income — a heavy concentration in the very top income brackets, much less to those below. There is currently a stirring discussion of inequality; I would like to see it intensified. When it is said, as it is, that we should protect the income of the rich, reduce taxes in order to encourage effort, I have an answer. Perhaps we should have a higher marginal rate of taxation to stimulate effort to maintain after-tax income. My plan is not widely applauded. I yield, but the equalizing effect of taxation must be strongly defended.

Inequality, poverty, has its grave international dimension as well. As we look at the achievements of our waning century, we must all pay tribute to the end of colonialism. Too often, however, the end of colonial rule has also meant the end of effective government. Particularly in Africa colonialism has frequently given way to corrupt government or no government at all. Nothing so ensures hardship, poverty and suffering as the absence of a responsible, effective, honest polity. In Latin America this was the result of an earlier escape from colonialism; so it is now in much of Africa and in lesser measure in Asia.

In a humane world order we must have a mechanism to suspend sovereignty when it becomes necessary to protect against human suffering and disaster. Let there be solid action by the United Nations to bring about an effective and humane independence. Economic aid is important, but without honest, competent government, it is of little consequence. We have here one of the major unfinished tasks of the century and the millennium.

My emphasis, you will have observed, is on the United Nations. I believe it should have had the dominant role in the recent tragedy in the Balkans. I am also far from enthusiastic about air power as there used, a matter on which, oddly enough, I claim major experience. There was nothing affirmative to be said for the Serbian rule of Kosovo, but neither was there for the basically indiscriminate nature of the bombing — of men, women, children and, one should add, foreign embassies.

VII

There is one final piece of unfinished business. In the United States we have a rigorous control of action in our foreign policy not by thought but by acceptance of the past. This keeps us from accommodating what we do to the realities of the world scene. Some Cuban migrants apart, no one now defends our adverse policies toward Cuba. Yet under the tyranny of that policy we continue an embargo on trade and a partial embargo on other communication that makes no sense whatever.

But this is a detail. There is a far more serious legacy of the last hundred years and particularly of the last fifty years. It is that we find ourselves facing a total end to civilized existence on the planet and perhaps to life itself. Available are the nuclear weapons which could accomplish precisely this. And there is a strong commitment to keeping and protecting these weapons even though we fully realize the threat. As long as we accept them in the nuclear countries, we are limited in our ability to persuade others to a policy of sanity and survival. When in the recent past India and Pakistan exploded nuclear bombs, we in the United States reacted adversely. Their natural answer was "What about you?"

The greatest unfinished business of the century now ending is the need to eliminate this weaponry. It need only fall into the hands of mentally vulnerable politicians or generals to bring a nuclear exchange, which, to repeat, could be the end of all civilized existence and, quite possibly, of all existence. This weaponry and the danger it poses is the most serious legacy of the twentieth century. The most urgent task now and of the years to come is to eliminate the threat of Armageddon, something on which there has been solemn comment over the centuries but which is now a reality. With that glowing thought, I end this discourse.

SOURCES

"Countervailing Power": in *American Capitalism* (Boston: Houghton Mifflin, 1956), pp. 108–134.

"The Concept of the Conventional Wisdom": in *The Affluent Society*, 40th anniversary ed. (Boston: Mariner/Houghton Mifflin, 1998), pp. 6–17.

"The Myth of Consumer Sovereignty" ("The Dependence Effect"): in *The Affluent Society*, 40th anniversary ed. (Boston: Mariner/Houghton Mifflin, 1998), pp. 124–131.

"The Case for Social Balance" ("The Theory of Social Balance"): in *The Affluent Society*, 40th anniversary ed. (Boston: Mariner/Houghton Mifflin, 1998), pp. 186–199.

"The Imperatives of Technology": in *The New Industrial State*, 3d ed., rev. (Boston: Houghton Mifflin, 1978), pp. 11–21.

"The Technostructure": in *The New Industrial State*, 3d ed., rev. (Boston: Houghton Mifflin, 1978), pp. 62–74.

"The General Theory of Motivation": in *The New Industrial State*, 3d ed., rev. (Boston: Houghton Mifflin, 1978), pp. 136–147.

"Economics and the Quality of Life": in *Economics, Peace and Laughter* (Boston: Houghton Mifflin, 1971), pp. 3–25.

"The Proper Purpose of Economic Development": in *Economics, Peace and Laughter* (Boston: Houghton Mifflin, 1971), pp. 201–210.

"The Valid Image of the Modern Economy": in *Annals of an Abiding Liberal* (Boston: Houghton Mifflin, 1979), pp. 3–19.

"Power and the Useful Economist": in *Annals of an Abiding Liberal* (Boston: Houghton Mifflin, 1979), pp. 353–371.

"The Founding Faith: Adam Smith's *Wealth of Nations*": in *Annals of an Abiding Liberal* (Boston: Houghton Mifflin, 1979), pp. 86–102.

"The Massive Dissent of Karl Marx" ("The Dissent of Karl Marx"): in *The Age of Uncertainty* (Boston: Houghton Mifflin, 1977), pp. 77–108.

"Who Was Thorstein Veblen?": in *Annals of an Abiding Liberal* (Boston: Houghton Mifflin, 1979), pp. 123–147.

"The Mandarin Revolution": in *The Age of Uncertainty* (Boston: Houghton Mifflin, 1977), pp. 197–226.

"How Keynes Came to America": in *Economics, Peace and Laughter* (Boston: Houghton Mifflin, 1971), pp. 43–59.

"The Speculative Episode": in *A Short History of Financial Euphoria* (New York: Whittle Direct Books, 1990), pp. 3–9.

"In Goldman, Sachs We Trust": in *The Great Crash, 1929,* collectors' ed. (Boston: Houghton Mifflin, 1995), pp. 43–65.

"The Crash": in *The Great Crash, 1929,* collectors' ed. (Boston: Houghton Mifflin, 1995), pp. 88–107.

"Things Become More Serious": in *The Great Crash, 1929,* collectors' ed. (Boston: Houghton Mifflin, 1995), pp. 108–127.

"The Unfinished Business of the Century": Speech given at special honorary degree convocation, London School of Economics, June 28, 1999.